Political Science Cracked 2020 Edition

ROGER LANG COHEN

ISBN: 978-19-885572-5-0

Published in New Zealand

A catalogue record for this book is available from the National Library of New Zealand.

Kei te pātengi raraunga o Te Puna Mātauranga o Aotearoa te whakarārangi o tēnei pukapuka.

Table of Contents

Chapter 1

The Basics of Political Science

Types of Government

As an introduction to the American Government, the question must be asked, "Who Governs?" This question rests on the answer regarding the type of political system the Government consists. For this book, there are five types of political systems explored.

The first political system is a Republic. A Republic is a government in which citizens rule indirectly and make government decisions through their elected representatives. The second system is the Pluralist Theory. In the Pluralist theory, the people of the country are the ones who directly influence the government and have access to the leaders of government. The third political system is the Elite Theory. In the Elite Theory, the power rests in the hands of wealthy and powerful individuals and not in the hands of the people. The is power control could be a small group of people. The fourth system is the Bureaucratic Theory. In the Bureaucratic Theory, the control lies with the workers of modern government, and the workers create all the policy and implement the policy. The final political system theory is the Social Movement Theory. In the Social Movement Theory, the citizens wield power when they organize and rise up in protest. This has the power of revolution and change held by the people themselves.

Types of Liberty

In the Political Theory of Liberty, there are two types of liberty that impact the freedoms people have in government. The first type of liberty is called Negative Liberty. In Negative Liberty, freedom is the absence of constraints. This is the most common type of limitation of liberty that people are familiar with. It involves laws and limitations that the government puts on people, and mainly the lack of government to intervene in one's life. In a society that espouses Negative Liberty, the function of society is to make sure that others do not interfere with individuals. This means that people are free to act as they wish without the limitations of government creating laws and rules regarding living and working in society. This is a limited government, and the government does not get involved in the day to day events of life.

The second type of Liberty is Positive Liberty. This type of liberty is the freedom to pursue one's goals. This could be that you are not constrained from the pursuit of one's goals, and it can be that you are fully equipped by the government to be able to seek such liberty. In this model of liberty, individuals cannot really be free if they lack the basic necessities of life. This includes the idea that every citizen should have food, shelter, healthcare, and educational opportunities. In a modern political environment, the question would be asked if the government has an obligation to provide housing, healthcare, college education, and other programs at the expense of the greater population.

Democracy

A democracy is a government in which citizens rule directly and make government decisions for themselves. This can be done through multiple methods of democratic representation. As well, there are methods in which in a democracy people can become involved beyond voting. In some democracies, like the Republic of California, two types of Democratic function allow for the people to become directly involved in the democratic process. The use of Referendum and Initiative allow for direct democracy.

The use of Referendum in an election allows for the citizens of a democracy to become directly involved on a single issue. A referendum in an election occurs when citizens vote directly on an issue that is of importance to the citizens. The use of the Initiative process is another tool that is used in a democratic nation. The Initiative process is one in which citizens propose new laws or amendments to the state constitution. This process allows the citizens of a nation to circumvent the politicians who are controlling and leading the democracy.

A Republic

In a Republic, the method of ruling for the citizens is through indirect rule. In the Republic, Government is ruled by citizens who rule indirectly and permit elected representatives to make decisions. People will choose to rule indirectly through elected representatives, who in tern will represent the will of the people. This is seen differently around the world. In the context of American constitutional law, the definition of republic refers specifically to a form of government in which elected individuals represent the citizen body and exercise power according to the rule of law under a constitution, including separation of powers with an elected head of state, referred to as a constitutional republic, or representative democracy.

Multiple Choice Questions

1) Lieutenant Russell Burgos was formerly a _____, prior to fighting in the Iraq War.

a. college student

b. attorney

*c. political science professor

d. construction worker

2) In a republic, who is in charge?

*a. the people

b. the president

c. the Supreme Court

d. the bureaucracy

3) The key to understanding our political decision making lies in four "I's." What are they?

a. imagination, institutions, ingenuity, and individuals

*b. ideas, institutions, interests, and individuals

c. intelligence, institutions, imagination, and individuals

d. impact, institutions, interests, and individuals

4) What does the theory of pluralist mean?

a. *Pluralist* is the ideal of multicultural coexistence.

*b. *Pluralist* suggests that people can influence government through the many interest groups that spring up to champion everything from fighting for energy independence to banning abortions.

c. *Pluralist* suggests that people can influence politicians by advocating their views on a large scale.

d. *Pluralist* is the idea that one can believe in both Christian and Muslim religious tenets.

5) According to pluralist theory, where is influence displayed in government?

a. religious groups

*b. interest groups

c. political groups

d. unions

6) Where does elite theory place the source of political influence?

a. "power elite" in government, the judicial branch, and the military

b. "power elite" in college institutions, business, and the Central Intelligence Agency

c. "power elite" in unions, corporations, and banks

*d. "power elite" in government, corporations, and the military

7) Where does elite theory place political power?

a. status based on economic influence and religious background

*b. status based on economic influence and leadership position

c. status based on economic influence and academic background

d. status based on economic influence and party affiliation

8) What does social movement theory identify as the source of influence?

a. controversial uprisings/movements

b. religious uprisings/movements

*c. popular uprisings/movements

d. economic uprisings/movements

9) Where does social movement theory locate political power?

*a. strength of mass demands

b. strength of student demands

c. strength of union demands

d. strength of private demands

10) More than ___ percent of all federal government spending goes to just four programs.

*a. 61

b. 50

c. 75

d. 80

11) What are the top four programs that the federal government spends a large percentage of its funding on?

a. education, human services, Social Security, and Medicare

*b. the military, Social Security, Medicare, and Medicaid

c. Social Security, Medicare, Medicaid, and education

d. the military, education, Medicare, and Medicaid

12) The expenditures of the biggest four programs of the federal government total over ___ trillion dollars.

*a. 3

b. 1.7

c. 5.0

d. 3.7

13) What is meant by the expression, "The United States is a nation of immigrants"?

a. America is a country where people from different countries can come to work and play on vacation and then return home.

b. The United States is a nation where people from a few countries can come to live.

*c. We are a country where individuals come to reinvent themselves.

d. all of the above

14) Studies show that members of Generation Y (millennials), on average, are more responsible, harder working, and more law-abiding than the generations that came before. Which of the following are they also have

a. low work ethic

b. fewer charitable inclinations

c. irresponsible

*d. high rates of religious faith

15) What is a republic?

*a. A system of government that rests ultimate governing power in its people, who may rule directly or via representatives.

b. A system of government that rests most governing power in the elite selected for authority based on obtaining superior education.

c. A system of government that rests none of the governing power in its people but instead allows a single individual to exercise sole political control to ensure the well-being of all people.

d. All of the above.

16) The principle of checks and balances ensures that which branch of government has the authority to block the other branches?

a. the executive branch

b. the judicial branch

c. the legislative branch

*d. all three branches

17) As _____ left the Constitutional Convention in 1787, a woman stopped him. "What kind of government have you given us?" she asked. He responded, "A republic, madam—if you can keep it."

a. Thomas Jefferson

*b. Benjamin Franklin

c. John Adams

d. none of the above

18) _____ was a republic that had collapsed during ancient times but became hugely influential on the Founders of the US in the development of the Constitution.

*a. Athens

b. Barcelona

c. London

d. Moscow

19) What does the political term *institutions* mean?

a. organizational establishments

*b. the organizations, norms, and rules that structure political action

c. the mindsets of a political environment

d. the establishments of the political elite

20) Which of the following is an example of an *institution*?

*a. Congress

b. Red Cross

c. Occupy Wall Street

d. all of the above

21) Which of the following is an example of an *institution*?

*a. the Supreme Court

b. United Way

c. families

d. all of the above

22) Which of the following is an example of an *institution*?

a. Parent-Teacher Association

b. Knights of Columbus

*c. Department of Homeland Security

d. all of the above

23) The federal government had an annual budget of ___ trillion.

a. $55.2

b. $27.3

*c. $4.4

d. $0.2

24) _____ provides health care for people over the age of sixty-five.

*a. Medicare

b. Welfare

c. Social Security

d. none of the above

25) ____ provides health care for some poor people; about half the program's spending also goes to people over the age of sixty-five.

a. Financial aid

*b. Medicaid

c. Social Security

d. none of the above

26) When did the colonies break away from England?

a. August 21, 1824

b. January 4, 1706

*c. July 4, 1776

d. July 4, 1781

27) American leaders issued a Declaration of Independence explaining their revolutionary actions. Which of the following encapsulated their ideas?

a. *"That all men and women are created equal, that they are endowed by their Creator with certain unalienable rights, that among these are life, liberty and the pursuit of happiness."*

b. *"That all men are created equal, that they are endowed by their God with certain unalienable rights, that among these are life, liberty and the pursuit of happiness."*

*c. *"That all men are created equal, that they are endowed by their Creator with certain unalienable rights, that among these are life, liberty and the pursuit of happiness."*

d. none of the above

28) The Declaration of Independence explained the role of government—securing each individual's three rights. Which of the following is one of those rights?

*a. life

b. freedom

c. success

d. none of the above

29) The Declaration of Independence explained the role of government—securing each individual's three rights. Which of the following is one of those rights?

a. wealth

b. land

*c. liberty

d. none of the above

30) The Declaration of Independence explained the role of government—securing each individual's three rights. Which of the following is one of those rights?

a. freedom of religion

*b. pursuit of happiness

c. property

d. none of the above

31) Which of the following is not one of the seven big ideas espoused in the Declaration of Independence?

a. liberty

b. individualism

*c. freedom of religion

d. freedom to bear arms

32) Which of the following is not one of the seven big ideas espoused in the Declaration of Independence?

*a. land ownership

b. self-rule (which is often called democracy)

c. limited government

d. freedom to own slaves

33) Which of the following IS one of the seven big ideas espoused in the Declaration of Independence?

a. the American dream

b. equality

c. faith in God

*d. all of the above

34) Why did eighty thousand slaves join the British during the Revolutionary War?

*a. The royal governor of Virginia promised them freedom.

b. The royal governor of Virginia paid them.

c. They did so out of loyalty.

d. They were forced to by King George III.

35) What was the motto for the slaves who fought in the Revolutionary War?

a. "Freedom for the slaves."

b. "Freedom for all."

*c. "Liberty for the slaves."

d. "Liberty and justice for slaves."

36) What is the definition of *freedom*?

a. It means that the government will protect your life, your liberty, and your property from the coercion of others (excluding government) in order to permit you to pursue the goals you define for yourself.

*b. It means that the government will protect your life, your liberty, and your property from the coercion of others (including government) in order to permit you to pursue the goals you define for yourself.

c. It means that the government will protect your life, your liberty, and your guns from the coercion of others (including government) in order to permit you to pursue the goals you define for yourself.

d. none of the above

37) What is the view of *negative liberty*?

a. Freedom is granted with limited restrictions.

*b. Freedom is the absence of constraints.

c. Freedom is the inclusion of constraints.

d. None of the above.

38) What is the definition of *positive liberty*?

a. The freedom to pursue one's goals with government restrictions.

b. The freedom to pursue one's goals with some exceptions.

*c. The freedom to pursue one's goals.

d. The freedom to pursue one's goals without government control.

39) President Franklin D. Roosevelt, as the nation prepared for World War II, proclaimed that the nation was fighting for four freedoms. Which of the following is not one of them?

a. freedom of speech

b. freedom of worship

*c. freedom of oppression

d. freedom from want

40) What does "freedom from want" mean?

a. helping people achieve a home

*b. helping needy people who have fallen on hard times

c. helping people obtain the American dream

d. none of the above

41) President Roosevelt adheres to which viewpoint?

a. negative liberty

*b. positive liberty

c. both

d. social democracy

42) _____ means that citizens participate directly in making government decisions.

a. Republic

*b. Democracy

c. Autocratic

d. Libertarian

43) When did Dr. Martin Luther King give his famous "I Have a Dream" speech?

a. 1962

b. 1955

*c. 1963

d. 1969

44) Which of the Founding Fathers was a big proponent of maximizing democracy?

*a. Thomas Jefferson

b. George Washington

c. James Madison

d. Benjamin Franklin

45) Which perspective stipulates that the Constitution's drafters were guided less by cultural values, rather, they were looking for organizational arrangements that would regulate political behavior?

a. political organizations

*b. political institutions

c. political culture

d. political dichotomy

46) The Family and Medical Leave Act (1993) requires employers with more than fifty workers to allow up to _____ of unpaid leave for pregnancy, adoption, illness, or military service.

a. one week

b. five weeks

*c. twelve weeks

d. fifteen weeks

47) What is the concept of *individualism*?

a. The idea that individuals, with some assistance from the government, are responsible for their own well-being.

b. The notion that individuals, with some assistance from the greater society, are responsible for their own well-being.

*c. The idea that individuals, not the society or the community or the government, are responsible for their own well-being.

d. None of the above.

48) What do *social democrats* believe?

a. Members of a society are responsible for one another with the exception of some assistance from the government.

b. Members of a society are responsible for one another and should support other developing countries.

*c. Members of a society are responsible for one another.

d. None of the above

49) Social democracies are based on ____, the idea that people have a tight bond and are responsible for one another.

*a. solidarity

b. social cohesiveness

c. interdependence

d. social collaboration

50) Which economist famously wrote, "The world runs on individuals pursuing their separate interests"?

a. Susan Richards

b. Michael Samuels

*c. Milton Friedman

d. Roger Hernandez

51) Individualism points toward limited government, faith in economic markets, and a strong emphasis on

*a. negative liberty.

b. positive liberty.

c. a mixture of positive and negative liberty.

d. none of the above

52) By 1860, how many black slaves were in America?

a. Two million

*b. Four million

c. Three million

d. One million

53) Benjamin Franklin perfected a classic American literary form—tips for getting rich. Which of the following was a slogan of his?

a. "A penny saved is a penny earned"

b. "No gains without pains"

c. "God helps those who help themselves"

*d. all of the above

54) Which president said, "as government expands, liberty contracts"?

a. George W. Bush

b. Bill Clinton

*c. Ronald Reagan

d. Jimmy Carter

55) Today, which of the following statements is a correct assessment of America's economic milieu?

a. The top 1 percent of Americans own more than the bottom 90 percent.

b. Three million people enjoy more wealth than 290 million others.

c. Sixty million Americans at the bottom of the charts own almost nothing—one-tenth of one percent of the national wealth.

*d. all of the above

56) President Franklin Roosevelt said, "If they teach us that our true ____ is . . . to minister . . . to our ____ man."

a. quest... fallen

*b. destiny... fellow

c. fate... brethren

d. none of the above

57) In comparison with other wealthy nations, our taxes are relatively ___, we regulate business less, we take ____ vacations, and we place more stress on getting ahead.

a. high... fewer

b. high... more

*c. low... fewer

d. low... more

58) The _____ is a belief that anyone who works hard can get ahead and grow wealthy.

a. social democracy

b. American democracy

*c. American dream

d. individualism

59) What does *equality* mean?

a. Every citizen, man or woman, enjoys the same privileges, status, and rights before the laws.

*b. Every citizen enjoys the same privileges, status, and rights before the laws.

c. Every male citizen enjoys the same privileges, status, and rights before the laws.

d. None of the above.

60) ____ means that all individuals enjoy the same status in society.

*a. Social equality

b. Democratic equality

c. Socialism

d. Equal opportunity

61) _____ means that every citizen has the same political rights and opportunities.

*a. Political equality

b. Social equality

c. Democratic equality

d. Political outcome

62) ____ focuses on differences in wealth.

a. Social equality

b. Political equality

*c. Economic equality

d. none of the above

63) The ____ is one measure of economic inequality.

a. economic coefficient

*b. Gini coefficient

c. social coefficient

d. Reagan coefficient

64) Today, American society has become far less equal than which of the following countries?

a. Japan

b. Sweden

c. Germany

*d. all of the above

65) We are now ____ the inequality levels of less-developed nations, like Argentina or South Africa.

*a. closer to

b. passing

c. moving away from

d. none of the above

66) _____ is the idea that every American has an equal chance.

a. American dream

b. Democracy

*c. Equal opportunity

d. Equal outcome

67) _____ is the idea that a society guarantees not just an opportunity but also the results. Some nations reserve a minimum number of seats in the national legislature (whether it be a parliament or Congress) for women or members of specific ethnic groups.

*a. Equal outcome

b. Equal opportunity

c. Social democracy

d. American liberty

68) Over time, the United States has gone from the most equal society in the world to one that is considerably less equal than other wealthy nations. The past _____ years, in particular, have seen a very sharp spike in inequality.

a. Twenty-five

*b. Thirty-five

c. Forty

d. Twenty

69) In the 1630s, a large contingent of_____ sailed to New England with an ambitious aim: to establish a biblical commonwealth that would serve as a Christian model for the rest of the world.

a. Catholics

b. Christians

*c. Puritans

d. Quakers

70) Governor John Winthrop called their settlement "a city upon a hill." Where did the verse "city upon a hill" derive from?

a. Governor John Winthrop.

b. A group of Puritan religious leaders.

*c. It is a quotation from the Sermon on the Mount in the New Testament.

d. None of the above.

71) As most nations grow wealthier, their religious fervor wanes. Which of the following countries tell pollsters that God is not very important in their lives?

a. Britain

b. France

c. Japan

*d. All of the above

72) Americans have a lot of religions to choose from. One recent survey found ____ different Christian denominations with more than a million members each.

a. Fifty

b. Twenty-five

*c. Sixteen

d. Thirty

73) In America, Jews number some ____million.

a. 1.5

*b. 6.7

c. 3.0

d. 5.1

74) In the United States, there are nearly ____ Muslims.

*a. 3 million

b. 1 million

c. 5 million

d. 2 million

75) There are ____ other non-Christian groups that have over 100,000 adherents each.

a. five

b. three

*c. seven

d. ten

76) Religious observance is not the same throughout the United States. For example, Texas and Georgia have ___ religiosity.

*a. high

b. medium-level

c. low

d. none of the above

77) Religious observance is not the same throughout the United States. For example, Florida and Missouri have ___ religiosity.

a. high

*b. medium-level

c. low

d. none of the above

78) Religious observance is not the same throughout the United States. Which of the following states is not especially religious?

a. Utah

b. Alabama

*c. Wisconsin

d. Maryland

79) The least religious state is

a. California

b. Florida

*c. Maine

d. Kansas

80) Which of the Founding Fathers described "a wall of separation between church and state"?

a. Benjamin Franklin

*b. Thomas Jefferson

c. John Adams

d. George Washington

81) When did Congress add "under God" to the Pledge of Allegiance?

*a. 1954

b. 1832

c. 1790

d. 1976

82) When did Congress add "In God We Trust" to paper money?

a. 1877

b. 1794

*c. 1955

d. 1991

83) Which of the following ideas are integral to portray the American *political culture*?

a. liberty

b. individualism

c. the American dream

*d. all of the above

84) Why did the framers add a Bill of Rights to the Constitution?

a. Their belief in a social democracy.

b. Their resolution in liberty.

*c. Their abiding faith in individualism.

d. All of the above.

85) Why are there so many checks and balances in our national government?

*a. Because of the old American fear of too much government.

b. Because of Congress's fear of power being usurped.

c. Because of the democratic way.

d. None of the above.

86) Why does the United States regulate and tax less than other nations?

a. Because Americans are too individualistic.

b. Because elected officials are afraid of voters.

*c. Because of the American dream's gospel of success.

d. Because of the American dream's belief of independence.

87) In bureaucratic theory where does control lie?

a. ordinary people

b. wealthy

c. powerful

*d. government workers

88) A classic definition of politics is

*a. who gets what, when, and how

b. live long and prosper

c. early to bed early to rise

d. economy is most important

89) A classic definition of politics is

*a. politics is how a society makes its collective decisions

b. live long and prosper

c. early to bed early to rise

d. economy is most important

90) According to rational-choice theory individuals will

a. work for the greater good

*b. maximize their own self-interest

c. vote for the best looking candidate

d. be hesitant to vote

91) When a driver stops at a red light they are allowing government to

a. snap their picture

b. monitor their driving

*c. set the rules for society

d. control the driving

92) According to the Declaration of Independence why do people form governments

a. to vote

b. to make decisions

c. to fight wards

*d. to secure rights

93) The right to an education is a

*a. positive freedom

b. negative freedom

c. Constitutional right

d. Declaration right

94) American history can be seen as a _____ toward greater liberty.

a. slow walk

*b. steady march

c. fast pace

d. marathon race

95) American history can be seen as a _____ toward greater liberty.

a. slow walk

b. fast pace

*c. back and forth

d. marathon race

96) The most often invoked American value is

a. self-rule

b. limited government

c. individualism

*d. liberty

97) When voters decide whether or not to enlarge the local city water plant they are using which democratic process

*a. referendum

b. initiative

c. sunshine law

d. voter prerogative

98) American government has elements of both

a. democracy and socialism

*b. democracy and a republic

c. socialism and a republic

d. socialism and Unitarianism

99) Another name for a Conservative is

*a. right wing

b. left wing

c. centrist

d. moderate

100) Another name for a Liberal is

a. right wing

*b. left wing

c. centrist

d. moderate

Chapter 2

The Constitution

The Constitution

The Constitution is the framework for the legal system of the United States. The Constitution is divided into Articles and Amendments. It has been added to over the years and courts continue to argue the applications of the Constitution. In terms of the Constitution in this course, it was the founding document for the democracy we live in.

The Preamble

The Preamble of the U.S. Constitution—the document's famous first fifty-two words—introduces everything that is to follow in the Constitution's seven articles and twenty-seven amendments. It proclaims who is adopting this Constitution: "We the People of the United States." It describes why it is being adopted—the purposes behind the enactment of America's charter of government. And it describes what is being adopted: "this Constitution"—a single authoritative written text to serve as fundamental law of the land.

The word "preamble," while accurate, does not quite capture the full importance of this provision. "Preamble" might be taken to imply that these words are merely an opening rhetorical flourish or frill without meaningful effect. To be sure, "preamble" usefully conveys the idea that this provision does not itself confer or delineate powers of government or rights of citizens. Those are set forth in the substantive articles and amendments that follow in the main body of the Constitution's text.

Article 1: Congress

Article 1 sets the framework for Congress. Signed in a convention on September 17, 1787. Ratified June 21, 1788. A portion of Article I, Section 2, was changed by the 14th Amendment; a portion of Section 9 was changed by the 16th Amendment; a portion of Section 3 was changed by the 17th Amendment; a portion of Section 4 was changed by the 20th Amendment

The text of the U.S. Constitution begins with a description of the legislative branch of the government or the "Congress." In fact, the first three articles of the Constitution deal in turn with the three branches of the federal government: legislative (Congress), executive (President), and judicial (Supreme Court). These branches were designed to compete with each other – to have overlapping and competing interests, so no single branch or person could possess complete authority. In the wake of the American Revolution, the founders were left with a distaste for the monarchy, and they created a system whose very structure lends toward a separation of powers. Article I is made up of ten sections, which can be thought generally of as answering three separate questions: What is the Congress (Sections 1-3)? How does Congress work (Sections 4-7)? What can Congress do or not do (Sections 8-10)? Below, is section one, which is uniquely short and straightforward.

Article 2: The President

Article 2 sets the framework for defining the role of the President. Signed in the convention on September 17, 1787. Ratified June 21, 1788. Portions of Article II, Section 1, were changed by the 12th Amendment and the 25th Amendment

Article 2 of the Constitution establishes the Executive branch of the federal government. It defines the office of President and Vice President, and an Electoral College to elect them. Article II also sets the requirements needed to be President, establishes the President's powers, and provides for a President's removal of office for high crimes and misdemeanors, as well as the removal of any civil officer for similar reasons.

Article 3: The Courts

Article 3 established the Court system and used four sections to define the role of the courts. Signed in the convention on September 17, 1787. Ratified June 21, 1788. A portion of Article III, Section 2, was changed by the 11th Amendment

Article III of the Constitution identifies the third branch of our separated government, empowering the courts to decide cases and limiting them to the exercise of a certain kind of authority. It establishes the Supreme Court of the United States and defines the crime of treason, the only crime listed in the Constitution.

Section 1.

The judicial power of the United States shall be vested in one Supreme Court, and in such inferior courts as the Congress may from time to time ordain and establish. The judges, both of the supreme and inferior courts, shall hold their offices during good behavior, and shall, at stated times, receive for their services, a compensation, which shall not be diminished during their continuance in office.

Section 2.

The judicial power shall extend to all cases, in law and equity, arising under this Constitution, the laws of the United States, and treaties made, or which shall be made, under their authority;--to all cases affecting ambassadors, other public ministers and consuls;--to all cases of admiralty and maritime jurisdiction;--to controversies to which the United States shall be a party;--to controversies between two or more states;--between a state and citizens of another state;--between citizens of different states;--between citizens of the same state claiming lands under grants of different states, and between a state, or the citizens thereof, and foreign states, citizens or subjects.

In all cases affecting ambassadors, other public ministers and consuls, and those in which a state shall be a party, the Supreme Court shall have original jurisdiction. In all the other cases before mentioned, the Supreme Court shall have appellate jurisdiction, both as to law and fact, with such exceptions, and under such regulations as the Congress shall make.

The trial of all crimes, except in cases of impeachment, shall be by jury; and such trial shall be held in the state where the said crimes shall have been committed; but when not committed within any state, the trial shall be at such place or places as the Congress may by law have directed.

Section 3.

Treason against the United States shall consist only in levying war against them, or in adhering to their enemies, giving them aid and comfort. No person shall be convicted of treason unless on the testimony of two witnesses to the same overt act, or on confession in open court.

The Congress shall have the power to declare the punishment of treason, but no attainder of treason shall work corruption of blood or forfeiture except during the life of the person attainted.

Section 4.

Signed in the convention on September 17, 1787. Ratified June 21, 1788. A portion of Article IV, Section 2, was changed by the 13th Amendment

The United States shall guarantee to every state in this union a republican form of government and shall protect each of them against invasion, and on the application of the legislature, or of the executive (when the legislature cannot be convened) against domestic violence.

Article 5: Amendments

Article 5 defines how amendments can be made to the Constitution. Article 5 was signed in the convention on September 17, 1787. Ratified June 21, 1788. Article 5 stipulates that

The Congress, whenever two thirds of both houses shall deem it necessary, shall propose amendments to this Constitution, or, on the application of the legislatures of two thirds of the several states, shall call a convention for proposing amendments, which, in either case, shall be valid to all intents and purposes, as part of this Constitution, when ratified by the legislatures of three fourths of the several states, or by conventions in three fourths thereof, as the one or the other mode of ratification may be proposed by the Congress; provided that no amendment which may be made prior to the year one thousand eight hundred and eight shall in any manner affect the first and fourth clauses in the ninth section of the first article; and that no state, without its consent, shall be deprived of its equal suffrage in the Senate.

Article 4: Relations Between the States

Article 4 defines the relationship between the States and uses three sections to do this. One of the major terminologies is called the "full faith and credit clause."

Section 1.

Full faith and credit shall be given in each state to the public acts, records, and judicial proceedings of every other state. And the Congress may by general laws prescribe the manner in which such acts, records, and proceedings shall be proved, and the effect thereof.

Section 2.

The citizens of each state shall be entitled to all privileges and immunities of citizens in the several states.

A person charged in any state with treason, felony, or other crime, who shall flee from justice, and be found in another state, shall on demand of the executive authority of the state from which he fled, be delivered up, to be removed to the state having jurisdiction of the crime.

No person held to service or labor in one state, under the laws thereof, escaping into another, shall, in consequence of any law or regulation therein, be discharged from such service or labor, but shall be delivered up on claim of the party to whom such service or labor may be due.

Section 3.

New states may be admitted by the Congress into this union; but no new states shall be formed or erected within the jurisdiction of any other state; nor any state be formed by the junction of two or more states, or parts of states, without the consent of the legislatures of the states concerned as well as of the Congress.

The Congress shall have the power to dispose of and make all needful rules and regulations respecting the territory or other property belonging to the United States, and nothing in this Constitution shall be so construed as to prejudice any claims of the United States or of any particular state.

Article 6: The Law of the Land

Article 6 defines the supremacy of the law of the land. Article 6 was signed in a convention on September 17, 1787 and it was ratified June 21, 1788.

All debts contracted and engagements entered into, before the adoption of this Constitution, shall be as valid against the United States under this Constitution, as under the Confederation.

This Constitution, and the laws of the United States which shall be made in pursuance thereof; and all treaties made, or which shall be made, under the authority of the United States, shall be the supreme law of the land; and the judges in every state shall be bound thereby, anything in the Constitution or laws of any State to the contrary notwithstanding.

The Senators and Representatives before mentioned, and the members of the several state legislatures, and all executive and judicial officers, both of the United States and of the several states, shall be bound by oath or affirmation, to support this Constitution; but no religious test shall ever be required as a qualification to any office or public trust under the United States.

Article 7: Ratification

Article 7 defines how the Consitution must be ratified. Article 7 was signed in the convention on September 17, 1787 and ratified June 21, 1788. Article 7 defines that the ratification of the conventions of nine states shall be sufficient for the establishment of this Constitution between the states so ratifying the same.

Multiple Choice Questions

1) The document America considers its "owners' manual" is

a. the Declaration of Independence.

b. the Articles of Confederation.

*c. the Constitution.

d. the Magna Carta.

2) The document that takes the ideas of the Declaration of Independence and turns them into laws and institutions is

a. the Articles of Confederation.

b. the Magna Carta.

c. the Mayflower Compact.

*d. the Constitution.

3) There are ___ articles in the United States Constitution and ____ amendments in the Bill of Rights.

*a. 7, 10

b. 7, 27

c. 10, 17

d. 7, 26

4) Article 7 requires ___ states to ratify the Constitution of 1787.

a. all

b. thirteen

c. six

*d. nine

5) All of the following are features that propelled the framers toward the Constitutional Convention of 1787, except

a. representation.

b. violent borders.

c. social mobility.

*d. abolitionism.

6) In England in the eighteenth century the notion that members of Parliament should be guided by their sense of "the general good" regardless of the district they represented was known as

a. constituency service.

*b. trustee representation.

c. delegate representation.

d. "better men" representation.

7) One Act of Parliament the colonists found particularly repugnant required them to house British troops in barns and warehouses; it was called the

a. Stamp Act.

b. Redcoat Accommodation Act.

*c. Quartering Act.

d. English Occupation Act.

8) The Boston Massacre was precipitated by the

a. Impoundment Act.

b. Tea Party.

*c. Townshend Act.

d. *Amistad.*

9) On a December night in 1773, fifty Boston colonists "dressed in the Indian manner" dumped 342 chests of____ into Boston Harbor.

a. whiskey

*b. tea

c. molasses

d. cotton

10) Due to continued requirements for the colonists to house, or "quarter," British soldiers at colonists' expense, they wrote into the Bill of Rights

a. the Fifth Amendment.

b. the Fourth Amendment.

*c. the Third Amendment.

d. the Second Amendment.

11) The key statement of American political philosophy is

a. the Constitution.

b. the Emancipation Proclamation.

c. the Mayflower Compact.

*d. the Declaration of Independence.

12) The colonists favored the model of representation where members of the legislature responded to constituents' desires, known as

a. the trustee model.

b. the parliamentary model.

*c. the delegate model.

d. the politico model.

13) The Declaration of Independence was adopted on

a. July 4, 1774.

b. July 4, 1775.

*c. July 4, 1776.

d. July 4, 1787.

14) The Declaration of Independence details all of the following American ideals except

a. life, liberty, and the pursuit of happiness.

*b. capitalism and the protection of private property.

c. all men are created equal.

d. people form governments to protect rights that they are "endowed" with and which cannot be taken away.

15) The political philosopher that had enormous impact on revolutionary America and the thinking of the framers was

a. Tocqueville.

b. Robespierre.

c. Hobbes.

*d. Locke.

16) The second half of the Declaration of Independence lists twenty-seven

a. God-given rights.

b. principles of government.

*c. grievances against the King George III.

d. principles of democracy.

17) Identify the three complaints against the English Crown that dominate the Declaration of Independence.

*a. representation, occupying army, loss of an independent court

b. representation, taxes, loss of an independent court

c. taxation without representation, the tax on tea, and British impressments of American sailors

d. taxation without representation, the quartering of soldiers, and the Stamp Act

18) The Declaration of Independence states that liberty is a right that is

a. quite important.

b. fundamental to happiness.

*c. unalienable.

d. subject to the whims of governments—it can be taken away.

19) In 1776, for the first time in world history, the American colonists made the claim that government

a. must be limited.

b. must protect private property.

*c. derives its power from the consent of the governed.

d. must be subject to frequent elections.

20) The Founding Father who stated "that laws and institutions must go hand in hand with the progress of the human mind" was

a. George Washington.

b. James Madison.

*c. Thomas Jefferson.

d. John Adams.

21) The Articles of Confederation were approved by the First Continental Congress in

a. 1620.

b. 1776.

*c. 1777.

d. 1787.

22) Under the Articles of Confederation, ___ votes were required on important matters.

a. thirteen

b. seven

c. four

*d. nine

23) Among the serious obstacles to the new government under the Articles of Confederation,

*a. Congress could not raise taxes and had no money of its own.

b. Virginia dominated all policy discussions.

c. The southern states were in open rebellion.

d. North Carolina had brokered treaties with foreign powers.

24) The provision that all thirteen states must approve any changes to the Articles of Confederation

a. facilitated the amendment process.

b. made it difficult to conduct foreign affairs.

c. gave the states too little power.

*d. made it virtually impossible to amend the Articles.

25) A major lesson learned from our experience under the Articles of Confederation

a. was that a strong confederation of states was impossible.

*b. was that a weak central government left the nation vulnerable.

c. was the need for a Supreme Court.

d. was the alliance between Rhode Island and South Carolina.

26) An event in 1786 that dramatized the problems of governing the new nation under the Articles of Confederation was

a. Benedict Arnold's treachery.

b. George Washington's refusal to run for president without a new Constitution.

*c. Shays's Rebellion.

d. the French and Indian War.

27) The constitutional deliberations were

a. open to the public

b. very quick

*c. secret

d. attended by delegates from only 8 states

28) The Articles showed the founding fathers that a weak government could

a. support rights

*b. Fail to protect rights

c. Create new rights

d. abuse power

29) The Founders adopted a federal system

a. because they hoped King George III would approve.

b. because they were inspired by John Locke, who advocated such a division of powers.

c. because the division of sovereignty between a strong central government and regional governments is a basic principle of all democratic governments.

*d. as a compromise between those who wanted a strong central government and those who wanted to retain strong state governments.

30) Which of the following is NOT a difference between the Virginia Plan and the New Jersey Plan?

a. The Virginia Plan created stronger state governments.

b. The New Jersey Plan created a single legislature, whereas the Virginia Plan called for a bicameral legislature.

*c. The Virginia Plan strengthened the national government, whereas the New Jersey Plan weakened the national government.

d. The New Jersey Plan had multiple chief executives, whereas the Virginia Plan created a one-person executive.

31) The Great, or Connecticut, Compromise

a. provided strong powers to state governments.

*b. established a legislature with equal state representation in the Senate and proportional representation in the House of Representatives.

c. limited the importation of slaves until 1808.

d. created a confederacy of state governments.

32) Some delegates at the Constitutional Convention were concerned that an executive would be

*a. too powerful.

b. too weak.

c. too subject to "the whims of the people."

d. someone who was not an American.

33) The delegates did not want people electing the president because they felt people

a. would be swayed by political parties

b. would not vote

*c. had enough information or wisdom

d. did not want to elect the president

34) Why did the framers not give the popular-vote winner the presidency?

*a. They did not trust the judgment of voters.

b. Women could not vote.

c. The country had a bad history of electing corrupt politicians.

d. The Electoral College was more efficient.

35) The number of electors in a state is based on

a. the number of people in the state.

b. the number of voters in the state.

*c. the number of senators plus the number of members of the House of Representatives.

d. the number of members in the state legislature.

36) In what year did no presidential candidate receive a majority in the Electoral College?

a. 2000

b. 2008

c. 1820

*d. 1824

37) How many times has the popular-vote winner not been elected president because he did not win a majority in the Electoral College?

a. Six times

*b. Five times

c. One time

d. Twelve times

38) For each power described in the Constitution for a branch of government,

a. there is an appropriation process independent of the other branches.

*b. there is a "countervailing" power.

c. there is a federal agency.

d. there is a way for the other branches to destroy that branch.

39) The president is the commander in chief, but Congress has the power to declare war. This is an example of

a. the imperial presidency.

b. the imperial Congress.

*c. checks and balances.

d. judicial neutrality.

40) How did the Founders treat slavery in the Constitution?

a. It was not important.

b. It was so divisive they had to tackle it head-on.

c. They were unified in their desire to eliminate it.

*d. It was so divisive they did not mention it directly.

41) The practice of counting slaves as fractional "persons" for representation in the House of Representatives is known as

a. the "Not-Quite" Compromise.

*b. the Three-Fifths Compromise.

c. the Two-Thirds Compromise.

d. the Three-Quarters Compromise.

42) During the Constitutional Convention, the state with the highest percentage of slaves out of the total population, at 43 percent, was

a. Virginia.

b. Massachusetts.

c. Texas.

*d. South Carolina.

43) If the institution of slavery had not been protected in the Constitution,

*a. the southern states would have walked out.

b. Massachusetts would have immediately abolished slavery.

c. North Carolina would have seceded from the Union.

d. Texas would have never been admitted to the Union.

44) The first three words of the Constitution are

a. "Fourscore and seven . . . "

b. "In order to . . . "

*c. "We the People . . . "

d. "My fellow Americans . . . "

45) In 1787, a member of the House of Representatives had around 30,000 constituents. Today that number is approximately

a. 50,000.

b. 150,000.

c. 350,000.

*d. 700,000.

46) A large-scale program like Social Security is constitutionally legitimate because

*a. Congress can write any law it deems "necessary and proper."

b. there is a need to protect old people.

c. old people vote.

d. the executive branch has extensive powers to make laws under article 2.

47) Far and away the longest and most detailed section of the Constitution is

a. the First Amendment.

*b. article 1.

c. article 2.

d. article 3.

48) Constitutionally, members of the US House of Representatives must be____ years of age.

a. 18

*b. 25

c. 30

d. 35

49) Constitutionally, members of the US Senate must be____ years of age.

a. 18

b. 25

*c. 30

d. 35

50) All of the following are powers granted to Congress under article 1, section 8, of the Constitution except

a. the power to declare war.

*b. the power to command the armed forces.

c. the power to collect taxes.

d. the power to coin money.

51) The necessary and proper clause

a. allows Congress to regulate commerce.

b. allows Congress to control the money supply.

*c. gives Congress a great deal of creative leeway.

d. it has defined boundaries.

52) According to article 1, section 9 of the Constitution, habeas corpus may not be suspended unless

a. Americans gather to protest for the overthrow of the government.

b. an election takes place.

c. a majority of Congress votes to suspend.

*d. in cases of rebellion or invasion the public safety requires it.

53) Originally, each state decided how it chose its electors for the Electoral College, but now

a. every state has the minority party select them.

b. Twenty-seven states have the people make the choice.

c. Seventeen states have the people make the choice.

*d. all states have the people make the choice.

54) Treaties made by presidents are constitutionally valid if

*a. two-thirds of the Senate approve.

b. two-thirds of the House of Representatives approve.

c. three-quarters of the Senate approve.

d. three-quarters of the House of Representative approve.

55) The case in which Chief Justice John Marshall established judicial review, giving the Supreme Court the power to overturn an act of Congress, was

a. *Wickard v. Fillburn.*

b. *Brown v. Topeka Board of Education.*

*c. *Marbury v. Madison.*

d. *Barron v. Baltimore.*

56) The section of the Constitution that deals with the relationship between the states is

a. article 1.

b. article 2.

c. article 3.

*d. article 4.

57) Two, and only two, provisions of the Constitution are expressly not amendable: the continuation of the slave trade until 1808 and

*a. the requirement that each state have equal representation in the United States Senate.

b. freedom of the press.

c. freedom of religion.

d. the House of Representatives will have 435 members elected for two-year terms.

58) Why is the Constitution the "supreme law of the land"?

a. Because the framers were divinely inspired.

b. Because states don't have constitutions.

*c. Because article 6 says so.

d. Because the Articles of Confederation coexisted with the new Constitution.

59) The only amendment to be ratified by state convention was

a. the Eleventh.

b. the Twelfth.

c. the Sixteenth.

*d. the Twenty-first.

60) The Bill of Rights was added to the Constitution in order to

a. pacify Rhode Island.

b. satisfy the demands of Thomas Jefferson.

*c. pacify Anti-Federalists.

d. pacify Federalists.

61) Federalists

a. were loyal to the Articles of Confederation.

*b. advocated the adoption of the Constitution of 1787.

c. were loyal to King George III.

d. wanted stronger states' rights.

62) During the ratification debate, which of the following was NOT a major criticism by the Anti-Federalists of the new Constitution?

a. The president looked too much like a king.

b. The national government was too powerful and citizens did not have enough influence.

*c. The Supreme Court had too much power.

d. There was no Bill of Rights.

63) The central goal of the delegates to the Constitutional Convention was to

a. increase the power of the states.

b. increase the power of the people.

c. increase the democratic nature of government.

*d. increase the power of the national government.

64) The Federalist Papers did NOT serve which of the following purposes?

a. pro-constitutional editorials

b. examples of American political theory

*c. partisan arguments for a George Washington presidency

d. guides to the thinking of the framers

65) In Federalist no. 10, James Madison is concerned about the dangers of factions because

a. he anticipated problems with campaign financing.

*b. powerful interests can capture government and expand their self-interest at the expense of minorities.

c. they would create political parties.

d. a charismatic leader might take over the government and refuse to recognize election outcomes.

66) In Madison's political thought, a large government

*a. will have many diverse interests, so no one interest will be able to dominate.

b. is always bad.

c. is inevitable.

d. is more likely to be oppressive.

67) The first ten amendments to the Constitution are known as

a. The Preamble

*b. Bill of Rights

c. Article 8

d. Necessary and Proper Clause

68) Virginia, the most powerful state, voted in favor of the Constitution

*a. 89–79.

b. unanimously.

c. after seventeen ballots.

d. Virginia did not approve the new Constitution.

69) In Federalist no. 51, Madison argues for what kind of government structure to ensure "ambition . . . be made to counteract ambition"?

a. a democracy

b. a direct democracy

*c. a separation of powers in the national government

d. a representative democracy

70) All of the following groups were excluded from voting rights under the original Constitution except

a. women.

b. African Americans.

c. Native Americans.

*d. property-owning white males.

71) The Bill of Rights were incorporated to the states through the

*a. Fourteenth Amendment

b. Fifteenth Amendment

c. Sixteenth Amendment

d. Bill of Rights did not need incorporating

72) How many nations in the eighteenth century had similar documents to the American Constitution?

a. 7

*b. 0

c. 4

d. 9

73) The first colonial legislature was elected in

a. 1776

b. 1736

*c. 1620

d. 1589

74) The signing of the Mayflower Compact helped lead the colonists to

a. more religious freedom

b. Bill of Rights

c. elected President

*d. Constitution

75) The American Revolution can be traced to what English War?

*a. French and Indian War

b. 100 Years War

c. War of the Roses

d. War of Quebec

76) Britain's demand for _____ provoked the colonists.

a. allegiance

*b. money

c. tea

d. cotton

77) An American ship that traded with Spanish colonists in Florida was guilty of

a. international trade

b. conscription

*c. smuggling

d. nationalism

78) A common way of raising money in England that set off a firestorm in the colonies was

a. taxing cotton

b. Quartering Act

c. taxing weapons

*d. Stamp Tax

79) The colonial authority which collected taxes was the

*a. American Board of Customs

b. English Board of Customs

c. Tax Authority of the Colonies

d. Parliamentary Representatives

80) The first blood to fall was that of

a. Nathan Hale

*b. Crispus Attucks

c. John Adams

d. Patrick Henry

81) The must have product of the eighteenth century that the British controlled for the colonists was

a. cotton

b. syrup

*c. tea

d. linen

82) The American revolutions was different rather than demanding new _____, they were fighting for _____ they had been exercising.

a. ideas; ideas

b. rights; ideas

c. ideas; rights

*d. rights; rights

83) The Second Continental Congress faced the job of

*a. declaring independence

b. paying the army

c. building a navy

d. creating a new government

84) An alliance of independent states is also known as a

a. democracy

*b. confederation

c. independent alliance

d. republic

85) What type of person did the delegates think should represent the public?

a. any male

b. family men

*c. educated, wealthy men

d. farmers

86) Which of the following could a member of the public vote for in 1788?

a. president

b. Virginia Senator

c. Supreme Court Justice

*d. Massachusetts Representative

87) The Articles of Confederation gave most power to the _____ while the new Constitution gave more power to the _____.

*a. states; national government

b. national government; states

c. states; states

d. national government; national government

88) _____ states wanted representation based on population.

a. small

*b. large

c. coastal

d. southern

89) The _____ Plan put forth a unicameral legislature.

a. Virginia

*b. New Jersey

c. Connecticut

d. Massachusetts

90) As a result of checks and balances when the president nominates a Supreme Court Justice the _____ must confirm them before they take office.

a. House

b. States

*c. Senate

d. voters

91) How many presidents have faced formal impeachment proceedings?

a. 0

b. 1

c. 2

*d. 3

92) According to the Constitution who organizes courts, aside from the Supreme Court?

*a. Congress

b. Supreme Court

c. President

d. States

93) According to the Constitution every state must have a _____ form of government.

a. Democratic

*b. Republican

c. Socialist

d. States can choose

94) One author of the Federalist Papers was

a. George Washington

b. Benjamin Franklin

*c. Alexander Hamilton

d. John Adams

95) The first state to ratify the Constitution was

a. Virginia

b. Georgia

c. South Carolina

*d. Delaware

96) The most recent right incorporated to the states is the

*a. Second

b. Fourth

c. Sixth

d. Eighth

97) Guaranteeing the right to vote to eighteen-year-olds is an example of

*a. extending rights

b. adjusting election rules

c. affecting government powers over individuals

d. changing government operations

98) Limiting the president to two terms is an example of

a. extending rights

*b. adjusting election rules

c. affecting government powers over individuals

d. changing government operations

99) Switching Inauguration Day from March to January is an example of

a. extending rights

b. adjusting election rules

c. affecting government powers over individuals

*d. changing government operations

100) Prohibiting alcohol is an example of

a. extending rights

b. adjusting election rules

*c. affecting government powers over individuals

d. extending rights

Chapter 3

Federalism and Nationalism

Commerce Clause

The Commerce Clause refers to Article 1, Section 8, Clause 3 of the U.S. Constitution, which gives Congress the power "to regulate commerce with foreign nations, and among the several states, and with the Indian."

Congress has often used the Commerce Clause to justify exercising legislative power over the activities of states and their citizens, leading to significant and ongoing controversy regarding the balance of power between the federal government and the states. The Commerce Clause has historically been viewed as both a grant of congressional authority and as a restriction on the regulatory authority of the States.

"Dormant" Commerce Clause

The "Dormant Commerce Clause" refers to the prohibition, implicit in the Commerce Clause, against states passing legislation that discriminates against or excessively burdens interstate commerce. Of particular importance here, is the prevention of protectionist state policies that favor state citizens or businesses at the expense of non-citizens conducting business within that state. In West Lynn Creamery Inc. v. Healy, 512 U.S. 186 (1994), the Supreme Court struck down a Massachusetts state tax on milk products, as the tax impeded interstate commercial activity by discriminating against non-Massachusetts business.

The Meaning Of "Commerce."

The meaning of the word "commerce" is a source of controversy, as the Constitution does not explicitly define the word. Some argue that it refers simply to trade or exchange, while others claim that the Framers of the Constitution intended to describe more broadly commercial and social intercourse between citizens of different states. Thus, the interpretation of "commerce" affects the appropriate dividing line between federal and state power. Moreover, what constitutes "interstate" commercial activity has also been subject to consistent debate.

Broad Interpretation

In Gibbons v. Ogden, 22 U.S. 1 (1824), the Supreme Court held that intrastate activity could be regulated under the Commerce Clause, provided that the activity is part of a larger interstate commercial scheme. In Swift and Company v. United States, 196 U.S. 375 (1905), the Supreme Court held that Congress had the authority to regulate local commerce, as long as that activity could become part of a continuous "current" of commerce that involved the interstate movement of goods and services.

From about 1905 until about 1937, the Supreme Court used a narrow version of the Commerce Clause. However, beginning with NLRB v. Jones & Laughlin Steel Corp, 301 U.S. 1 (1937), the Court recognized broader grounds upon which the Commerce Clause could be used to regulate state activity. Most importantly, the Supreme Court held that activity was commerce if it had a "substantial economic effect" on interstate commerce or if the "cumulative effect" of one act could have an effect on such commerce. Decisions such as NLRB v. Jones, United States v. Darby, 312 U.S. 100 (1941) and Wickard v. Filburn, 317 U.S. 111 (1942) demonstrated the Court's willingness to give an unequivocally broad interpretation of the Commerce Clause. Recognizing the development of a dynamic and integrated national economy, the Court employed a broad interpretation of the Commerce Clause, reasoning the even local activity will likely affect the larger interstate commercial economic scheme.

Shift To A Stricter Interpretation

From the NLRB decision in 1937 until 1995, the Supreme Court did not invalidate a single law on the basis of the Commerce Clause. In 1995, the Supreme Court attempted to curtail Congress's broad legislative mandate under the Commerce Clause by returning to a more conservative interpretation of the clause in United States v. Lopez, 514 U.S. 549 (1995). In Lopez, the defendant, in this case, was charged with carrying a handgun to school in violation of the federal Gun-Free School Zones Act of 1990. The defendant argued that the federal government had no authority to regulate firearms in local schools, while the government claimed that this fell under the Commerce Clause, arguing that possession of a firearm in a school zone would lead to violent crime, thereby affecting general economic conditions. The Supreme Court rejected the government's argument, holding that Congress only has the power to regulate the channels of commerce, the instrumentalities of commerce, and action that substantially affects interstate commerce. The Court declined to further expand the Commerce Clause, writing that "[t]o do so would require us to conclude that the Constitution's enumeration of powers does not presuppose something not enumerated and that there never will be a distinction between what is truly national and what is truly local. This we are unwilling to do."

In Gonzales v. Raich, 545 U.S. 1 (2005), however, the Court did return to its more liberal construction of the Commerce Clause in relation to intrastate production. In Gonzales, the Court upheld federal regulation of intrastate marijuana production.

Recently, the Supreme Court addressed the Commerce Clause in NFIB v. Sebelius, 567 US. 519 (2012). In Sebelius, the Court addressed the individual mandate in the Affordable Cart Act (AFA), which sought to require uninsured individuals to secure health insurance in an attempt to stabilize the health insurance market. Focusing on Lopez's requirement that Congress regulate only commercial activity, the Court held that the individual mandate could not be enacted under the Commerce Clause. The Court stated that requiring the purchase of health insurance under the AFA was not the regulation of commercial activity so much as inactivity and was, accordingly, impermissible under the Commerce Clause.

Necessary and Proper Clause

The "Necessary and Proper Clause," formally drafted as Clause 18 of Article 1 of the U.S. Constitution, is one of the most powerful and important clauses in the Constitution. Clauses 1–17 of Article 1 enumerate all of the powers that the government has over the legislation of the country. Clause 18 gives Congress the ability to create structures organizing the government, and to write new legislation to support the explicit powers enumerated in Clauses 1–17.

Article I, Section 8, Clause 18 allows the Government of the United States to:

> "make all laws which shall be necessary and proper for carrying into execution the foregoing powers, and all other powers vested by this constitution."

The definitions of "necessary," "proper," and "carrying into execution" have all been debated since the words were written during the Constitutional Convention in Philadelphia in 1787. There is a strong possibility that it was kept purposefully vague.

Necessary and Proper Clause

The Necessary and Proper clause of the U.S. Constitution provides Congress the power to fulfill its legal powers. Also known as the "elastic clause," it was written into the Constitution in 1787. The first Supreme Court case against the clause was in 1819 when Maryland objected to Alexander Hamilton's formation of a National Bank. The Necessary and Proper clause has been used in cases about many things, including challenges about Obamacare, legalizing marijuana, and collective bargaining.

Purpose of the Elastic Clause

In general, the main purpose of this "elastic" clause, also known as the "sweeping" or "general clause," is to give Congress the flexibility to get the other 17 enumerated powers achieved. Congress is limited in its power over the American people, to only those powers specifically written into the Constitution, such as determine who can be a citizen, collect taxes, establish post offices, and set up a judiciary. The existence of that list of powers implies that Congress can make laws necessary to ensure that those powers can be carried out. Clause 18 makes that explicit.

For example, the government could not collect taxes, which power is enumerated as Clause 1 in Article 1, Section 8, without passing a law to create a tax-collecting agency, which is not enumerated. Clause 18 has been used for all sorts of federal actions including requiring integration in the states—for instance, whether a National Bank can be created (implied in Clause 2), to Obamacare and the ability of states to legalize the growing and distribution of marijuana (both Clause 3).

In addition, the elastic clause allows the Congress to create the hierarchical structure to enact the other 17 clauses: to build a lower court (Clause 9), to set up an organized militia (Clause 15), and to organize a post office distribution method (Clause 7).

The Powers of Congress

According to Article 1, section 8, of the Constitution, Congress has the following 18 powers and only the following powers:

- To lay and collect Taxes, Duties, Imposts, and Excises, to pay the Debts and provide for the common Defence and general Welfare of the United States; but all Duties, Imposts and Excises shall be uniform throughout the United States;
- To borrow Money on the credit of the United States;
- To regulate Commerce with foreign Nations, and among the several States, and with the Indian Tribes;
- To establish a uniform Rule of Naturalization, and uniform Laws on the subject of Bankruptcies throughout the United States;
- To coin Money, regulate the Value thereof, and of foreign Coin, and fix the Standard of Weights and Measures;
- To provide for the Punishment of counterfeiting the Securities and current Coin of the United States;
- To establish Post Offices and post Roads;
- To promote the Progress of Science and useful Arts, by securing for limited Times to Authors and Inventors the exclusive Right to their respective Writings and Discoveries;

- To constitute Tribunals inferior to the Supreme Court;
- To define and punish Piracies and Felonies committed on the high Seas, and Offences against the Law of Nations;
- To declare War, grant Letters of Marque and Reprisal, and make Rules concerning Captures on Land and Water;
- To raise and support Armies, but no Appropriation of Money to that Use shall be for a longer Term than two Years;
- To provide and maintain a Navy;
- To make Rules for the Government and Regulation of the land and naval Forces;
- To provide for calling forth the Militia to execute the Laws of the Union, suppress Insurrections and repel Invasions;
- To provide for organizing, arming, and disciplining, the Militia, and for governing such Part of them as may be employed in the Service of the United States, reserving to the States respectively, the Appointment of the Officers, and the Authority of training the Militia according to the discipline prescribed by Congress;
- To exercise exclusive Legislation in all Cases whatsoever, over such District (not exceeding ten Miles square) as may, by Cession of particular States, and the Acceptance of Congress, become the Seat of the Government of the United States, and to exercise like Authority over all Places purchased by the Consent of the Legislature of the State in which the Same shall be, for the Erection of Forts, Magazines, Arsenals, Dock-Yards, and other needful Buildings;—And
- To make all Laws which shall be necessary and proper for carrying into Execution the foregoing Powers, and all other Powers vested by this Constitution in the Government of the United States, or in any Department or Officer thereof.

The Elastic Clause and the Constitutional Convention

The 18th clause was added to the Constitution by the Committee on Detail without any previous discussion at all, and it was not the subject of debate in Committee, either. That was because the original intent and wording of the Section was not to enumerate Congress's powers at all, but instead to provide an open-ended grant to Congress to "legislate in all cases for the general interests of the Union, and also to those to which the States are separately incompetent, or in which the harmony of the United States may be interrupted by the exercise of individual legislation." Proposed by Delaware politician Gunning Bedford, Jr., that version was roundly rejected by the Committee, who instead enumerated the 17 powers and the 18th to help them get the other 17 completed.

However, Clause 18 was hotly debated in the ratification stage. Opponents objected to the 18th clause saying it was evidence that the Federalists wanted unlimited and undefined powers. The Anti-Federalist delegate from New York, John Williams, said with alarm that it is "perhaps utterly impossible fully to define this power," and "whatever they judge necessary for the proper administration of the powers lodged in them, they may execute without any check or impediment." The Federalist delegate from Virginia George Nicholas said "the Constitution had enumerated all the powers which the general government should have but did not say how they should be exercised. The 'sweeping clause' should only be extended to the enumerated powers."

What Do "Necessary" and "Proper" Mean?

In his finding over the 1819 McCulloch v. Maryland case, Supreme Court Chief Justice John Marshall defined "necessary" to mean "appropriate and legitimate." In the same court case, Thomas Jefferson interpreted that it meant "essential"—an enumerated power would be pointless without the proposed action. James Madison said there had to be an obvious and precise affinity between the power and any implementing law, and Alexander Hamilton said that it meant any law that might be conducive to the implemented power. Notwithstanding the long-term debate over what "necessary" means, the Supreme Court has never found a congressional law unconstitutional because it was not "necessary."

However, more recently, the definition of "proper" was brought up in Printz v. the United States, which challenged the Brady Handgun

Multiple Choice Questions

1) The complex interplay between state, local, and national governments stretches all the way back to the debates between

a. Federalists and Whigs.

*b. Federalists and Anti-Federalists.

c. Republicans and Democrats.

d. Anti-Federalists and Whigs.

2) Which form of government favors a central government exercising all or most political authority?

*a. unitary

b. confederation

c. loosely coupled federation

d. federal

3) Which type of government did the US rebel against?

*a. unitary

b. confederation

c. loosely coupled federation

d. federal

4) When the federal power is weak providing defense and economic benefits it may be a

*a. confederation

b. federation

c. republic

d. democracy

5) Which level(s) of government is/are responsible for regulating business?

a. federal

b. state

c. local

*d. federal and state

6) The hybrid developed by the delegates at the Constitutional Convention was a _____ system.

a. confederal

*b. federal

c. unitary

d. socialist

7) Which of the following is NOT a weakness of a confederation?

*a. more local control over policy

b. weak central authority

c. a variety of contradictory state actions

d. unclear individual rights

8) Public education would be a good example of what kind of power or powers?

a. federal

*b. state

c. concurrent

d. local

9) Which of the following is NOT an advantage of federalism?

*a. coordination across levels of government

b. protecting individual rights

c. providing sources of innovation

d. responsiveness to local needs

10) "Laboratories of democracy" relates to which advantage of federalism?

a. choosing between communities

b. protecting individual rights

*c. providing sources of innovation

d. responsiveness to local needs

11) Spreading policy ideas from one city to another is an example of

a. introduction

*b. diffusion

c. infusion

d. sharing

12) Citizens in Massachusetts desiring greater government involvement in social policies than those in Montana reflect which advantage of federalism?

a. choosing between communities

b. protecting individual rights

c. providing sources of innovation

*d. responsiveness to local needs

13) Which of the following is NOT a disadvantage of federalism?

a. coordination

*b. individual rights

c. poor policies

d. inequalities across layers

14) Which of the following describes competition between states and localities, where providing better social services for poor people will drive out businesses and attract poor people?

a. coordination

*b. race to the bottom

c. poor policies

d. inequalities across layers

15) Which of the following is not a granted power to Congress?

*a. organizing state elections

b. handling US foreign policy

c. establishing post offices

d. raising an army

16) What is the name for a power that is explicitly found in the Constitution?

*a. enumerated

b. necessary and proper

c. implied

d. informal

17) ____ powers could be thought of as those implied by, but not specifically named in, the Constitution.

*a. Inherent

b. Enumerated

c. Expressed

d. Concurrent

18) Which amendment to the Constitution provides the foundation for states' rights?

a. Fourth

*b. Tenth

c. Twelfth

d. Fourteenth

19) The Tenth Amendment is most likely favored by

a. big-government advocates.

b. those favoring dual federalism.

*c. small-government advocates.

d. those with a strong liberal ideology.

20) The Tenth Amendment relates to and demonstrates best which type of powers?

*a. reserved

b. concurrent

c. inherent

d. implied

21) Which of the following is not an example of a reserved power?

a. organizing state elections

*b. coining money

c. public education

d. public health

22) Being able to use your driver's license in any state is an example of the _____ clause.

a. necessary and proper

*b. full faith and credit

c. supremacy

d. inherent powers

23) Which clause to the Constitution says that each state should recognize and uphold laws passed by any other state?

a. necessary and proper

*b. full faith and credit

c. supremacy

d. inherent powers

24) Building railways, borrowing money, and regulating business are examples of ______ powers.

a. police

b. reserved

c. inherent

*d. concurrent

25) The layer cake model demonstrates which era of federalism?

a. cooperative federalism

*b. dual federalism

c. New Federalism

d. "New" New Federalism

26) Under dual federalism, which of the following is NOT one of the three major areas of responsibility for the federal government?

a. international relations

b. internal improvements

c. regulating commerce between the states

*d. providing public education in the states

27) ____ federalism argues for the clear division of governing authority between national and state governments.

*a. Dual

b. Cooperative

c. Coaptive

d. New

28) If Virginia law conflicts with federal law, which clause argues for federal law to be superior?

*a. supremacy

b. full faith and credit

c. elasticity

d. inherent powers

29) The ______ clause says that the national government may wield powers "necessary and proper" to support its function.

a. supremacy

b. full faith and credit

*c. elasticity

d. inherent powers

30) Cooperative federalism is most often attributed to the policies of which president?

a. T. Roosevelt

b. B. Clinton

c. W. Wilson

*d. F. Roosevelt

31) What historical event gave rise to greater cooperation between levels of government?

a. Dust Bowl

*b. Great Depression

c. Civil War

d. Revolutionary War

32) Which of the following is NOT an example of a concurrent power?

a. education

b. transportation

c. taxation

*d. national defense

33) Block grants provide funds for

a. elections

b. any use

*c. specific use

d. urban growth

34) Which of the following is a key feature of New Federalism?

a. grants in aid

*b. heavy use of block grants

c. limited state income tax

d. increased income tax

35) ____ is defined as the transfer of authority from national to state or local governments.

a. Supremacy

*b. Devolution

c. Elastic

d. Power-seeking theory

36) When the federal government requires all schools hire new teachers but does not provide funding for the teachers this is a(n)

a. funded mandate

b. taxable mandate

c. check mandate

*d. unfunded mandate

37) Who is more likely to prefer state control of an issue?

*a. Republicans

b. Democrats

c. Socialists

d. Communists

38) Which of the following is NOT a good example of an unfunded mandate?

a. reducing federal funding for food stamps

*b. first responders subsidies

c. No Child Left Behind Act

d. increasing the minimum wage

39) Republicans continue to urge _____ control on most issues.

a. federal

b. federal and state

*c. state and local

d. federal and local

40) Democrats continue to urge ______ control on most issues.

*a. federal

b. federal and state

c. state and local

d. federal and local

41) The federal government can invalidate a state law that conflicts with federal law through the power of

a. veto

b. diffusion

c. federalism

*d. preemption

42) Which era of federalism favors high levels of national funding and a high degree of national supervision?

a. dual federalism

*b. cooperative federalism

c. New Federalism

d. "New" New Federalism

43) ____ federalism is characterized by clear responsibilities between state and national governments.

*a. Dual

b. Cooperative

c. New

d. "New" New

44) The era when state governments wielded as much authority as the federal government was

a. New Federalism

*b. Dual Federalism

c. Cooperative Federalism

d. Progressive Federalism

45) President Obama's approach to federalism can best be described as falling into which period of the development of federalism?

a. dual federalism

b. cooperative federalism

*c. New Federalism

d. dual cooperative federalism

46) When the national government sets goals for programs and expects the state to achieve them they are practicing

a. cooperative federalism

*b. progressive federalism

c. new federalism

d. original federalism

47) The states and federal government are _____ in progressive federalism.

*a. partners

b. competitors

c. separate

d. alienated

48) The Trump Administration is returning to

*a. New Federalism

b. Progressive Federalism

c. Cooperative Federalism

d. Constitutionalism

49) Through the Court's interpretation of the necessary and proper clause, which institution of government is most affected?

a. the presidency

*b. Congress

c. the bureaucracy

d. independent commissions

50) The Rehnquist Court is famous for emphasizing the rights of which level(s) of government?

a. federal

b. federal and state

*c. state and local

d. federal and local

51) Which Supreme Court case extended to individuals the right to challenge federal statutes on the grounds that they interfere with powers reserved to the states?

a. *Medellin v. Texas*

b. *Citizens United v. Clinton*

c. *Gonzales v. Oregon*

*d. *Bond v. United States*

52) Feelings of nationalism help maintain the federal balance by instilling loyalty to which level(s) of government?

a. federal

b. state

c. local

*d. all of the above

53) In recent years, the Supreme Court has trended toward power to which level(s) of government?

a. federal and state

*b. state and local

c. state

d. federal and local

54) The Supreme Court's review of a law passed by Congress best demonstrates which principle of American government and relates to federalism?

*a. checks and balances

b. supremacy clause

c. nationalism

d. unfunded mandates

55) The juxtaposition that shapes American politics, governing practices, and policy making is best demonstrated by the phrase:

a. relatively strong nation, relatively weak national government.

b. weak nation, strong national government.

*c. strong nation, weak national government.

d. relatively weak nation, relatively strong national government.

56) How does the US government's spending compare to the spending of governments in other developed democracies?

a. It is about the same.

b. It is more.

*c. It is less.

d. It is much larger than all others.

57) Federalism operates along a _____ dimension.

*a. vertical

b. horizontal

c. lateral

d. multidimensional

58) The United States has always emphasized

*a. community participation over centralized administration.

b. centralized administration over community participation.

c. community participation over decentralized administration.

d. decentralized administration over community participation.

59) Which group best demonstrates civic voluntarism?

a. members of Congress

*b. local school board members

c. district court judges

d. local police officers

60) According to the authors, ________ is defined as participation in public life without government involvement.

*a. civic voluntarism

b. bounded rationality

c. volunteer-appreciation

d. civic responsibility

61) What two layers of government interacted to define dual federalism?

*a. national and state

b. state and local

c. national and local

d. national and the nonprofit sector

62) Which "cake" metaphor was introduced during the New Deal?

a. layer cake

b. Bundt cake

*c. marble cake

d. none of the above

63) According to the authors, Americans ________________ and ________________ governing power more extensively than any other modern country.

*a. separate, divide

b. combine, distribute

c. decentralize, divide

d. none of the above

64) A large, diverse and fragmented nation can be bound together through

*a. nationalism

b. federalism

c. voting

d. borders

65) A reason for historical shifts in the Supreme Court can be traced to

a. state courts

b. the bureaucracy

*c. the party in power

d. the president

66) Federalism is the relationship between different levels of

*a. government

b. people

c. bureaucracies

d. states

67) Which government is likely to have the most trust of the American people?

*a. City of Detroit

b. US Congress

c. Nebraska state legislature

d. US Senate

68) In the federal system, allowing lower level governments to "try out" new policies on a local level is generally referred to as "____________ of democracy."

a. group think tanks

b. think tanks

*c. laboratories

d. dry run institutions

69) Powers necessary for the President to fulfil their duties but not named in the Constitution are known as _____ powers.

*a. inherent

b. concurrent

c. diffused

d. mixed

70) Congress's authority to establish a national bank exemplifies its ________ powers.

a. concurrent

*b. inherent

c. reserved

d. granted

71) The "____________ and proper clause" provides Congress's power over issues not specifically found in the Constitution.

*a. necessary

b. useful

c. immediate

d. utilized

72) The federal government gives a fixed amount to states for infrastructure repair with no further instruction. This is an example of

a. grants in aid

b. tax breaks

*c. block grants

d. welfare

73) Unlike their counterparts, _______ provide a fixed amount of funds for specific government programs, thus not automatically covering everyone who qualifies.

a. grants-in-aid

*b. block grants

c. specific-use grants

d. categorical grants

74) The increased use of block grants by recent presidents best exemplifies which principle of federalism?

a. redistribution

*b. devolution

c. welfare state

d. incrementalism

75) The program Race to the Top encouraged states to _____ for national dollars without national regulations.

*a. compete

b. bid for

c. lobby for

d. segregate schools

76) Which kind of grants have low levels of national supervision and high levels of national funding?

a. grants-in-aid

*b. block grants

c. specific-use grants

d. categorical grants

77) The spreading of policy ideas from state to state is typical of

a. Democracy

b. Confederalism

*c. Federalism

d. Unitary Government

78) A city in which the police do not ask about legal status during encounters is known as a

a. free life city

b. legal city

c. state city

*d. sanctuary city

79) There are _____ state governments and _____ national governments.

*a. 50;1

b. 1;50

c. 13;50

d. 50;13

80) Early Americans had two choices of how to organize politics: unitary and _____.

a. democracy

*b. confederation

c. republic

d. federalist

81) Immigration control by the federal government and police control by local government in sanctuary citizens is an example of

a. democracy

b. confederation

*c. federalism

d. republic

82) When states grant their local governments broad powers that is known as

a. local rule

b. town rule

c. citizen rule

*d. home rule

83) A state with more government services is

*a. Alaska

b. Mississippi

c. Florida

d. Oregon

84) Federal minimum wage is an example of how national policy is often more

a. even

*b. fair

c. controversial

d. unfair

85) New Jersey national guard helping out at a hurricane in Alabama is an example of how the national government can

a. be more equitable

b. take care of citizens

*c. equalize resources

d. use the military as they see fit

86) Taking a state policy that works well and creating a national policy is an example of how the federal government

a. creates fairness

b. equalizes resources

c. resolves problems of coordination

*d. standardizes best practices

87) The most important question in federalism is

*a. where to place responsibility

b. who pays

c. who taxes

d. who benefits

88) The rules for federalism have evolved _____ and are _____ clear.

a. quickly; always

*b. over time; not always

c. over time; always

d. slowly; always

89) Powers that are set out in black and white are known as _____ powers.

a. inherent

b. national

*c. delegated

d. listed

90) Federal authority over merchandise shipped to Alabama from Wisconsin is found in the

a. implied clause

b. Bill of Rights

c. full faith and credit clause

*d. commerce clause

91) The necessary and proper clause creates _____ powers.

*a. implied

b. specified

c. commerce

d. banking

92) The Constitution is the final law of the land based on the

a. necessary and proper clause

*b. supremacy clause

c. full faith and credit clause

d. commerce clause

93) Most American court cases are adjudicated in

a. federal courts

b. military courts

*c. state courts

d. international courts

94) The power to tax is a

a. state power

b. federal power

c. local power

*d. both state and federal power

95) It is unconstitutional for a state to

*a. enter into a treaty with Canada

b. tax private vehicles

c. assign polling places

d. issue drivers licenses

96) The first type of federalism practiced in the United States was

a. cooperative federalism

*b. dual federalism

c. progressive federalism

d. new federalism

97) Which of the following is the federal government responsible for?

a. education

b. town governments

*c. internal improvements

d. establishing election policy

98) Dual federalism collapsed in the

*a. 1930s

b. 1970s

c. 1990s

d. 2000s

99) Money became standardized in the United States with the passage of the

a. Currency Act

b. Money Act

c. Federal Reserve Act

*d. Banking Act

100) Federal funds that came with specific instructions about how to spend the money were known as

*a. grants in aid

b. block grants

c. Pell grants

d. specified grants

Chapter 4

Civil Liberties

Civil Liberties

Libel

Definition

Libel is a method of defamation expressed by print, writing, pictures, signs, effigies, or any communication embodied in physical form that is injurious to a person's reputation, exposes a person to public hatred, contempt or ridicule, or injures a person in his/her business or profession.

Overview

Traditionally, libel was a tort governed by state law. State courts generally follow the common law of libel, which allows recovery of damages without proof of actual harm. Under the traditional rules of libel, injury is presumed from the fact of publication. However, the U.S. Supreme Court has held that the First Amendment's protection of freedom of expression limits a State's ability to award damages in actions for libel.

In New York Times Co. v. Sullivan, the Court held that proof of actual malice is required for an award of damages in an action for libel involving public officials or matters of public concern. See New York Times Co. v. Sullivan, 376 U.S. 254 (1964). The Court reasoned that speech related to matters of public concern is at the heart of the protections guaranteed by the First Amendment, and outweighs the State's interest in compensating individuals for damage to their reputations. This "actual malice" test created a national judicial standard for whether speerecch qualifies as libel.

In Curtis Publishing Co. v. Butts (1967), the Supreme Court decided that, in addition to public officials, public figures must also prove that actual malice had been the intent of libelous claims against them.

In Gertz v. Robert Welch, Inc. (1974), the Court refused to extend the New York Times standard to actions for libel involving private individuals even where the matter is of public concern. In Gertz, the Court recognized a strong and legitimate state interest in compensating private individuals for injury to reputation, but cautioned that this interest extends no further than compensation for actual injury. The Gertz Court held that with in a case regarding a public concern, recovery of presumed or punitive damages is not permitted without a showing of malice. The only exception to this is when the liability is based on a showing of knowledge of falsity or a reckless disregard for the truth.

In Dun & Bradstreet, Inc. v. Greenmoss Builders, Inc. (1985), the Supreme Court held that in actions for libel involving private individuals and matters of purely private concern, presumed and punitive damages may be awarded on a lesser showing than actual malice. The Court determined that the First Amendment was not violated by permitting recovery of presumed and punitive damages without a showing of malice, as long as the defamatory statements do not involve issues of public concern.

Obscenity Test and Obscenity Law

Obscenity is a category of speech unprotected by the First Amendment. Obscenity laws are concerned with prohibiting lewd, filthy, or disgusting words or pictures. Indecent materials or depictions, normally speech or artistic expressions, may be restricted in terms of time, place, and manner, but are still protected by the First Amendment. There are major disagreements regarding obscene material and the government's role in regulation. All fifty states have individual laws controlling obscene material.

A comprehensive, legal definition of obscenity has been difficult to establish. Yet, key components of the current obscenity test stem from the U.S. Court of Appeals decision in United States v. One Book Entitled Ulysses, which determined that a work investigated for obscenity must be considered in its entirety and not merely judged on its parts.

Currently, obscenity is evaluated by federal and state courts alike using a tripartite standard established by Miller v. California. The Miller test for obscenity includes the following criteria: (1) whether 'the average person, applying contemporary community standards' would find that the work, 'taken as a whole,' appeals to 'prurient interest' (2) whether the work depicts or describes, in a patently offensive way, sexual conduct specifically defined by the applicable state law, and (3) whether the work, 'taken as a whole,' lacks serious literary, artistic, political, or scientific value.

Prior to Miller, judges testing for obscenity invoked the wisdom handed down by the Court in Roth v. United States. A landmark case, Roth ruled that obscene material was not protected by the First Amendment and could be regulated by the States rather than by a singular, Federal standard. Also, Roth established a new judicial standard for defining obscenity that invoked the average person's application of contemporary community standards to judge whether or not the dominant theme of the material taken as a whole appeals to prurient interest. A test for obscenity derived from Roth that included the following five-part structure: (1) the perspective of evaluation was that of an ordinary, reasonable person, (2) community standards of acceptability were to be used to measure obscenity, (3) works whose predominant theme was questionable were the only target of obscenity law, (4) a work, in order to be evaluated for obscenity, had to be taken in its entirety, and (5) an obscene work was one that aimed to excited individuals' prurient interest. Miller revised Roth's emphasis on creating a uniform Federal standard. Instead, it touted reliance on community standards of a more local nature, which threw the arduous task of defining obscenity back upon the States.

The Supreme Court has repeatedly grappled with problematic elements of the Miller test for obscenity. However, to date, no standard has replaced it.

In 1997, Reno v. American Civil Liberties Union ("ACLU I") addressed obscenity in the field of new media. The ACLU challenged the Communications Decency Act (CDA), a portion of the 1996 Telecommunications Act aimed at protecting children by restricting transmissions sent over the Internet. After the Supreme Court ruled the CDA was overly broad in its approach to regulating obscenity online, Congress passed the Children's Online Privacy Protection Act (COPPA) in 1998.

The ACLU again filed suit, which became Ashcroft v. Civil Liberties Union ("ACLU II"). Aschcroft, upheld the Constitutionality of COPPA and deemed its use of "'community standards' to identify 'material that is harmful to minors'" an acceptable practice under the First Amendment. However, the Court also demanded that COPPA be enjoined and the case be remanded to the Third Circuit, where the Court found COPPA created a content-ban on adult transmissions that was overly broad, intrusive, and restrictive in its efforts to protect children from adult speech. The details of the case were finally resolved in January 2009, when the Supreme Court denied certiorari to ACLU v. Mukasey, a case that could have broadened obscenity law beyond the parameters of the Miller test.
Fourth Amendment: Search and Seizure Laws

FOURTH AMENDMENT: AN OVERVIEW

I. INTERESTS PROTECTED

The Fourth Amendment of the U.S. Constitution provides that "[t]he right of the people to be secure in their persons, houses, papers, and effects, against unreasonable searches and seizures, shall not be violated, and no Warrants shall issue, but upon probable cause, supported by Oath or affirmation, and particularly describing the place to be searched, and the persons or things to be seized."

The ultimate goal of this provision is to protect people's right to privacy and freedom from unreasonable intrusions by the government. However, the Fourth Amendment does not guarantee protection from all searches and seizures, but only those done by the government and deemed unreasonable under the law.

To claim a violation of Fourth Amendment as the basis for suppressing a relevant evidence, the court had long required that the claimant must prove that he himself was the victim of an invasion of privacy to have a valid standing to claim protection under the Fourth Amendment. However, the Supreme Court has departed from such requirement, issue of exclusion is to be determined solely upon a resolution of the substantive question whether the claimant's Fourth Amendment rights have been violated, which in turn requires that the claimant demonstrates a justifiable expectation of privacy, which was arbitrarily violated by the government.

In general, most warrantless searches of private premises are prohibited under the Fourth Amendment, unless specific exception applies. For instance, a warrantless search may be lawful, if an officer has asked and is given consent to search; if the search is incident to a lawful arrest; if there is probable cause to search and there is exigent circumstance calling for the warrantless search. Exigent circumstances exist in situations where a situation where people are in imminent danger, where evidence faces imminent destruction, or prior to a suspect's imminent escape.

On the other hand, warrantless search and seizure of properties are not illegal, if the objects being searched are in plain view. Further, warrantless seizure of abandoned property, or of properties on an open field do not violate Fourth Amendment, because it is considered that having an expectation of privacy right to an abandoned property or to properties on an open field is not reasonable.

However, in some states, there are some exception to this limitation, where some state authorities have granted protection to open fields. States can always establish higher standards for searches and seizures protection than what is required by the Fourth Amendment, but states cannot allow conducts that violate the Fourth Amendment.

Where there was a violation of one's fourth amendment rights by federal officials, A bivens action can be filed against federal law enforcement officials for damages, resulting from an unlawful search and seizure. Under the Bivens action, the claimant needs to prove that there has been a constitutional violation of the fourth amendment rights by federal officials acting under the color of law.

However, the protection under the Fourth Amendment can be waived if one voluntarily consents to or does not object to evidence collected during a warrantless search or seizure.

II. SEARCHES AND SEIZURES UNDER FOURTH AMENDMENT

The courts must determine what constitutes a search or seizure under the Fourth Amendment. If the conduct challenged does not fall within the Fourth Amendment, the individual will not enjoy protection under Fourth Amendment.

A. Search

A search under Fourth Amendment occurs when a governmental employee or agent of the government violates an individual's reasonable expectation of privacy.

Strip searches and visual body cavity searches, including anal or genital inspections, constitute reasonable searches under the Fourth Amendment when supported by probable cause and conducted in a reasonable manner.

A dog-sniff inspection is invalid under the Fourth Amendment if the inspection violates a reasonable expectation of privacy. Electronic surveillance is also considered a search under the Fourth Amendment.

B. Seizure of a Person

A seizure of a person, within the meaning of the Fourth Amendment, occurs when the police's conduct would communicate to a reasonable person, taking into account the circumstances surrounding the encounter, that the person is not free to ignore the police presence and leave at his will.

Two elements must be present to constitute a seizure of a person. First, there must be a show of authority by the police officer. Presence of handcuffs or weapons, the use of forceful language, and physical contact are each strong indicators of authority. Second, the person being seized must submit to the authority. An individual who ignores the officer's request and walks away has not been seized for Fourth Amendment purposes.

An arrest warrant is preferred but not required to make a lawful arrest under the Fourth Amendment. A warrantless arrest may be justified where probable cause and urgent need are present prior to the arrest. Probable cause is present when the police officer has a reasonable belief in the guilt of the suspect based on the facts and information prior to the arrest. For instance, a warrantless arrest may be legitimate in situations where a police officer has a probable belief that a suspect has either committed a crime or is a threat to the public security. Also, a police officer might arrest a suspect to prevent the suspect's escape or to preserve evidence. A warrantless arrest may be invalidated if the police officer fails to demonstrate exigent circumstances.

The ability to make warrantless arrests are commonly limited by statutes subject to the due process guaranty of the U.S. Constitution. A suspect arrested without a warrant is entitled to prompt judicial determination, usually within 48 hours.

There are investigatory stops that fall short of arrests, but nonetheless, they fall within Fourth Amendment protection. For instance, police officers can perform a terry stop or a traffic stop. Usually, these stops provide officers with less dominion and controlling power and impose less of an infringement of personal liberty for individual stopped. Investigatory stops must be temporary questioning for limited purposes and conducted in a manner necessary to fulfill the purpose.

An officer's reasonable suspicion is sufficient to justify brief stops and detentions. To determine if the officer has met the standard to justify the seizure, the court takes into account the totality of the circumstances and examines whether the officer has a particularized and reasonable belief for suspecting the wrongdoing. Probable cause gained during stops or detentions might effectuate a subsequent warrantless arrest.

C. Seizure of Property

A seizure of property, within the meaning of the Fourth Amendment, occurs when there is some meaningful interference with an individual's possessory interests in the property.

In some circumstances, warrantless seizures of objects in plain view do not constitute seizures within the meaning of Fourth Amendment. When executing a search warrant, an officer might be able to seize an item observed in plain view even if it is not specified in the warrant.

III. WARRANT REQUIREMENT

A search or seizure is generally unreasonable and illegal without a warrant, subject to only a few exceptions.

To obtain a search warrant or arrest warrant, the law enforcement officer must demonstrate probable cause that a search or seizure is justified. A court-authority, usually a magistrate, will consider the totality of circumstances to determine whether to issue the warrant.

The warrant requirement may be excused in exigent circumstances if an officer has probable cause and obtaining a warrant is impractical in the particular situation. For instance, in State v. Helmbright, 990 N.E.2d 154, Ohio court held that a warrantless search of probationer's person or his place of residence is not violation of the Fourth Amendment, if the officer who conducts the search possesses "reasonable grounds" to believe that the probationer has failed to comply with the terms of his probation.

Other well-established exceptions to the warrant requirement include consensual searches, certain brief investigatory stops, searches incident to a valid arrest, and seizures of items in plain view.

There is no general exception to the Fourth Amendment warrant requirement in national security cases. Warrantless searches are generally not permitted in exclusively domestic security cases. In foreign security cases, court opinions might differ on whether to accept the foreign security exception to the warrant requirement generally and, if accepted, whether the exception should extend to both physical searches and to electronic surveillances.

IV. REASONABLENESS REQUIREMENT

All searches and seizures under the Fourth Amendment must be reasonable. No excessive force shall be used. Reasonableness is the ultimate measure of the constitutionality of a search or seizure. Searches and seizures with the warrant must also satisfy the reasonableness requirement.

On the other hand, warrantless searches and seizures are presumed to be unreasonable, unless they fall within the few exceptions.

In cases of warrantless searches and seizures, the court will try to balance the degree of intrusion on the individual's right to privacy and the need to promote government interests and special needs in exigent circumstances. The court will examine the totality of the circumstances to determine if the search or seizure was justified. When analyzing the reasonableness standard, the court uses an objective assessment and considers factors including the degree of intrusion by the search or seizure and the manner in which the search or seizure is conducted.

V. EXCLUSIONARY RULE

Under the exclusionary rule, any evidence obtained in violation of the Fourth Amendment will be excluded from criminal proceedings. There are a few exceptions to this rule.

VI. ELECTRONIC SURVEILLANCE

In recent years, the Fourth Amendment's applicability in electronic searches and seizures has received much attention from the courts. With the advent of the internet and increased popularity of computers, there has been an increasing amount of crime occurring electronically. Consequently, evidence of such crime can often be found on computers, hard drives, or other electronic devices. The Fourth Amendment applies to the search and seizure of electronic devices.

Many electronic search cases involve whether law enforcement can search a company-owned computer that an employee uses to conduct business. Although the case law is split, the majority holds that employees do not have a legitimate expectation of privacy with regard to information stored on a company-owned computer. In the 2010 case of City of Ontario v. Quon (08-1332), the Supreme Court extended this lack of an expectation of privacy to text messages sent and received on an employer-owned pager.

Lately, electronic surveillance and wiretapping has also caused a significant amount of Fourth Amendment litigation.

VII. THE USA PATRIOT ACT

Following the September 11, 2001 attacks on the World Trade Center and the Pentagon, Congress and the President enacted legislation to strengthen the intelligence gathering community's ability to combat domestic terrorism. Entitled the USA Patriot Act, the legislation's provisions aimed to increase the ability of law enforcement to search email and telephonic communications in addition to medical, financial, and library records.

One provision permits law enforcement to obtain access to stored voicemails by obtaining a basic search warrant rather than a surveillance warrant. Obtaining a basic search warrant requires a much lower evidentiary showing. A highly controversial provision of the Act includes permission for law enforcement to use sneak-and-peak warrants. A sneak-and-peak warrant is a warrant in which law enforcement can delay notifying the property owner about the warrant's issuance. In an Oregon federal district court case that drew national attention, Judge Ann Aiken struck down the use of sneak-and-peak warrants as unconstitutional and in violation of the Fourth Amendment. See 504 F.Supp.2d 1023 (D. Or. 2007).

The Patriot Act also expanded the practice of using National Security Letters (NSL). An NSL is an administrative subpoena that requires certain persons, groups, organizations, or companies to provide documents about certain persons. These documents typically involve telephone, email, and financial records. NSLs also carry a gag order, meaning the person or persons responsible for complying cannot mention the existence of the NSL. Under the Patriot Act provisions, law enforcement can use NSLs when investigating U.S. citizens, even when law enforcement does not think the individual under investigation has committed a crime. The Department of Homeland Security has used NSLs frequently since its inception. By using an NSL, an agency has no responsibility to first obtain a warrant or court order before conducting its search of records.

Another aspect of the Patriot Act, which has been highly confidential was the Telephone Metadata program, which under § 215 of the Patriot Act, had allowed the NSA to collect data about Americans' telephone calls in bulk, was reviewed by the Second Circuit in ACLU v. Clapper, in which the court held the Telephone Metadata program illegal under the Congress' original intent under the §215.

The Patriot Act has expired in mid-2015, and since June 2nd, 2015 has been repackaged under the USA Freedom Act. Although it remains to be seen how the Freedom Act will be interpreted, with respect to the Fourth Amendment protections, the new Act selectively re-authorized the Patriot Act, while banning the bulk collection of data of American's telephone records and internet metadata and limited the government's data collection to the "greatest extent reasonably practical" meaning the government now cannot collect all data pertaining to a particular service provider or broad geographic region.

VIII. FOURTH AMENDMENT AND SUPERVISED RELEASE/PAROLE

Probationers—convicted criminal offender who is released into the community under supervision of a probation officer in lieu of incarceration; or parolees—convicts who have served a portion of his judicially imposed sentence in penal institutions, and is released for the remainder of the sentence under supervision of a parole officer for good behavior—can also assert fourth amendment rights, creating a potential confrontation between fundamental constitutional guarantee and the society's legitimate interest in correctional programs to prevent the convicts from lapsing back into a crime.

Traditionally, courts have struggled with various theories of parole and probation to justify the complete denial of fourth amendment rights to the convicts on supervised release or probation. The most prevalent of the theories was the "Custody Theory," under which an offender was said to be entitled to no more liberty than he would have enjoyed had he been incarcerated. Recently, however, this rationale was rejected by Morrissey v. Brewer, which emphasized that the parolee's status more closely resembles that of an ordinary citizen than a prisoner. While the Court noted that since parole revocation only changed the type of penalty imposed on an already-convicted criminal, the Court need not afford the parolees "the full panoply of rights" available under the fourteenth amendment to a free man facing criminal prosecution, the Court held that certain procedural protections must be guaranteed to the parolees facing revocation of the parole. In general, the released offenders now have been afforded full Fourth Amendment protection with respect to searches performed by the law enforcement officials, and warrantless searches conducted by correctional officers at the request of the police have also been declared unlawful.

However, in reviewing the searches undertaken by the correctional officers on their own initiative, some courts have modified the traditional Fourth Amendment protections to accommodate the correctional officers' informational needs, developing a modified "Reasonable Belief" standard, under which the correctional officer is permitted to make a showing of less than probable cause in order to justify the intrusion of privacy into the released offender.

Multiple Choice Questions

1) ______are the limits on government so that people can freely exercise their rights.

*a. Civil liberties

b. Civil rights

c. Selective incorporation

d. Civil controls

2) According to the text, we always weigh the rights of individuals against the concerns and ______ of the community.

*a. safety

b. morals

c. income

d. standard of living

3) Civil ______ require government action to help secure individual rights.

*a. rights

b. liberties

c. freedoms

d. laws

4) Civil ______ restrict government action to protect individual rights.

a. rights

*b. liberties

c. freedoms

d. laws

5) Initially, the Court ______ the requirement for students to recite the Pledge of Allegiance, even if it violated a student's faith.

*a. upheld

b. failed to address

c. overturned

d. rejected

6) Initially, the Bill of Rights protected against violations of citizens' rights from ______ government(s).

a. state

*b. federal

c. state and federal

d. state and local

7) The *Barron v. Baltimore* case demonstrates the selective incorporation of what civil liberty?

*a. seizing property

b. search and seizure

c. right to bear arms

d. free-exercise clause

8) ______ incorporation is defined as extending protections from the Bill of Rights to the state governments, one right at a time.

a. Concurrent

b. Majority

*c. Selective

d. Applicable

9) The Fourteenth Amendment is often the basis for what process?

a. concurrent incorporation

b. majority incorporation

c. applicable incorporation

*d. selective incorporation

10) The Fourteenth Amendment is known as the ________________ clause.

*a. due process

b. clear and present danger

c. free-exercise

d. necessary and proper

11) In what year did the Supreme Court make a classic statement of civil liberties?

a. 1940

b. 1941

*c. 1943

d. never

12) What case provides for the selective incorporation of the free exercise of religion?

a. *Miranda v. Illinois*

b. *Benton v. Maryland*

*c. *Cantwell v. Connecticut*

d. *Powell v. Alabama*

13) What case provides for the selective incorporation of the right to free speech?

a. *Miranda v. Illinois*

b. *Benton v. Maryland*

*c. *Gitlow v. New York*

d. *Powell v. Alabama*

14) What case provides for the selective incorporation of the right to remain silent?

*a. *Miranda v. Illinois*

b. *Benton v. Maryland*

c. *Gitlow v. New York*

d. *Powell v. Alabama*

15) What case provides for the selective incorporation of the right to counsel in felony cases?

a. *Miranda v. Illinois*

*b. *Gideon v. Wainright*

c. *Gitlow v. New York*

d. *Powell v. Alabama*

16) Which of the following rights is not found in the Constitution or Bill of Rights?

a. bear arms

*b. abortion

c. cruel and unusual punishment

d. free speech

17) Which Supreme Court case granted women a right to contraceptives?

*a. *Griswold v. Connecticut*

b. *Gideon v. Wainright*

c. *Gitlow v. New York*

d. *Powell v. Alabama*

18) Which Supreme Court case established a woman's right to choose?

a. *Gideon v. Wainright*

*b. *Roe v. Wade*

c. *Gitlow v. New York*

d. *Powell v. Alabama*

19) *Roe v. Wade* overturned a(n) ______ law banning abortion.

*a. Texas

b. South Carolina

c. Alabama

d. Mississippi

20) In what year was the *Roe v. Wade* decision rendered?

a. 1982

*b. 1973

c. 1994

d. 1984

21) In 1980, the Court ________ a congressional ban on federal funding for abortions.

*a. upheld

b. overturned

c. did not address in the ruling

d. none of these

22) With the *Planned Parenthood v. Casey* decision, the Court left much discretion in abortions to (the) ______ government(s), so long as they did not go against the *Roe* decision.

*a. state

b. federal

c. local

d. none of these

23) The *Planned Parenthood v. Casey* decision established a judicial __________, guiding principles that help governments make judgment calls.

*a. standard

b. rule

c. opinion

d. regulation

24) A judicial ________ can be found in the *Roe v. Wade* case.

a. standard

*b. rule

c. opinion

d. regulation

25) The state that passed the law struck down by *Roe v. Wade* was

a. Oklahoma

b. California

*c. Texas

d. Arkansas

26) What right did the *Lawrence v. Texas* case address?

*a. privacy

b. right to bear arms

c. free exercise

d. cruel and unusual punishment

27) Which case relates to same-sex couples?

a. *Gideon v. Wainright*

*b. *Lawrence v. Texas*

c. *Gitlow v. New York*

d. *Powell v. Alabama*

28) Which of the following is not one of the clauses relating to freedom of religion?

a. free exercise/practice

*b. necessary and proper

c. establishment

d. none of these

29) Where are the rights to freedom of religion found?

*a. First Amendment

b. Second Amendment

c. Eighth and Ninth Amendments

d. Fourth Amendment

30) Which clause says that government may not interfere in religious practice?

*a. free exercise/practice

b. necessary and proper

c. establishment

d. none of these

31) Which president called for a "wall of separation" between church and state?

*a. Jefferson

b. Washington

c. Adams

d. Lincoln

32) The wall of separation permitting religious freedoms relates to which clause?

a. free exercise/practice

b. necessary and proper

*c. establishment

d. none of these

33) Which Court case said starting the school day with a prayer violated the establishment clause?

a. *Williams v. Ohio*

*b. *Engel v. Vitale*

c. *Lemon v. Kurtzman*

d. none; the Court ruled it is constitutional

34) The _______case set a test for judging what government actions are permissible relating to the establishment clause.

*a. Lemon

b. Engel

c. Williams

d. Miranda

35) Which of the following is NOT part of the Lemon test?

a. secular purpose

b. neither advancing nor inhibiting religion

c. not excessively entangling government in religion

*d. none; these are all parts of the Lemon test

36) Which of the following is allowable, thus not violating the freedom of religion?

a. children reciting "under God" during the Pledge of Allegiance

b. prayer at graduation

c. public school minute of silent prayer or meditation

*d. Christmas displays with secular displays as well

37) Which faith has been predominant in the United States since its founding?

a. Catholicism

b. Jewish

c. Islam

*d. no predominant religion

38) The Lemon test is an example of what perspective on judging violations of the establishment clause?

a. accommodation

*b. strict separation

c. strict entanglement

d. none of these

39) Which test applies to the free exercise clause?

a. Lemon

b. Engel

*c. Sherbert

d. Miranda

40) In the Sherbert case, the Court ruled denying unemployment benefits to someone who was fired for refusing to work on Saturdays for religious reasons was

a. constitutional.

*b. unconstitutional.

c. the right thing to do.

d. none of these

41) Which Court case replaced the Sherbert test with a neutrality test?

a. *Lawrence v. Texas*

*b. *Employment Division v. Smith*

c. *Miranda v. Illinois*

d. *Ohio v. Smith*

42) __________ speech is hostile statements based on someone's personal characteristics.

a. First degree

b. Second degree

c. Culturally insensitive

*d. Hate

43) When the right to speak out clashes with other rights, like protecting minorities from abusive language, free speech usually

*a. wins.

b. loses.

c. ties.

d. fails to be upheld.

44) In what amendment is the right to free speech guaranteed?

*a. First

b. Third

c. Sixth

d. Seventh

45) Freedom of speech holds a ____________ position among rights.

a. deferential

b. subsidiary

*c. preferred

d. none of these

46) The Alien and Sedition Acts relate to which individual freedom?

*a. freedom of speech

b. freedom of religion

c. unreasonable search and seizure

d. no quartering of troops

47) Under the Alien and Sedition Act criticizing the government would lead to

a. new legislation

b. changes in laws

c. right to assembly

*d. prosecution

48) What test was the result of the *Schenck v. US* case?

a. necessary and proper

*b. clear and present danger

c. constitutional determination of legitimacy

d. none of these

49) Which Supreme Court justice articulated the clear and present danger test?

*a. Holmes

b. Roberts

c. Warren

d. O'Connor

50) The clear and present danger test applies to which civil liberty?

*a. speech

b. bear arms

c. cruel and unusual punishment

d. right to a grand jury

51) The ____________ test says that speech is not protected if officials believe that the speech will lead to prohibited action like violence or terrorism.

a. necessary and proper

*b. clear and present danger

c. constitutional determination of legitimacy

d. none of these

52) Which of the following is NOT a form of protected symbolic speech?

a. burning the flag

*b. banners advocating drugs at schools

c. wearing armbands to school

d. burning a cross to express views

53) What war was the basis for the *Tinker* decision?

*a. Vietnam

b. Korean

c. World War I

d. World War II

54) The Nixon administration attempting to stop publication of the Pentagon Papers demonstrates what principle in the freedom of the press?

*a. prior restraint

b. prior constraint

c. reactive restraint

d. reactive constraint

55) What Court case formed the basis for the test for obscenity in regulating free speech?

a. *Mapp v. Ohio*

*b. *Miller v. California*

c. *Engel v. Vitale*

d. *Michigan v. Jones*

56) At least how many of the three characteristics for judging obscene speech must be met in order for the speech to be declared obscene?

a. 1

b. 2

*c. 3

d. none

57) What are defined as spoken untruths or falsehoods that, with the exception of public officials, are not protected under free speech?

a. libel

*b. slander

c. both libel and slander

d. none of these

58) What are defined as written untruths or falsehoods that, with the exception of public officials, are not protected under free speech?

*a. libel

b. slander

c. both libel and slander

d. none of these

59) It is generally __________ to prove slander or libel against a public official than an average citizen.

a. less difficult

*b. more difficult

c. about the same difficulty

d. none of these

60) For slander or libel against a public official, what must be proven in the speech?

a. knowledge

*b. malice

c. poor fact checking

d. none of these

61) In what amendment is the right to bear arms found?

*a. Second

b. Third

c. Fifth

d. Seventh

62) What government was at issue in a recent (2008) Supreme Court decision, which struck down a rule restricting guns to people's homes?

a. Illinois

b. Virginia

*c. District of Columbia

d. South Carolina

63) What case provided for the incorporation of the Second Amendment to lower-level governments?

*a. *McDonald v. Chicago*

b. *DC v. Heller*

c. *Michigan v. Arnold*

d. *Mapp v. Ohio*

64) Which amendment does not apply to the rights of the accused?

a. Fourth

b. Fifth

*c. Seventh

d. Eighth

65) Relating to the rights of the accused, the courts are generally moving away from individual protections and toward __________ law enforcement powers.

*a. enhanced

b. limited

c. neutral

d. none of these

66) Which country leads in the number of incarcerated individuals?

a. Italy

b. Denmark

c. Mexico

*d. US

67) Which case provides the foundation for the exclusionary rule?

*a. *Mapp v. Ohio*

b. *Miranda v. Arizona*

c. *Lawrence v. Texas*

d. *Roe v. Wade*

68) Which amendment does the exclusionary rule relate to most prominently?

a. First

b. Third

*c. Fourth

d. Seventh

69) The ____________ rule says that evidence obtained in an illegal search may not be introduced in a trial.

*a. exclusionary

b. limited approach

c. limited inclusion

d. false pretense

70) The case out which came the exclusionary rule was

a. Roe v. Wade

b. Griswold v. Connecticut

c. Baron v. Baltimore

*d. Mapp v. Ohio

71) The Fourth Amendment is generally referred to as preventing

a. trials without attorneys.

b. reading of rights well after arrest.

*c. unlawful search and seizure.

d. none of the above

72) Which amendment relates to the rights of individuals at trials?

a. Fourth

*b. Fifth

c. Seventh

d. Ninth

73) A citizen's right to a grand jury before a trial is found in what amendment?

a. Fourth

*b. Fifth

c. Seventh

d. Ninth

74) A(n) ____________ jury is one that does not decide on guilt or innocence but only on whether there is enough evidence for the case to go to trial.

*a. grand

b. arraignment

c. attainment

d. "golden"

75) The O.J. Simpson case demonstrates the principle of being tried twice for the same crime, once in criminal court and once in civil court. Since these were separate proceedings, they did not violate which principle of the Fifth Amendment?

a. first past the post

b. Miranda indictment

*c. double jeopardy

d. Mapp indictment

76) "You have the right to remain silent" is a famous introduction to what warnings, based in interpretation of the Fifth Amendment?

*a. Miranda

b. Mapp

c. Lawrence

d. Engale

77) Through the *Miranda* decision, if a police officer acquires evidence before reading your Miranda warnings, such evidence ________ be admitted in court.

a. could

b. sometimes could

*c. could not

d. none of the above

78) One's right to an attorney in felony cases is based in what amendment?

a. Fourth

b. Fifth

*c. Sixth

d. Ninth

79) Originally, one's right to an attorney was only provided in what kind of case?

a. civil

*b. capital

c. felony

d. misdemeanor and above

80) Which case granted citizens' rights to an attorney in all felony cases?

*a. *Gideon v. Wainwright*

b. *Powell v. Alabama*

c. *Lawrence v. Texas*

d. *Jones v. Ohio*

81) Debates surrounding the death penalty center around which amendment?

a. Sixth

b. Seventh

*c. Eighth

d. none of the above

82) The Eighth Amendment is typically associated with

a. unlawful search and seizure.

b. quartering of troops.

*c. cruel and unusual punishment.

d. states' rights.

83) How many countries have abolished the death penalty?

*a. 101

b. 80

c. 77

d. none

84) How many people were executed in the United States in 2017?

*a. 23

b. 33

c. 233

d. 366

85) What did the Supreme Court rule about lethal injections?

a. They constitute cruel and unusual punishment.

b. They do not constitute cruel and unusual punishment, but they should be outlawed.

*c. They do not constitute cruel and unusual punishment.

d. none of these

86) What act is often criticized for trampling individual civil liberties in the name of enhancing national security?

a. USA ARMOR Act

*b. USA Patriot Act

c. USA DOD Act

d. none of these

87) The USA Patriot Act enhanced security by removing

a. weapons from schools

*b. restrictions on law enforcement

c. Miranda Rights

d. Courts

88) Which president permitted the NSA to conduct international surveillance without a search warrant?

a. George W. Bush

b. Barack Obama

c. Donald Trump

*d. All of the above

89) Immigration laws apply to

*a. non-citizens

b. citizens

c. government employees

d. state employees

90) Rights in immigration laws are

a. less restricted

*b. more restricted

c. monitored by states

d. monitored by counties

Chapter 5

The Struggle for Civil Rights

Dred Scott v. Sandford (1857)

In Dred Scott v. Sandford (argued 1856 -- decided 1857), the Supreme Court ruled that Americans of African descent, whether free or slave, were not American citizens and could not sue in federal court. The Court also ruled that Congress lacked power to ban slavery in the U.S. territories. Finally, the Court declared that the rights of slaveowners were constitutionally protected by the Fifth Amendment because slaves were categorized as property.

The controversy began in 1833, when Dr. John Emerson, a surgeon with the U.S. Army, purchased Dred Scott, a slave, and eventually moved Scott to a base in the Wisconsin Territory. Slavery was banned in the territory pursuant to the Missouri Compromise. Scott lived there for the next four years, hiring himself out for work during the long stretches when Emerson was away. In 1840, Scott, his new wife, and their young children moved to Louisiana and then to St. Louis with Emerson. Emerson died in 1843, leaving the Scott family to his wife, Eliza Irene Sanford. In 1846, after laboring and saving for years, the Scotts sought to buy their freedom from Sanford, but she refused. Dred Scott then sued Sanford in a state court, arguing that he was legally free because he and his family had lived in a territory where slavery was banned. In 1850, the state court finally declared Scott free. However, Scott's wages had been withheld pending the resolution of his case, and during that time Mrs. Emerson remarried and left her brother, John Sanford, to deal with her affairs. Mr. Sanford, unwilling to pay the back wages owed to Scott, appealed the decision to the Missouri Supreme Court. The court overturned the lower court's decision and ruled in favor of Sanford. Scott then filed another lawsuit in a federal circuit court claiming damages against Sanford's brother, John F.A. Sanford, for Sanford's alleged physical abuse against him. The jury ruled that Scott could not sue in federal court because he had already been deemed a slave under Missouri law. Scott appealed to the U.S. Supreme Court, which reviewed the case in 1856. Due to a clerical error at the time, Sanford's name was misspelled in court records.

The Supreme Court, in an infamous opinion written by Chief Justice Roger B. Taney, ruled that it lacked jurisdiction to take Scott's case because Scott was, or at least had been, a slave. First, the Court argued that they could not entertain Scott's case because federal courts, including the Supreme Court, are courts of "peculiar and limited jurisdiction" and may only hear cases brought by select parties involving limited claims. For example, under Article III of the U.S. Constitution, federal courts may only hear cases brought by "citizens" of the United States. The Court ruled that because Scott was "a negro, whose ancestors were imported into this country, and sold as slaves," and thus "[not] a member of the political community formed and brought into existence by the Constitution," Scott was not a citizen and had no right to file a lawsuit in federal court.

Second, the Court argued that Scott's status as a citizen of a free state did not necessarily give him status as a U.S. citizen. While the states were free to create their own citizenship criteria and had done so before the Constitution even came into being, the Constitution gives Congress exclusive authority to define national citizenship. Moreover, the Court argued that even if Scott was deemed "free" under the laws of a state, he would still not qualify as an American citizen because he was black. The Court asserted that, in general, U.S. citizens are only those who were members of the "political community" at the time of the Constitution's creation, along with those individuals' heirs, and slaves were not part of this community. Finally, the Court argued that, in any case, Scott could not be defined as free by virtue of his residency in the Wisconsin Territory, because Congress lacked the power to ban slavery in U.S. territories. The Court viewed slaves as "property," and the Fifth Amendment forbids Congress from taking property away from individuals without just compensation. Justice Benjamin Curtis issued a strong dissent.

The decision in Dred Scott v. Sandford exacerbated rising sectional tensions between the North and South. Although the Missouri Compromise had already been repealed prior to the case, the decision nonetheless appeared to validate the Southern version of national power, and to embolden pro-slavery Southerners to expand slavery to all reaches of the nation. Unsurprisingly, antislavery forces were outraged by the decision, empowering the newly formed Republican Party and helping fuel violence between slaveowners and abolitionists on the frontier. Following the Civil War, the Reconstruction Congress passed, and the states ratified, the Thirteenth, Fourteenth, and Fifteenth Amendments, all of which directly overturned the Dred Scott decision. Today, all people born or naturalized in the United States are American citizens who may bring suit in federal court.

Brown v. Board of Education of Topeka, 347 U.S. 483 (1954)

Facts of the case

This case was the consolidation of cases arising in Kansas, South Carolina, Virginia, Delaware, and Washington D.C. relating to the segregation of public schools on the basis of race. In each of the cases, African American students had been denied admittance to certain public schools based on laws allowing public education to be segregated by race. They argued that such segregation violated the Equal Protection Clause of the Fourteenth Amendment. The plaintiffs were denied relief in the lower courts based on Plessy v. Ferguson, which held that racially segregated public facilities were legal so long as the facilities for blacks and whites were equal. (This was known as the "separate but equal" doctrine.)

Question

Does the segregation of public education based solely on race violate the Equal Protection Clause of the Fourteenth Amendment?

Conclusion

Separate but equal educational facilities for racial minorities is inherently unequal violating the Equal Protection Clause of the Fourteenth Amendment Separate but equal educational facilities for racial minorities is inherently unequal, violating the Equal Protection Clause of the Fourteenth Amendment.

Chief Justice Earl Warren delivered the opinion of the unanimous Court. The Supreme Court held that "separate but equal" facilities are inherently unequal and violate the protections of the Equal Protection Clause of the Fourteenth Amendment. The Court reasoned that the segregation of public education based on race instilled a sense of inferiority that had a hugely detrimental effect on the education and personal growth of African American children. Warren based much of his opinion on information from social science studies rather than court precedent. The decision also used language that was relatively accessible to non-lawyers because Warren felt it was necessary for all Americans to understand its logic.

Multiple Choice Questions

1) With what act were Chinese immigrants deemed ineligible for citizenship?

a. Civil Rights Act

*b. Chinese Exclusion Act

c. California Alien Land Law

d. they were never deemed ineligible

2) When did Congress outlaw sex discrimination in the Civil Rights Act?

*a. 1964

b. 1966

c. 1965

d. 1968

3) Which minority group was forbidden from becoming American citizens?

a. blacks

b. women

*c. Chinese

d. all of the above

4) How many African Americans served in the Senate during the entire twentieth century?

a. eight

b. ten

c. two

*d. three

5) Asians have won full rights, but which minority group has not?

a. Puerto Ricans

*b. Native Americans

c. blacks

d. women

6) African Americans are almost ___ times as likely to be poor as the rest of the population. They have a life expectancy ___ years shorter than whites.

a. five . . . three

b. ten . . . five

*c. three . . . nine

d. ten . . . two

7) What was the number of black mayors in 1965?

*a. 0

b. 5

c. 10

d. 12

8) What is the poverty rate of white Americans today?

a. 5.5

*b. 8.8

c. 10

d. 12.6

9) What is the poverty rate of Hispanic Americans today?

a. 15

b. 17.5

*c. 19.4

d. 33

10) What is the poverty rate of black Americans today?

*a. 22

b. 10.5

c. 17

d. 12.7

11) What is the poverty rate of Native Americans today?

a. 10

b. 25

c. 15

*d. 28.3

12) What is the number of women elected to full Senate terms between 1920 and 1970?

*a. 3

b. 5

c. 7

d. 12

13) What is the number of women serving in the Senate today?

a. 33

b. 50

*c. 21

d. 10

14) What year did the Supreme Court strike down laws forbidding marriage between blacks and whites?

a. 1905

*b. 1968

c. 1868

d. 1999

15) What are rules issued by the president that have the force of law but do not require congressional approval?

a. presidential orders

*b. executive orders

c. White House decrees

d. none of the above

16) Which president desegregated the army in 1948?

a. Wilson

b. Roosevelt

c. Ford

*d. Truman

17) In 2012, Barack Obama gave undocumented individuals protection, these individuals were known as

*a. dreamers

b. field workers

c. college students

d. free workers

18) Few groups in American history have suffered worse treatment than African Americans. Which of the following horrific actions did they experience?

a. Men and women chained in the holds of slave ships.

b. Raped at will.

c. Murdered for challenging their oppression.

*d. all of the above

19) What was the Missouri Compromise of 1820?

a. Slavery was abolished in the Louisiana Territory.

*b. A line was drawn through the Louisiana Territory: territories north of the line except Missouri would be free; everything south of the line would be open to slavery.

c. Slavery would be allowed only in some states in the South.

d. none of the above

20) What was the Compromise of 1850?

*a. Permitted territories to vote on whether they would be slave or free.

b. Local governments would decide whether they would be slave or free.

c. Slavery was allowed only in the western states.

d. all of the above

21) Which 1857 Supreme Court case ruled that the federal government did not have the power to give a black man rights?

a. *Brown v. Board of Education*

*b. Dred Scott v. Sandford

c. *Roe v. Wade*

d. none of the above

22) Which war in American history caused more Americans to lose their lives than in all the other American wars put together?

a. World War I

*b. Civil War

c. Korean War

d. Vietnam War

23) The Fifteenth Amendment excluded which group?

*a. women

b. blacks

c. Chinese

d. none of the above

24) Southern state and local governments reacted to slaves' freedom by passing

a. anti-sovereignty codes.

b. nonwhites codes.

c. black regulations.

*d. black codes.

25) For a time, Congress supported the former slaves. In an effort known as _____, it tried to rebuild the South around a vision of racial justice.

a. the Fourteenth Amendment

*b. Reconstruction

c. the Civil Rights Act

d. none of the above

26) The Civil Rights Act of 1866 guaranteed African Americans which of the same rights as white Americans?

*a. property rights

b. right to participate in politics

c. limited private racial discrimination in hotels, restaurants, and theaters

d. all of the above

27) ___ were allegedly a requirement that voters were literate. In reality, they were a way to restrict black suffrage.

*a. Literacy tests

b. Intelligence tests

c. Black voters' tests

d. none of the above

28) In the Civil Rights Cases of 1883, the Supreme Court struck down the Civil Rights Act of 1875, ruling that Congress did not have the authority to stop private discrimination. In what year did Congress finally find a way around this barrier?

a. 1901

b. 2011

*c. 1964

d. 1887

29) The white majority built a system of segregation known as ______.

a. Ku Klux Klan

b. James Crow

*c. Jim Crow

d. none of the above

30) In what year did the Supreme Court rule, in *Plessy v. Ferguson*, that there was nothing inherently discriminatory in separating the races?

a. 1843

b. 1851

*c. 1896

d. 1954

31) The percentage of southern students in integrated schools eight years after *Brown v. Board of Education* was

a. 74

b. 6

*c. 1

d. none

32) What was the plot of the 1915 movie *Birth of a Nation*?

a. Social equality for all in America.

*b. Lust-filled black men

c. The framers of the Constitution.

d. The Puritans' quest for religious freedom.

33) Beginning in the 1920s, many African Americans left southern agriculture and moved to more lucrative factory jobs in the northern cities—a journey known as the

a. Northern Migration.

b. Extradition.

*c. Great Migration.

d. Great Movement.

34) In 1909, black leaders formed the NAACP. What does this abbreviation stand for?

a. National Association for the Advancement of Celebrated People

b. National Association for the Advancement of Christian Patrons

*c. National Association for the Advancement of Colored People

d. National Association for the Advancement of Christian People

35) In 1961, activists came up with a new tactic. Groups of young people rented Greyhound buses as _____ to protest segregated interstate bus lines and terminals.

a. Desegregation Riders

*b. Freedom Riders

c. Freedom for Blacks

d. freedom activists

36) Which of the following activists was instrumental in the success of the civil rights movement?

a. Martin L. King

b. Rosa Parks

c. A. Philip Randolph

*d. all of the above

37) Martin L. King delivered his famous "I Have a Dream" speech in _____ in Washington, DC.

*a. 1963

b. 1968

c. 1995

d. 1866

38) The Civil Rights Act was passed in what year?

a. 1991

b. 1962

*c. 1964

d. 1865

39) Congress passed the Voting Rights Act in what year?

*a. 1965

b. 1992

c. 1967

d. 1866

40) What is the American ideal often expressed as *equality of opportunity*?

a. Give every individual a fair chance at achieving success with the aid of government assistance.

b. Give every individual a fair chance at achieving success if they can access seed money from parents.

*c. Give every individual a fair chance at achieving success if they are talented and hardworking.

d. all of the above

41) When did the new approach of affirmative action emerge in America?

a. 1850s and 1860s

*b. 1960s and 1970s

c. 1970s and 1980s

d. 1980s and 1990s

42) Which of the following could a woman do in the early nineteenth century?

a. vote

b. serve on a jury

c, enter into a contract

*d. none of the above

43) When was the first convention for woman suffrage, held at Seneca Falls, that grew directly from the abolition movement?

*a. 1848

b. 1891

c. 1898

d. 1937

44) By 1916, an effective political campaign had won full suffrage in fifteen states and partial suffrage in twenty-three others. Women voted in every state of the West and Midwest except

a. Utah.

b. Wyoming.

c. Idaho.

*d. New Mexico.

45) President Woodrow Wilson put aside his condescension and supported women's suffrage as a

*a. "wartime measure."

b. "morally right thing to do."

c. "form of appeasement."

d. all of the above

46) After the 1970 election how many women were in the House of Representatives?

a. 36

b. 23

*c. 11

d. 4

47) Hispanics make up what percentage of the American population?

a. 10.3

*b. 17.3

c. 27.5

d. 45.9

48) Latinos took many of the tactics of the black civil rights movement and adapted them to their own needs. They organized which of the following organizations in 1929?

a. League of United Hispanic American Citizens

*b. League of United Latin American Citizens

c. United Latin American League

d. Hispanic League of Freedom

49) Immigrants often trigger the same fears. Which of the following corresponds to those fears?

a. They will undermine American values and culture.

b. They will remain loyal to their own languages and their home countries.

c. They will take away jobs.

*d. all of the above

50) Which of the following groups has the highest education level and the highest median personal income among American population groups?

a. European Americans

b. African Americans

*c. Asian Americans

d. Hispanics

51) The common language of Asian immigrants is

a. Japanese

b. Chinese

c. Vietnamese

*d. none

52) The third largest minority in the United States is

a. Blacks

*b. Asians

c. Hispanics

d. Native Americans

53) Congress passed the ______ in 1882 barring ______ immigrants and declaring them ineligible for citizenship.

a. Japanese Exclusion Act . . . Japanese

*b. Chinese Exclusion Act . . . Chinese

c. Vietnamese Exclusion Act . . . Vietnamese

d. Korean Exclusion Act . . . Korean

54) After the Pearl Harbor attack in 1941, President Roosevelt ordered the army to round up Japanese Americans and place them in internment camps. What did they lose as a result of this act of injustice?

a. their liberty

b. their jobs

c. their property and their bank accounts

*d. all of the above

55) San Francisco established separate schools for who?

a. Hispanics

*b. Chinese

c. Irish

d. Miners

56) By the time the United States stretched from coast to coast, only about ______ million of the ten million Native Americans remained.

*a. one

b. three

c. five

d. seven

57) In 1831, the Supreme Court ruled that Indian tribes were _______.

a. domestic indigenous tribes

*b. domestic dependent nations

c. independent countries

d. none of the above

58) The civil rights protests inspired some Native Americans, just as they did so many other groups, to organize a political movement. Which is one such movement?

a. American Indian Sovereignty

b. American Indian United

*c. American Indian Movement

d. American Indian Justice

59) Section 504 of the 1973 Rehabilitation Act benefited the disabled. Which piece of legislation did this bill borrow from?

*a. the Civil Rights Act of 1964

b. the Constitution

c. the Bill of Rights

d. Civil Rights Act of 1866

60) The movement for same-sex rights began with a riot. In 1969, police raided a _______ gay bar named the Stonewall Inn.

a. San Francisco

*b. New York City

c. Los Angeles

d. Salt Lake City

61) When did the American Psychiatric Association remove homosexuality from its list of mental disorders?

a. 1949

b. 1961

*c. 1973

d. 1999

62) In the early 1980s, AIDS plagued the gay community. This deadly disease pushed them into local politics. Which political action did they take?

a. They established links to the medical community.

b. They established connections with local governments.

c. They prodded politicians and drug companies into action.

*d. all of the above

63) Which president promised to open the military to gay men and women?

a. Ronald Reagan

b. Jimmy Carter

c. Gerald Ford

*d. Bill Clinton

64) Which president ended the "don't ask, don't tell" policy?

a. Ronald Reagan

b. George W. Bush

*c. Barack Obama

d. Richard Nixon

65) Which state became the first state to permit gay marriage?

a. California

b. New York

c. Vermont

*d. Massachusetts

66) Which state was the first to recognize civil unions between same sex partners?

*a. Vermont

b. Massachusetts

c. New York

d. California

67) The plague upon the gay community of the early 1980s was

*a. AIDS

b. marriage laws

c. military rules

d. Illegal drug use

68) How many LGBTQ Americans report serious employment discrimination?

*a. one in four

b. one in six

c. one in twelve

d. one in 32

69) In ______ the courts ruled that denying same-sex couples the right to marry violated equal protection, and in ______ the state legislature approved same-sex marriage. In both states, the public promptly voted to reject the practice.

a. Texas . . . Utah

b. Florida . . . Alabama

*c. California . . . Maine

d. none of the above

70) The freedom to participate in the full life of the community is also known as

a. civil liberties

b. legal rights

c. executive mandates

*d. civil rights

71) Once civil rights are won what is the next job of the public?

*a. protecting them

b. codifying them

c. ignoring them

d. there is no next step

72) The most powerful story in American history is

a. political parties

*b. battle to win civil rights

c. interest groups

d. power of the presidency

73) One way to view the history of civil rights is as a(n)

a. easy path

b. slow march

*c. steady march

d. fast run

74) Which of the following is a civil right?

a. voting

b. using public facilities

c. equal economic opportunity

*d. all of the above

75) One way to view the history of civil rights is as

*a. expanding and contracting

b. moving forward rapidly

c. moving forward slowly

d. moving backward slowly

76) The first step to political equality is

a. challenging society

*b. defining the group

c. changing the story

d. bring Federalism into play

77) Challenging society involves entering the

a. economic arena

b. international arena

*c. political arena

d. public space

78) Changing the view of immigrants from job taker to job creators is an example of

a. challenging society

b. employing Federalism

c. group definition

*d. changing the stories

79) Civil rights involve what area of government?

*a. local, state and federal

b. federal only

c. state only

d. civil rights does not involve government

80) The branch of government that normally makes the great changes regarding Civil Rights is

a. executive

*b. legislative

c. judicial

d. bureaucracy

81) The ultimate arbiters of civil rights are the

a. bureaucrats

b. executives who make changes

*c. courts

d. states

82) "Equal protection of the laws" is guaranteed by the

a. Bill of Rights

b. Twelfth Amendment

c. Thirteenth Amendment

*d. Fourteenth Amendment

83) When the court asks if the government has a compelling interest in singling out a race or an ethnicity they are applying

*a. strict scrutiny

b. suspect scrutiny

c. quasi-suspect scrutiny

d. rights consideration

84) A law that singles out an ethnicity is likely to have what court decision?

a. moved forward

*b. struck down

c. refused

d. sent back to be rewritten

85) A special category for gender is

a. suspect

b. strict scrutiny

*c. quasi-suspect

d. non-suspect

86) Legislation that mandates retirement at age 72 would fall under which category

a. suspect

b. strict scrutiny

c. quasi-suspect

*d. non-suspect

87) The group that developed the tactics other groups would use in battling for civil rights were

*a. African Americans

b. Asian Americans

c. Native Americans

d. Hispanics

88) Slaves found leadership and organization in their

a. homes

*b. churches

c. businesses

d. government

89) The legislation that enabled Maine to enter the union in 1820 as a free state was the

a. Compromise of 1850

b. Civil War

*c. Missouri Compromise

d. Emancipation Proclamation

90) Reading and interpreting a constitutional passage in order to vote is an example of a(n)

a. voting test

b. enrollment test

c. citizenship test

*d. literacy test

91) Discrimination that is codified in law is known as

*a. de jure discrimination

b. de facto discrimination

c. political discrimination

d. social discrimination

92) Discrimination that exists without a legal basis is

a. de jure discrimination

*b. de facto discrimination

c. political discrimination

d. social discrimination

93) The first racially integrated federal institution in the United States was the

a. House of Representatives

b. West Wing

*c. military

d. FBI

94) Segregated schools were ruled unconstitutional in

a. *Marbury v Madison*

b. *Plessy v Ferguson*

c. *Citizens United*

*d. Brown v Board of Education

95) Segregation was finally defeated by

*a. ordinary American people

b. military involvement

c. Executive order

d. court rulings

96) An approach that involves direct, positive steps to increase representation is

a. civil rights

*b. affirmative action

c. civil liberties

d. judicial review

97) When companies create policies that discriminate, even unintentionally, they are guilty of

a. affirmative action

b. equal opportunity

*c. disproportionate impact

d. proportional impact

98) School busing was meant to

a. fill school desks

b. bring rural children to urban schools

c. balance student numbers

*d. integrate public schools

99) The word added to the Civil Rights Act of 1964 that changed women's rights was

*a. sex

b. gender

c. female

d. woman

100) Phyllis Schlafly stopped what amendment by reframing the issue

a. Civil Rights

*b. Equal Rights

c. Equal Employment

d. Voting Age

CHAPTER 6

Public Opinion and Political Participation

1) Which perspective on public opinion's influence could be related to the American system's design to avoid the dangers of mob rule?

*a. ignorant masses

b. self-governing people

c. rational public

d. none of these

2) *Public Opinion,* an influential book, was written by

a. Ronald Reagan

*b. Walter Lippmann

c. John Kennedy

d. Karl Marx

3) Lippmann saw the typical American as distracted by

*a. minor scandals

b. voting records

c. party politics

d. none of the above

4) __________ described the science of public opinion as undeserving of the name.

a. Mills

*b. Lippmann

c. Goodnow

d. Lawrence

5) Lippmann saw the typical American as distracted by

*a. celebrity shenanigans

b. voting records

c. party politics

d. none of the above

6) Lippmann felt the typical American

a. was interested in politics

b. voted every election

*c. rarely understood policy details

d. was highly motivated

7) With what university were the authors of *The American Voter* affiliated?

*a. University of Michigan

b. University of California

c. Arizona State University

d. Harvard University

8) The publication of what text showed that those surveyed for the book's research knew little about the positions either political party stood for, or about the main policy issues at the time?

a. *Voting in the States after Landslides*

b. *The Constant Majority*

*c. The American Voter

d. none of these

9) In *The American Voter*, the authors argued citizens knew ________ about the positions either political party stood for, or about the main policy issues at the time.

*a. little

b. a moderate amount

c. a great deal

d. none of these

10) *The American Voter* presented the foundation for what concept known as the lack of a stable perspective in opinion surveys?

*a. nonattitudes

b. response bias

c. margin of error

d. scientific inquiry

11) ____ can be described as people changing their responses or opinions often randomly, not necessarily because of new information.

*a. Nonattitudes

b. Response bias

c. Margin of error

d. Shifting alignments

12) Which publication says the public is wise and reasonable in its opinions?

a. *The American Voter*

b. *The Informed Public*

*c. The Rational Public

d. none of these

13) ____ opinion is the key to assessing popular preferences, according to *The Rational Public*.

a. Minority

b. Majority

*c. Collective

d. Cascading

14) Which of the following is not one of the three basic propositions in *The Rational Public?*

a. Collective opinion is key to assessing popular preferences.

*b. Majority opinion is key to assessing popular preferences.

c. Individuals might be vague on policy specifics or even government basics.

d. Collective opinion is useful only when public officials are attentive to it.

15) To which of the three propositions in *The Rational Public* does the idea of information shortcuts relate?

a. Collective opinion is key to assessing popular preferences.

b. Majority opinion is key to assessing popular preferences.

*c. Individuals might be vague on policy specifics or even government basics.

d. Collective opinion is useful only when public officials are attentive to it.

16) ____ shortcuts are cues about candidates and policies drawn from everyday life.

a. Preference

*b. Information

c. Access

d. Temporary restraint

17) A homeowner grasping the importance of interest-rate changes demonstrates what type of shortcut relating to *The Rational Public*?

a. preference

*b. information

c. access

d. temporary restraint

18) The basic argument behind the publication of *The Rational Public* is that the _________ public has rational views and the government should pay closer attention to them.

a. minority

b. majority

*c. collective

d. cascading

19) Which book makes the argument that, taken together, the views of a random collection of people adds up to a rational public?

*a. The Wisdom of Crowds

b *The American Voter*

c. *The Informed Public*

d. *The Rationale of Crowds*

20) What term describes the tendency among a small group of decision makers to converge on a shared set of views?

a. like-mindedness

*b. groupthink

c. shared outlook

d. none of these

21) All of the following encourage creative thinking or solutions to policy problems except

*a. groupthink.

b. random selection of participants.

c. open dialogue.

d. none of these

22) In order for public opinion to guide government, according to the authors, how many conditions must be met?

*a. three

b. four

c. five

d. six

23) Public views are __________ those which politicians follow blindly.

*a. rarely

b. almost always

c. always

d. never

24) A(n) _____________ is political authority claimed by an election winner as reflecting the approval of the people.

a. ideological adjustment

*b. mandate

c. winner-take-all system

d. none of these

25) Those elected with mandates can experience ________ getting legislation passed in the policy area for which they claimed their election demonstrated a mandate.

a. ease

b. acceptance when

*c. difficulty

d. none of these; this does not relate to electoral mandates

26) ______ research is defined as the systematic study of a defined population analyzing a representative sample's views to draw inferences about the larger public's views.

*a. Survey

b. Qualitative

c. In-person

d. Random-digit dialing

27) Approximately how much is spent on campaign polling annually in the US?

a. $10 million

b. $100 million

c. $750 million

*d. $1 billion

28) "80% of Americans support the president" is an example of what type of rating?

a. campaign

*b. approval

c. establishment

d. none of these

29) Public opinion is often viewed as

*a. unreliable

b. reliable

c. changeable

d. available for purchase

30) Presidents claim to have the approval of the people when through

a. winning elections

b. legislative control

*c. mandates

d. judicial nominations

31) Polls help set the _________, or the issues that the public considers important.

*a. agenda

b. framework

c. legitimation of policy

d. evaluation of policy

32) Members of Congress are often _______________ to legislate in the face of strong popular opposition.

*a. reluctant

b. open

c. willing

d. none of these

33) President Trumps tweets are followed by millions and help shape

a. congressional votes

b. political campaigns

*c. supporters' views

d. opponents voting patterns

34) A sampling ____________ is defined as a designated group of people from whom a set of poll respondents is randomly selected.

*a. frame

b. error

c. measure

d. statistic

35) The sampling frame in a public survey should represent diverse aspects and characteristics of the _______, for conclusions to be drawn about this group.

*a. population

b. sample

c. random sample

d. stratified sample

36) ____ voters can be defined as those identified as more probable to turn out in an upcoming election.

*a. Likely

b. Registered

c. Campaign-friendly

d. Probable

37) Generally, the closer to Election Day the poll about electoral behaviors is taken, the ___ accurate it is.

a. less

*b. more

c. least

d. none of these

38) According to the text, ________ voters more accurately predict the outcome of most elections.

*a. likely

b. registered

c. campaign-friendly

d. probable

39) Calling respondents to a poll on a Friday night demonstrates lack of consideration for which principle of polling?

a. location

*b. timing

c. proximity

d. courteousness

40) Framing effects relate to the ________ of a question.

*a. wording

b. punctuation

c. spelling

d. none of these

41) ____ effects are the influences on the respondent of how a polling question is asked.

*a. Framing

b. Scaling

c. Sampling

d. Falsifying

42) In local political races, respondents to surveys typically favor the first candidate named in a list, demonstrating the ________ effect.

*a. framing

b. scaling

c. sampling

d. falsifying

43) A ________ poll is a form of negative campaigning that masquerades as a regular opinion survey.

a. survey research

b. partial

*c. push

d. none of these

44) What is considered the polling gold standard?

*a. random sample

b. self-selected sample

c. semi random sample

d. weighted sample

45) Samples of the population should be ___________ of that population.

*a. representative

b. indicative

c. short

d. none of these

46) Today, more than ________ of Americans rely on mobile phones.

*a. 47%

b. 50%

c. 54%

d. 65%

47) What is the typical margin of error for polls?

a. 2%

*b. 3%

c. 5%

d. 10%

48) A margin of sampling ________ is a statistical calculation for how accurate a poll's results are.

*a. error

b. residual

c. frame

d. framework

49) As a general rule, the larger the sample size, the ________ the margin of sampling error.

a. larger

*b. smaller

c. less affected

d. none of these

50) The margin of sampling error is the degree of __________ in any poll.

a. accuracy

*b. inaccuracy

c. representativeness

d. none of these

51) If you surveyed every individual in a population, the margin of error would be

*a. 0%.

b. 1%.

c. 3%.

d. 5%.

52) _____ bias is the tendency of poll respondents to misstate their views, frequently to avoid "shameful" opinions.

a. Selection

*b. Response

c. Sampling error

d. none of these

53) What bias reflects a respondent's desire to answer a question in a way that is "acceptable"?

a. random error

*b. response bias

c. sampling error

d. selection

54) The Bradley effect is a response bias based on

a. age.

*b. race.

c. income.

d. sexual orientation.

55) The apparent inclination of some survey respondents to avoid appearing racist or racially motivated is known as the _______ effect.

a. Bradford

*b. Bradley

c. Miranda

d. poor sampling

56) What magazine used polling to predict presidential elections and predicted the wrong winner in 1936?

*a. Literary Digest

b. *Readers Digest*

c. *Good Housekeeping*

d. *Political Digest*

57) The *Literary Digest* started polling to predict presidential elections in what year?

a. 1910

*b. 1920

c. 1950

d. 1951

58) Pollsters predicted who would win the presidential race in 2016?

*a. Clinton

b. Trump

c. Sanders

d. Obama

59) The *Literary Digest* incorrectly predicted who would lose in 1936?

*a. Franklin D. Roosevelt.

b. Woodrow Wilson.

c. Warren Harding.

d. John Kennedy.

60) What contributed to the incorrect prediction from the *Literary Digest* poll during President Franklin Roosevelt's election?

*a. sampling frame

b. response bias

c. oversampling

d. none of these

61) Converse found that when people were asked same question at different times their answers tended to

*a. change

b. remains similar

c. reverse direction

d. remains exactly the same

62) Cues gained from everyday life are known as

*a. information shortcuts

b. details

c. information cues

d. none of these

63) Savvy message consultants can use public opinion for

*a. manipulation

b. voting behavior

c. agenda setting

d. policy creation

64) What percentage of the "Silent Generation" approve of marijuana legalization?

a. 71

*b. 35

c. 20

d. 25

65) What percentage of millennials believe abortions should be legal?

a. 82

b. 78

*c. 62

d. 54

66) What effect is demonstrated by people wanting to hold the same views as a majority?

*a. bandwagon

b. boomerang

c. tiled-floor

d. "golden"

67) What effect is demonstrated by candidates who are leading in the polls tending to pick up support from voters who were undecided?

*a. bandwagon

b. boomerang

c. tiled-floor

d. underdog

68) What effect is described as the discrepancy between candidates' high poll ratings and election performance?

a. bandwagon

*b. boomerang

c. tiled-floor

d. "golden"

69) People not voting because they saw polls indicating their candidate was in the lead, resulting in their candidate losing the election, demonstrates the ________effect.

a. bandwagon

*b. boomerang

c. tiled-floor

d. "golden"

70) On average, women prefer ____________ candidates.

a. Republican

*b. Democratic

c. Libertarian

d. Women do not demonstrate systematic preferences.

71) Political __________ are individuals who control significant wealth, status, power, or visibility and consequently have significant influence over public debate.

*a. elites

b. partisans

c. beginners

d. none of these

72) __________ public is the best source of democratic decision making.

a. Irrational

b. Innovative

*c. Rational

d. Voting

73) Which of the following is most likely subject to groupthink?

*a. experts

b. independent voters

c. registered voters

d. none of these

74) How easy is it for people to convey their views to policymakers?

a. easy

*b. difficult

c. complicated

d. impossible

75) ______ polls are conducted by a campaign as the race begins, and these provide a basis for comparison.

*a. Benchmark

b. Response

c. Straw

d. Brushfire

76) What types of polls are informal polls carried out by local party organizations or news outlets, and involve actual nonbinding votes cast by party members?

a. benchmark

*b. straw

c. brushfire

d. response

77) Once an election begins campaigns are conduct internal surveys called ______ polls.

a. benchmark

b. straw

*c. brushfire

d. response

78) Polls taken on Election day are known as _______ polls.

a. benchmark

*b. exit

c. brushfire

d. response

79) Media often relies on _______ polls to call results.

a. benchmark

b. straw

c. brushfire

*d. exit

80) When a party has members vote unofficially to help determine who would win a primary it is known as a _______ poll.

a. benchmark

*b. straw

c. brushfire

d. response

81) The first poll conducted by a campaign will likely be a _______ poll.

*a. benchmark

b. straw

c. brushfire

d. response

82) Bad news from a poll is referred to as a

a. benchmark

b. straw

*c. brushfire

d. response

83) A 3 percent margin of error on a 50 percent approval rating means the actual rating could be as high as

a. 150%

*b. 53%

c. 47%

d. 15%

84) A 3 percent margin of error on a 50 percent approval rating means the actual rating could be as low as

a. 150%

b. 53%

*c. 47%

d. 15%

85) An internet poll where respondents choose to respond or not respond is how accurate?

a. very accurate

*b. not very accurate

c. depends on the website

d. depends on the questions

86) As the number of respondents decreases the margin of error

a. decreases

*b. increases

c. remains the same

d. number of respondents does not affect margin of error

87) The Bradley Effect was first seen in

a. Florida

*b. California

c. Oregon

d. Vermont

88) When survey respondents answer in a way to avoid appearing racist they are showing the

a. West Coast Effect

*b. Bradley Effect

c. California Effect

d. Los Angeles Effect

89) When a citizen donates funds simply by pointing their mouse at a computer screen they are practicing

a. Clicktocracy

*b. Clicktivism

c. Clicktocratic

d. Clicktic

90) The first step in the voting process is

a. choosing a candidate

*b. registering

c. choosing a party

d. casting a vote

91) How many states allow same day voting?

a. 13

b. 15

*c. 17

d. 19

92) If you fill out your ballot and mail it in along with most other voters in your state you likely live in

a. New Hampshire

b. Montana

c. California

*d. Oregon

93) Sitting at a table and verifying voter addresses is an example of

*a. political participation

b. direct action

c. volunteer voting

d. institutional participation

94) Standing on a street corner holding a political sign and waving at traffic is an example of

a. direct action

*b. electoral activities

c. institutional participation

d. political voice

95) Writing a letter to a State Senator after the election is an example of

a. direct action

b. electoral activities

*c. political voice

d. institutional participation

96) Which of the following topics can citizens use their political voice to contact government officials?

a. potholes

b. immigration policy

c. nuclear-weapons agreements

*d. all of the above

97) When contacting government officials, it is important to

*a. contact the right official

b. word the letter professionally

c. use enough postage

d. send the letter via email

98) Alexis de Tocqueville was impressed with American's propensity to

a. vote

b. write letters to the editor

*c. get involved

d. ignore party politics

99) The most active group in U.S. history for volunteering their time are the

a. Baby Boomers

b. Generation X

c. Silent Generation

*d. Millennials

100) Taking time on Thanksgiving to sever food at a local women's shelter is an example of

*a. Voluntary engagement

b. Direct Action

c. Institutional engagement

d. Clicktocracy

Chapter 7

Media, Technology and Government

1) In what year did the American Medical Association enlist Ronald Reagan to help fight President John F. Kennedy's health care program?

a. 1963

b. 1981

c. 1980

*d. 1961

2) During the health care debate in the early 1960s, Ronald Reagan cut a record (on vinyl) that the medical association sent (by snail mail) to

a. every member of Congress.

b. every member of the Senate.

*c. every physician's office.

d. every hospital.

3) What did Ronald Reagan warn about health care reform in the early 1960s?

*a. "One day we will awake to find that we have socialism."

b. "One day we will awake to find that we have fascism."

c. "One day we will awake to find that we have capitalism."

d. "One day we will awake to find that we have communism."

4) Congress turned down health care reform in the early 1960s, although four years later another version of the law was passed and is now known as

a. Medicaid.

b. food stamps.

*c. Medicare.

d. disability insurance.

5) The Health Insurance Association of American aired television ads opposing President Clinton's health plan, these were known as the ________ ads.

a. Bill and Hillary

b. Ron and Nancy

c. Joe and Mary

*d. Harry and Louise

6) What new tool did Donald Trump utilize in 2016 to air his views on government health care?

*a. Twitter

b. Facebook

c. Instagram

d. Snapchat

7) ______ is all the ways people get information about politics and the wider world.

a. Twitter

b. Tumblr

*c. Media

d. World Wide Web

8) A major change in media over the past fifty years is

a. information comes slower

*b. more formats

c. public is less active in new media

d. new media is less popular

9) Facebook is an example of

a. newspaper

b. magazine

c. old media

*d. new media

10) A role of media in a democratic system is

*a. public watchdog

b. electing candidates

c. broadcasting the political agenda

d. sharing candidate ideology

11) Media can help make informed voters through the role of

a. public watchdog

*b. providing information

c. shaping the political agenda

d. showing candidate mistakes

12) In the 1830s, ______ became the first mass media.

a. letters

b. radio

c. telegrams

*d. newspapers

13) What is the textbook's definition of mass media?

a. Facebook for all.

b. Internet access for all.

c. Media for you and me.

*d. Information and entertainment for audiences

14) In the 1830s, what newspaper hired reporters to dig up facts and give readers stories?

a. the *Washington Post*

b. the *Chicago Tribune*

*c. the New York Herald

d. *USA Today*

15) Which war was known as the first media war?

a. Korean War

*b. Spanish-American War

c. World War I

d. Vietnam War

16) People with strong opinions are affected by new information in what way?

a. they change their opinion

b. they look for similar information

*c. existing opinion is reinforced

d. they ignore it

17) Between 2000 and 2015, American newspapers slashed what percentage of their staffs?

*a. 40

b. 13

c. 3

d. 47

18) During the 1930s, who delivered a weekly radio address known as the "Fireside Chat"?

a. Theodore Roosevelt

b. Karl Marx

c. Walt Whitman

*d. Franklin Roosevelt

19) What is the main demographic for talk radio?

*a. middle-aged white male and conservative

b. middle-aged African American and liberal

c. age forty-five to sixty-four white female and conservative

d. age forty-five to sixty-four Hispanic male and liberal

20) What percentage of the American public calls radio its main news source?

*a. 15

b. 47

c. 26

d. 12

21) Which president gave the first live press conference in February 1961?

a. Dwight Eisenhower

b. Ronald Reagan

c. Lyndon Johnson

*d. John F. Kennedy

22) Which two networks monopolized the television news business during the 1960s and 1970s?

a. Fox and MSNBC

b. CNN and Fox

*c. CBS and NBC

d. CBS and ABC

23) In what year did Rupert Murdoch launch Fox News?

a. 1978

b. 1999

*c. 1996

d. 1995

24) The corporate setting helps blur the line between news, politics, and entertainment, a phenomenon now described as

a. minor media.

b. global information.

*c. infotainment.

d. entertainment.

25) In new media who chooses the material to be seen?

a. Newspaper editor

b. Director

c. Producer

*d. Reader

26) How long does it take a reader to respond to story on digital media?

*a. immediately

b. 24 hours

c. 48 hours

d. 3-4 days

27) Who does the reporting for new media?

a. Readers

*b. Traditional organization reporters

c. Web-based reporters

d. Editors

28) How long has it been since three networks and the local newspaper, basically, provided all of the news?

*a. about 30 years

b. not since the early 1900s

c. only about the last 10 years

d. about 50 years

29) Which of the following is NOT considered "new media"?

a. Facebook

b. Twitter

c. Internet

*d. cable news

30) What type of story attracts young viewers?

*a. sensational

b. educational

c. local interest

d. routine

31) One of the ways the Internet could enhance democracy is by

*a. making everyone a potential news reporter.

b. raising the bar for entry into politics.

c. exposing fallacious points of view.

d. allowing more people to stay at home with no need to attend public rallies.

32) Which media form is likely to include a variety of viewpoints?

a. Facebook page

*b. Newspaper

c. Personal Twitter

d. Instagram

33) What was the top-visited news website in 2010?

*a. Reddit

b. FoxNews

c. CNN

d. www.nytimes.com

34) An example of perceived fake news is

a. report on number of injuries in an auto accident

*b. Global Warming is not a scientific fact

c. Dow Jones went down 40 points

d. The president is visiting China

35) An example of a citizen turned into a news provider is

a. Citizen interviewed for the news

b. Television cameraman catching an auto accident on tape

*c. Passerby filming an accident on a cellphone

d. President answer questions at a press conference

36) Which type of media bias is most obvious to academics?

*a. commercial

b. liberal

c. conservative

d. realism

37) Which group is most likely to claim the media is biased?

a. liberals

*b. Republicans

c. Democrats

d. the public as a whole

38) What percentage of Americans believe the media separate fact from opinion?

a. 12 percent

b. 23 percent

*c. 32 percent

d. 58 percent

39) Which of the following is a complaint a Republican might make about traditional news organizations?

a. "Corporate owned media is biased against change"

b. "Media is a corporate powerhouse"

*c. "Media donations go to the Democratic Party"

d. "Media donations go to the Republican Party"

40) Which of the following is a media reporter likely to identify as?

a. Republican

b. Libertarian

c. Democrat

*d. Independent

41) More conservative communities usually get

*a. more conservative newspapers.

b. more libertarian newspapers.

c. less news coverage.

d. more news coverage.

42) What classic "rule of thumb" guides local TV news?

a. "short stories are better than long"

b. "cover the person not the event"

c. "make 'em squirm"

*d. "if it bleeds it leads"

43) According to studies how much favoritism is there in campaign coverage?

*a. none

b. over half of the stories

c. three-quarters of the stories

d. almost all of the stories

44) At the end of an election campaign, the media tends to focus on

*a. what mistakes the loser made.

b. mending the two sides so the winner can effectively govern.

c. the candidates' families.

d. the winner's most effective strategies.

45) Newspapers tend to run content with what form of bias?

a. Geographical

*b. Toward advertisers

c. Conservative

d. Liberal

46) What is the bias that is found in all news media?

a. Conservative

b. Liberal

*c. Need to attract a large audience

b. Corporate

47) What does media sell?

a. airtime

b. journalist availability

c. backdrop of the newsroom

*d. audience

48) How does a "fairness bias" corrupt news reporting?

a. It forces news outlets to give equal time to people on both sides of an issue.

b. It prevents news reporters from being able to report on both sides of an issue.

*c. It causes news reporters to present two sides of an issue when the truth is represented better by one side of the debate.

d. all of the above

49) Which statement is true about public ownership of the media?

*a. European countries have a much higher level of public ownership than the United States.

b. Americans pay more in taxes for government-owned media than is paid in most other countries.

c. Public ownership of the media is against the law in the United States.

d. Public ownership of the media is against the law in many European countries.

50) What government agency was created in the FDR administration to referee the airwaves?

a. Environmental Protection Agency

b. Federal Election Commission

*c. Federal Communications Commission

d. Federal Fairness Doctrine Board

51) What did the Fairness Doctrine attempt to accomplish?

a. It tried to make American elections fairer for third parties.

*b. It regulated the mass media so that different viewpoints would have to be presented on each television station.

c. It tried to make capital accumulation in the United States a fairer process.

d. It created fairness guidelines for the mass media to voluntarily follow.

52) Who was president when the FCC repealed the Fairness Doctrine?

a. George H. W. Bush

b. William Jefferson Clinton

*c. Ronald Reagan

d. Jimmy Carter

53) What did the Telecommunications Act of 1996 accomplish?

a. It caused a repeal of the Fairness Doctrine.

*b. It allowed for cross-ownership of media outlets by media conglomerates.

c. It led to the development of the Internet.

d. It caused the demise of newspapers.

54) To what extent has the US Supreme Court upheld the First Amendment protection of a free press?

a. Not at all there; have been numerous instances where the free press has been violated by government censorship.

b. Only a little; it has allowed some government censorship but not too much.

c. Quite a bit, but government censorship has occurred routinely throughout US history.

*d. There has been very little (almost no) censorship of the print media.

55) What percentage of the TV market share in Great Britain goes to the publicly owned BBC?

a. 10

*b. 32

c. 19

d. 58

56) What percentage of the TV market share in the United States goes to the publicly owned PBS?

a. 10

b. 38

*c. barely 2

d. about 6

57) News media is likely to pitch a story toward which political slant?

a. Conservative

b. Liberal

c. Corporate view

*d. Center

58) The prime directive of the news media is to

*a. Expand the audience

b. Predict the winner in elections

c. Be on the scene in less than a minute

d. Charge over $1 million dollars for advertising

59) Why do people complain about news media bias?

a. Stories are fact pitched to center

b. Stories are to the left of conservatives

c. Stories are to the right of liberals

*d. All of the above

60) Which of the following news stories are most likely to generate excitement?

a. Local school board meeting

*b. Miners trapped below the earth

c. Healthcare proposal

d. County commissioner meeting

61) Local news gets much of its drama from

a. School board meetings

b. Auto accidents

*c. Crime

d. Mayor's weekly message

62) The lead story on local news is likely to be which of the following

a. Mayor's press conference

b. Local Principal talking about extended school day

c. Road construction that backs up traffic

*d. Four car accident with three fatalities

63) What is an election report likely to focus on?

*a. The candidate's bankruptcy

b. The candidate's stance on taxes

c. The candidate's political party

d. The candidate's birthday party

64) Because people generally consume media that reinforces their existing beliefs, it takes broad coverage with an unambiguous message to change peoples' minds. What does the textbook call this phenomenon?

a. a "broken record"

*b. a "loud signal"

c. a "perfect ideal"

d. a "norm-breaker"

65) One of the most direct ways the media affects politics is via its __________ role.

a. socialization

b. entertainment

*c. agenda-setting

d. infomercial

66) Which of the following is the most subtle manner in which the media affects politics?

a. editorializing

b. framing

c. agenda-setting

*d. priming

67) In short, the __________ define(s) the nature of the problem, organize(s) potential solutions, and wipe(s) out alternative policies.

*a. frame

b. agenda

c. newsmakers

d. media schema

68) If people's minds are generally made up, what effect do news stories usually have on the way people think about politics?

a. depends if it is television or radio

*b. very little or none

c. depends if it is new media or old media

d. quite a bit if the news story is well written

69) In media jargon, what is a small clip from a candidate speech referred to as?

a. a "tidbit"

b. a "huge mistake"

*c. a "sound bite"

d. a "little morsel"

70) Sometimes politicians try to manipulate media sound bites by providing

*a. dramatic visuals.

b. full text of the speech.

c. guidelines on what part of the speech to use.

d. their own interpretation of the speech.

72) Which of the following is NOT an emphasis of media attention in election campaign coverage?

a. who's winning

b. conflict

*c. issues

d. drama

74) What makes mass media in the United States so unique?

a. It focuses on principles over personalities.

*b. It has always been a commercial enterprise.

c. It employs attention to detail and an issue-based focus.

d. nothing

75) Although crime is ______, media coverage has audiences believing crime is ______.

a. dropping; dropping

b. rising; dropping

*c. dropping; rising

d. rising; rising

76) Which president was involved in the Watergate scandal?

a. John F. Kennedy

b. Lyndon Johnson

c. Barry Goldwater

*d. Richard Nixon

77) Which of the following events transformed the media's stance toward the powerful?

*a. Civil Rights Movement

b. Cuban Missile Crisis

c. Iraq War

d. End of Cold War

78) After the Watergate scandal reporters redefined their roles and became

a. chummy insiders

*b. skeptics

c. professional

d. paid

79) The reporter's newest mission is to

a. help citizens make the right choice in the voting booth

*b. uncover lies

c. help presidents cover their mistakes

d. hiding bad behavior

80) The freedoms that the media enjoys come from which amendment?

*a. First

b. Third

c. Fifth

d. Seventh

81) Which of the following is NOT declining as a source of news?

a. television

*b. Internet

c. radio

d. newspapers

82) Prior restraint is an aspect of

a. early printing

b. sharing information

*c. censoring

d. editing

83) Saying the president is mentally unstable is an example of

a. libel

b. prior restraint

c. censoring

*d. slander

84) News media regulated from the beginning is

*a. television

b. newspapers

c. social media

d. journals

85) In exchange for a broadcasting frequency radio stations were required to be

a. unbiased

*b. socially responsible

c. unionized

d. publicly owned

86) The Fairness Doctrine led stations to avoid

a. advertising

b. corporate leadership

*c. political controversies

d. local news

87) The Reagan administration promoted media as a

a. public commodity

b. political tool

c. governmental agency

*d. private commodity

88) Government regulation of media evolves as

*a. media evolves

b. elections occur

c. directors change

d. nations become more involved

89) When the FCC established "net neutrality" it prohibited

a. public ownership of Internet providers

*b. Internet providers form charging more for certain content

c. Internet providers from being foreign owned

d. private ownership of Internet providers

90) One of the top two radio companies is

a. ABC

b. NBC

*c. CBS

d. CNN

91) Consolidation is a threat to

a. free press

b. public radio

c. public television

*d. free speech

92) The _____ allows companies to won multiple media markets.

*a. Telecommunications Act of 1996

b. Fairness Doctrine

c. Federal Communications Commission

d. First Amendment

93) The United States does not typically rely on which model of media organization?

a. Regulation

*b. Government Ownership

c. International

d. Markets

94) The public radio station in the United States is

a. CBS

b. PBS

*c. NPR

d. BBC

95) The largest network in Britain is

a. CBS

b. PBS

c. NPR

*d. BBC

96) In authoritarian nations who controls the media?

*a. government

b. private citizens

c. free market

d. large corporations

97) The media influence on politics is on display during which event?

a. market rises

*b. elections

c. depressions

d. natural disasters

98) Research has shown that reporting on terrorist acts leads to

a. fewer terrorist acts

b. bloodier terrorist acts

*c. more terrorist acts

d. no effect on terrorist acts

99) Media's prime concern in an election campaign is

a. who is running

b. poll numbers

c. political affiliation

*d. who will win

100) Sound bites have gone from over ______ seconds to under ______ seconds.

*a. 40; 8

b. 8; 40

c. 20; 5

d. 5; 20

Chapter 8

Campaigns and Elections

1) Which of the following candidates in 2016 broke all the rules?

*a. Donald Trump

b. Ted Cruz

c. Hilary Clinton

d. Marco Rubio

2) How much free media coverage is it estimated Donald Trump received in the 2016 campaign?

a. $500 million

b. $1 billion

*c. $2 billion

d. none, he paid for all coverage

3) Which of the following candidates in 2016 broke all the rules?

a. Donald Trump

b. Ted Cruz

c. Hilary Clinton

*d. Bernie Sanders

4) The long race for president takes a large number of candidates. How many Republicans candidates ran in 2016?

a. Ten

*b. Seventeen

c. Fifteen

d. Twenty

5) Americans vote more often and for more officers _______ than the people of almost any other nation.

a. on the local level of government

*b. on every level of government

c. on the national level of government

d. on the state level of government

6) What percentage of the US population is white, as of 2017?

a. 39

b. 57.5

*c. 61.3

d. 90.2

7) What percentages of Iowa's and New Hampshire's populations are white?

a. 65.0, 89.3

*b. 86, 91

c. 38.5, 49.0

d. 18.1, 79.8

8) The first presidential caucus of the season is held in

a. New Hampshire

b. Massachusetts

*c. Iowa

d. California

9) The first presidential primary of the season is held in

a. Iowa

*b. New Hampshire

c. Massachusetts

d. California

10) What was the year when women in all states could vote?

*a. 1920

b. 1821

c. 1929

d. 1963

11) What was the first state to allow women to voter?

a. Virginia

b. Wyoming

c. North Carolina

*d. New Jersey

12) How many Americans did NOT vote in the 2016 presidential race?

*a. 100 million

b. 50 million

c. 25 million

d. 3000

13) What was the percentage of voting-age population who turned out in 1912?

*a. 58.8

b. 54.8

c. 67.4

d. 89.7

14) What was the percentage of voting-age population who turned out in 2016?

a. 58.8

*b. 54.8

c. 67.4

d. 89.7

15) What would be a reason for a special election?

*a. office holder dies

b. President does not like office holder

c. voters ask for one

d. governor asks for one

16) What percentage of the House is elected every two years?

a. 33%

b. 50%

c. 75%

*d. 100%

17) How often is the president elected?

*a. every 4 years

b. every 6 years

c. every 8 years

d. when he calls an election

18) Why do Iowa and New Hampshire get the first crack at deciding each party's presidential nominee?

*a. State officials are empowered to decide their own election calendars—with the consent of the two parties.

b. Congress established this in 1792.

c. The citizens of these two states voted this into law.

d. none of the above

19) The state governs the ________ and ________ of elections.

*a. "place"... "manner"

b. "time"... "day"

c. "practice"... "application"

d. none of the above

20) The state governs the ________ and ________ of elections.

*a. "time"... "manner"

b. "time"... "day"

c. "practice"... "application"

d. none of the above

21) The date of the primary is set by the

*a. state

b. political party

c. president

d. Congress

22) When was the date of elections set?

*a. 1845

b. 1951

c. 1917

d. 1983

23) In parliamentary democracies what is the usual time period in which an election must be held?

a. 3 years

b. 4 years

*c. 5 years

d. 6 years

24) What month are Senate elections held?

a. March

*b. November

c. January

d. September

25) What day of the week do Americans vote for House members?

a. Saturday

b. Friday

c. Wednesday

*d. Tuesday

26) In what year are House elections held?

*a. even-numbered years

b. years divisible by three

c. years divisible by five

d. odd-numbered years

27) When is election day for House members?

*a. first Tuesday after first Monday in November of every even-numbered year

b. first Wednesday after first Monday in November of every even-numbered year

c. first Tuesday after first Thursday in November of every even-numbered year

d. first Tuesday after first Monday in November of every odd-numbered year

28) How much of the Senate is elected every two year?

a. 100%

b. half

c. one-fourth

*d. one-third

29) United States senators' term is ________ years; that's one of the ________ elected terms in the world.

a. two... shortest

b. four... quickest

*c. six... longest

d. none of the above

30) All American national elections are on a fixed cycle (except when an officeholder resigns or dies). Which of the following dire situations would affect this schedule?

a. war

b. economic collapse

c. terrorist attacks

*d. none of the above

31) A prime minister once remarked: "In your system, you guys campaign for 24 hours a day, every day for two years. You know, politics is one thing, but we have to run a government." Which country was this politician from?

a. Belgium

b. France

*c. Canada

d. Great Britain

32) The United States was the ________ nation to choose its chief executive by popular election.

*a. first

b. second

c. twentieth

d. fourth

33) American judges were ________ to face the voters, more than a century ago.

*a. the first

b. the fifth

c. the twenty-third

d. the fourth

34) Today how many states elect judges?

a. 20

*b. 39

c. 50

d. 10

35) Candidates for national office (presidency and Congress) spent more than ________ on their campaigns in 2016.

a. $1.5 billion

*b. $6.5 billion

c. $18 billion

d. $100 million

36) The 2018 midterms had the Democrats outraising the Republican by more than

a. $13 million

b. $434 million.

c. $1 billion.

*d. $100 million.

37) In 2016 Comcast gave ________ to Democrats and ________ to Republicans.

a. $1 million; $1 million

b. $1.8 million; $2.5 million

*c. $1.9 million; $2.1 million

d. $2.1 million; $1.9 million

38) The US system sets strict limits on individual donations: no one may contribute more than ________ to any individual candidate.

*a. $2,700

b. $3.5 million

c. $45,000

d. $500

39) How much can one individual contribute to an old fashioned PAC?

a. $2,700

b. $3,000

*c. $5,000

d. unlimited

40) Onetime candidate Morris "Mo" Udall said, afterward, "You have to be a little crazy to run for president." Which presidential election did he vie for?

a. 1875

*b. 1976

c. 1997

d. 1796

41) Parties generally nominate candidates from which office for president?

a. attorney general

b. secretary of state

*c. governor

d. House

42) The last president to come directly out of the House of Representatives was James Garfield, back in what year?

a. 1806

b. 1857

*c. 1880

d. 1959

43) ___ is the date on the primary calendar when the most states hold primaries and caucuses on the same day.

*a. Super Tuesday

b. Super Election Day

c. Super Primaries and Caucuses Day

d. none of the above

44) Because President Obama ran unopposed in 2012, Democrats had ________ contested primaries or caucuses.

*a. no

b. two

c. four

d. six

45) Which states have the first presidential caucus and primary contests every four years?

a. Idaho and California

*b. Iowa and New Hampshire

c. New Hampshire and Connecticut

d. New York and Maryland

46) ________ refers to the spike in the polls that follows an event.

a. *Polls bounce*

*b. Electoral bounce

c. *Voters bounce*

d. all of the above

47) Which event normally has the effect of creating an increase in the poll numbers for a presidential candidate?

*a. political party convention

b. rock concert

c. graduation ceremony

d. none of the above

48) ________ refers to a system under which the winning candidate receives all the delegates for that state.

*a. Winner-take-all system

b. Proportional representation

c. Demographic system

d. none of the above

49) A system of ________ allocates delegates based on the proportion of the vote a candidate wins.

a. winner-take-all

b. demographics

*c. proportional representation

d. none of the above

50) Traditionally, which party has adhered to the winner-take-all system?

*a. Republicans

b. Democrats

c. Green Party

d. none of the above

51) Traditionally, which party has adhered to the proportional representation system?

a. Republicans

b. Social Party

*c. Democrats

d. all of the above

52) In 2016, ________ primaries shifted to proportional representation before mid-March.

*a. GOP

b. Democratic

c. Green Party

d. Social Party

53) In 2016 the GOP allowed states to determine how to allocate their delegates after mid-March, what was the reasoning?

a. states requested it

b. candidates request it

*c. did not want candidate chosen too early

d. did not want candidate chosen too late

54) During the primary season candidates must

a. raise as much money as possible

b. visit as many states as possible

*c. make a strong first impression

d. avoid television commercials

55) Which Democratic presidential candidate in 1992 featured a whiteboard displaying a reminder to campaign staffers: "It's the Economy, Stupid"?

a. George H. W. Bush

b. George W. Bush

*c. Bill Clinton

d. Ronald Reagan

56) When members of a political party get together before a general election to choose delegates to the convention, they are attending a

a. primary

b. general election meeting

*c. caucus

d. convention planning meeting

57) When only party members can cast a vote in the primary it is known as a(n)

a. caucus

b. open primary

*c. closed primary

d. private vote

58) When any eligible voter can vote in a primary it is known as a(n)

a. caucus

b. closed primary

c. public vote

*d. open primary

59) Party officials hope to have a candidate by

a. Labor Day

*b. Super Tuesday

c. Fourth of July

d. Memorial Day

60) Donald Trump dominated what media which helped him win the Republican nomination?

*a. news feeds

b. editorials

c. print news

d. foreign newspapers

61) According to Donald Trump, "Controversy, in short, ________"?

*a. sells

b. should be avoided

c. is costly

d. is immoral

62) Which of the following voting blocks was Trump able to mobilize?

*a. white voters with low education

b. black voters with low education

c. white voters with high education

d. black voters with high education

63) Candidates running in the primary are talking to more ________ voters and then to more ________ voters in the general election.

a. centrist; ideologically driven

*b. ideologically driven; centrist

c. liberal; conservative

d. conservative; liberal

64) ________ refers to the tendency for members of Congress to win reelection in overwhelming numbers.

a. *Nepotism advantage*

*b. Incumbency advantage

c. *Insider advantage*

d. none of the above

65) Running for Congress is not only a rich person's club. Which of the following famous or wealthy people mounted a run but did not win?

a. David Trone

b. Linda McMahon

c. Jerry Springer

*d. all of the above

66) What are *midterm elections*?

a. Elections held in the middle of the year.

b. Elections held in the middle of each term.

*c. Elections held in a nonpresidential election year.

d. none of the above

67) In 1995, the Supreme Court ruled that ________ could not be the predominant factor in creating congressional districts.

*a. race

b. socioeconomic status

c. gender

d. all of the above

68) In what state did the Supreme Court permit partisan districts?

a. California

b. Texas

*c. North Carolina

d. Georgia

69) In what state did the Supreme Court permit partisan districts?

a. California

b. Texas

c. Alabama

*d. Maryland

70) ________ refers to a political system where individual candidates decide to run, raise their own money, and design their own strategy.

a. *Independent-centered elections*

*b. Candidate-centered elections

c. *Individual-centered elections*

d. all of the above

71) ________ focus on the person running for office, not the party the person is from.

*a. Candidate-centered elections

b. Party-centered elections

c. Platform-centered elections

d. Issue-centered elections

72) What decade saw the spread of primaries?

*a. 1970s

b. 1950s

c. 1930s

d. 1820s

73) In most advanced democracies, ________ remain the primary engines of campaigns and elections.

*a. political parties

b. candidates

c. general members of the populace

d. none of the above

74) In the last forty midterm elections the president's party picked up seats in Congress how many times?

a. 1

b. 3

*c. 5

d. 7

75) In the last forty midterm elections how often did the president's party lose House seats?

*a. 8

b. 10

c. 12

d. 14

76) Who usually wins during midterm congressional elections following a war's outbreak?

a. Democrats

b. Republicans

*c. Opposition

d. No difference

77) Which factor contributes to winning a congressional election?

a. money

b. organization

c. strategy and message

*d. all of the above

78) Typically how much money is needed to mount a legitimate challenge in a House district?

a. up to $100,000

b. up to $300,000

c. up to $500,000

*d. up to $2 million

79) How much money would a candidate need to run for Senate?

a. $6-8 million

b. $8-10 million

*c. $10-12 million

d. $12-14 million

80) Where does all the money go?

a. media/direct mailing

b. database and demographic data

c. phone banks

*d. all of the above

81) ________ refers to a long list of potential donors that candidates must phone.

a. *Donor list*

b. *Green list*

c. *Potential hit list*

*d. Call list

82) ________ refers to a seat in Congress without an incumbent running for reelection.

a. *Vacancy seat*

*b. Open seat

c. *Incumbent opening seat*

d. *Congressional seat*

83) ________ refers to an automated phone call used to contact thousands of voters simultaneously; may feature a recorded message by the candidate or a popular party leader—or an attack on the opponent.

*a. Robocall

b. *Automated call*

c. *Voters call*

d. none of the above

84) ________ refers to campaign staffers who arrive at major event sites—e.g., for an announcement speech—a day or more ahead of time, to organize the site and build crowds.

a. *Campaign staffers team*

b. *Motivational team*

*c. Advance team

d. none of the above

85) ________ refers to running for office by attacking the opponent. An unpopular tactic that is, nevertheless, very effective.

*a. Negative campaigning

b. *Trash talking*

c. *Tactical campaigning*

d. none of the above

86) ________ refers to attracting supporters or votes one by one, through door-to-door visits or small meetings.

a. *Individual campaigning*

b. *Door-to-door campaigning*

*c. Retail campaigning

d. *Supporters campaigning*

87) ________ refers to the use of text messages to donate funds to a campaign.

*a. Text-to-donate

b. *Text campaigning*

c. *Text-to-fund*

d. *Dial-to-cash*

88) A common rookie mistake is

a. not collecting enough money

b. hiring too many people

c. hiring too few people

*d. lack of a campaign strategy

89) Where does all the money go?

a. media/direct mailing

b. database and demographic data

c. phone banks

*d. all of the above

90) An element of a successful campaign strategy is

*a. building a coalition of supporters

b. lots of television commercials

c. phone banks

*d. good demographic information

91) An element of a successful campaign strategy is

a. phone banks

*b. connecting with voters

c. demographic data

d. direct mailings

92) The primary way candidates reach voters is through

a. party meetings

b. debates

*c. media

d. churches

93) Old fashioned politicking such as ________ is still the best way to win votes.

a. running television ads

b. writing letters to the editor

c. debates

*d. knocking on someone's door

94) A good message will

*a. give people a good reason to vote for you.

b. show how you feel about government.

c. give good biographical information.

d. show the opposition you are serious.

95) First year members of Congress are referred to as

a. newbies

*b. freshman

c. new recruits

d. freshies

96) As a new member of Congress when should you start planning your reelection campaign?

a. six months after the election

b. the following year

c. eighteen months after the election

*d. immediately

97) Why does the United States hold frequent elections?

a. to change government

b. to get the party they want in charge

*c. to hold public officials accountable

d. to keep public officials busy

98) How many states require a photo ID to vote?

*a. 8

b. 10

c. 12

d. 14

99) How many states allow same day voter registration?

a. 12

*b. 14

c. 16

d. 18

100) Americans ________ the rising tide of campaign cash, but the issue is a ________ priority.

a. favor; low

b. favor; high

*c. oppose; low

d. oppose; high

Chapter 9

Interest Groups and Political Parties

1) What is the street in downtown Washington, DC, that is home to the headquarters of many lobbying firms and interest groups?

a. I Street

*b. K Street

c. M Street

d. P Street

2) James Madison warns against interest groups in Federalist no. ________

a. 5.

b. 7.

*c. 10.

d. 25.

3) Madison refers to interest groups in the Federalist no. 10 as

a. lobbyists.

*b. factions.

c. special interests.

d. political parties.

4) Which of the following terms does NOT refer to a group that is primarily interested in gaining the support of government to pursue its specific policy goals?

*a. allied group

b. special interest group

c. faction

d. interest group

5) An interest group is defined as

a. an organization whose goal is to influence citizens.

b. an organization whose goal is to get members elected to office.

c. an organization whose goal is to disrupt the lawmaking process.

*d. an organization whose goal is to influence government.

6) The two important elements in the definition of an interest group are

a. membership and money.

*b. organization and influence.

c. bribery and blackmail.

d. persuasion and information.

7) A ________ is an individual who contacts government officials on behalf of a particular cause or issue.

*a. lobbyist

b. constituent

c. member of Congress

d. specialist

8) One of the threats of strict or strong partisanship is that it could lead to

a. increased participation.

b. effective conflict.

c. a decrease in ideological thinking.

*d. increased apathy.

9) According to the text, which of the following is an example of a membership group?

*a. AARP

b. Lockheed-Martin

c. American Israel Public Affairs Committee

d. US Chamber of Commerce

10) Which of the following is NOT a primary function of interest groups?

a. Informing members about political developments.

*b. Buying the votes of members of Congress.

c. Communicating members' views to government officials.

d. Mobilizing the public.

11) Which branch of government do lobbyists contact to convey their opinions and push their policy priorities?

a. executive branch

b. legislative branch

c. judicial branch

*d. all of the above

12) In order for an interest group to be successful, it must

a. inform members about political developments.

b. communicate members' views to government officials.

c. mobilize the public.

*d. all of the above

13) Since 2000, spending by registered lobbyists has

a. roughly stayed the same.

b. decreased greatly.

*c. consistently increased.

d. increased in some years and decreased in other years.

14) In 2017, spending by registered lobbyists totaled how much?

a. $200 million

b. $1.5 billion

c. $2.87 billion

*d. $3.37 billion

15) When an issue arises in Washington that is of interest to a group, the group tends to

a. Gain more members.

*b. Boost its spending.

c. Get ignored by legislators.

d. both a and c

16) On high-profile issues like climate change, lobbying

*a. Has little effect on the views of members of Congress.

b. Has great potential to change the views of members of Congress.

c. Has an effect on some members and no effect on other members of Congress, regardless of party.

d. Has little effect on members of Congress who are Democrats, but great effect on members of Congress who are Republicans.

17) The 1946 Regulation of Lobbying Act required lobbyists to

a. register with Congress.

b. report the amount and sources of income derived from lobbying.

*c. both a and b

d. none of the above

18) In the first half of the twentieth century, lobbyists were

*a. not really regulated.

b. regulated about the same as they are today.

c. regulated more than they are today.

d. not present in Washington, DC.

19) The lobbying restrictions imposed in 1995 limited

a. the number of members of Congress a lobbyist can contact.

*b. the gifts that lobbyists can give members of Congress.

c. lobbyists' activities so much that the total number in Washington, DC declined by half.

d. the total number of lobbyists able to work in Washington, DC.

20) The 2007 lobbying reforms did all of the following EXCEPT

a. prohibit former members from lobbying their former colleagues for two years after leaving office.

b. close loopholes from the 1995 restrictions.

*c. allow lobbyists to give unlimited amounts of money as gifts.

d. tighten the ban on gift giving.

21) Beginning in the mid-1960s, the number of lobbyists

*a. increased dramatically.

b. decreased dramatically.

c. stayed the same as pre-1960s.

d. decreased only slightly.

22) In Federalist no. 10, Madison suggests the way to prevent factions from killing off popular government is to

a. outlaw them.

*b. increase the number of them.

c. ignore them.

d. limit how many there can be.

23) Interest groups today represent

*a. virtually every political or social topic and concern.

b. a limited number of political or social groups.

c. a tiny number of wealthy individuals.

d. none of the above

24) About how many interest groups are active in American politics today?

a. 20,000

*b. 200,000

c. 2,000,000

d. 3,000,000

25) "An interest group primarily organized with voluntary members, often with a non-profit or public advocacy focus" is a good definition for a

*a. membership group.

b. lobbying coalition.

c. special interest.

d. faction.

26) A ___________ is a group of lobbyists working on related topics or a specific legislative proposal.

a. special interest

b. faction

c. membership group

*d. lobbying coalition

27) When interest groups mobilize the public to do something on their behalf, this includes actions such as

a. letter writing.

b. protesting.

c. contributing funds.

*d. all of the above

28) When interest groups mobilize the public, they typically reach out through

a. TV ads.

b. Facebook posts.

c. mailgram alerts.

*d. all of the above

29) Pluralism is defined as

*a. an open, participatory style of government in which many different interests are represented.

b. a closed system of government in which only a handful of individuals may participate.

c. a system that can only benefit the wealthy.

d. an open style of government in which only a few individuals are represented.

30) Which of the following theories best explains the bank bailouts of 2008–2009?

a. demosclerosis

*b. power elite theory

c. hyperpluralism

d. both a and c

31) The interest group lobbying reform of 2007 worked to

*a. close loopholes in previous lobbying reform laws.

b. decrease the number of interest groups in Washington, DC.

c. allow unrepresented segments of the public to form interest groups.

d. all of the above

32) The cozy relationship in one issue area between interest group lobbyists, congressional staffers, and an executive branch agency is called

a. a bill group.

*b. an iron triangle.

c. a congressional watchdog group.

d. an issue network.

33) According to the textbook, what always flows between interest groups, Congress, and the executive branch bureaucracy?

a. ill will

b. nonhuman resources (office supplies)

c. personnel policies

*d. money

34) What is an issue network?

*a. A shifting alliance of public and private interest groups, lawmakers, and other stakeholders all focused on the same policy area.

b. The cozy relationship in one issue area between interest group lobbyist, congressional staffer, and executive branch agency.

c. An organization run by the White House staff.

d. The relationship between the president and the cabinet.

35) What are attempts by public officials in one part of the government to influence their counterparts elsewhere—in another branch or at a different (state or local) level of government?

a. judicial precedent

b. reverse lobbying

*c. intergovernmental lobbying

d. bureaucratic rule making

36) Which term refers to attempts by government officials to influence interest groups on behalf of their preferred policies?

*a. reverse lobbying

b. bureaucratic rule making

c. judicial precedent

d. intergovernmental lobbying

37) What kind of lobbying did President Obama use in the early stages of health care reform?

a. intergovernmental lobbying

b. independent lobbying

c. social lobbying

*d. reverse lobbying

38) How much access do lobbyists have to Supreme Court justices?

a. The same amount of access they have to the president and Congress.

b. Nearly unlimited.

*c. Meager, almost nonexistent.

d. Lobbyists feel they do not need to try to influence the Court.

39) The most important aspect of interest groups within the judicial system is

*a. sponsoring class-action lawsuits.

b. appointing judges.

c. pushing for members to become judges.

d. writing appellate court decisions.

40) Which political party is known as the Grand Old Party?

a. Democrats

*b. Republicans

c. independents

d. Whigs

41) Which political party is known for its strong environmental policy positions?

a. Republicans

b. independents

*c. Greens

d. Democrats

42) Which Green Party candidate in the 2000 presidential election upset the results in the state of Florida?

a. Al Gore

b. Jeb Bush

*c. Ralph Nader

d. Jerry Brown

43) Who or what determines ballot access in American elections?

a. Supreme Court

b. Federal Elections Commission

c. federal laws

*d. state laws

44) What type of party system does the United States have today?

a. A two-and-a-half party system.

b. A single-party system.

*c. A two-party system.

d. A multiparty system.

45) How many members are in the United States House of Representatives?

*a. 435

b. 471

c. 443

d. 376

46) In United States history, who is the only third-party candidate to ever finish second in a presidential election?

a. Woodrow Wilson

b. William Howard Taft

*c. Theodore Roosevelt

d. Ross Perot

47) The ________ provide(s) support for a party's candidates and elected officials.

a. standing committees in Congress

b. party planks

*c. party organizations

d. Electoral College

48) What do the initials RNC stand for as they relate to political party organizations?

a. Republican National Conference

b. Republican Notoriety Committee

c. Republicans Never Commit

*d. Republican National Committee

49) What is the document called that contains a political party's core convictions and issue priorities?

a. the party privileges

b. the party constitution

*c. the party platform

d. the party compact

50) Which is the least organized part of the tripartite party structure?

a. party organizations

b. party-in-government

*c. party in the electorate

d. all three parts are equally disorganized

51) For approximately how many years have political parties existed in the United States?

a. 75

b. 150

*c. 225

d. 300

52) During the first party system, who was more inclined to advocate for a strong national government?

a. Thomas Jefferson

b. James Madison

c. Thomas Payne

*d. Alexander Hamilton

53) During the first party system, who was more inclined to advocate for a weaker national government and more states' rights?

a. George Washington

*b. Thomas Jefferson

c. Alexander Hamilton

d. John Adams

54) Which party system witnessed the birth of modern party politics?

*a. the second

b. the third

c. the fourth

d. the fifth

55) The Whig Party in the United States got its name from the British, where the term stood for opposition to

a. monarchy.

b. authoritarian rule.

*c. tyranny or mob rule.

d. the House of Lords.

56) Which of the following was an issue position of the Radical Republicans in the aftermath of the Civil War?

a. Higher tariffs to promote Southern agriculture.

*b. Political rights for former slaves.

c. An end to western expansion.

d. Giving back a certain amount of land to Native Americans.

57) "A hierarchical arrangement of party workers, often organized in an urban area to help integrate immigrants and minority groups into the political system" is the textbook's definition of what?

a. party boss

b. national party organization

*c. party machine

d. state party organization

58) Who won the election of 1896, which marks the beginning of the fourth party system in the United States?

a. William Jennings Bryan

*b. William McKinley

c. William Howard Taft

d. Woodrow Wilson

59) A primary tension during the fourth party system was between

*a. big business and progressive reform in the form of fair pay and better working conditions.

b. pro-slavery and anti-slavery factions.

c. those advocating the admission of new states and those who felt the country had grown too large.

d. all of the above

60) Who was president during the New Deal?

*a. Franklin D. Roosevelt

b. Theodore Roosevelt

c. William McKinley

d. Woodrow Wilson

61) Prior to the New Deal, which political party was considered the most progressive in the promotion of civil rights and social justice?

*a. Republicans

b. Democrats

c. Populists

d. Know-Nothings

62) Which political party dominated in the fifth party system?

a. Republicans

*b. Democrats

c. Populists

d. Know-Nothings

63) What statement best characterizes party electoral competition in the sixth party system?

*a. Too close to call.

b. Democratic Party dominance.

c. Republican Party dominance.

d. What competition?

64) Which two Republican presidential candidates developed a "southern strategy" that, in the end, converted the South to a Republican region of the country?

*a. Nixon and Reagan

b. Goldwater and Nixon

c. Reagan and Bush I

d. Dole and Bush II

65) How long have the Democratic and Republican Parties basically stood for the issues they identify with today?

*a. Since the 1980s.

b. Since the 1960s.

c. Since the 1920s.

d. Since the late nineteenth century.

66) Around what year did the sixth, and current, party system begin?

*a. 1972

b. 1964

c. 1984

d. 2002

67) Which group, on average, is more likely to support the Republican Party?

a. Puerto Rican Americans

b. women

*c. men

d. Mexican Americans

68) People who are more open and agreeable tend to be strong

a. independents.

*b. Democrats.

c. Republicans.

d. Libertarians.

69) "Party members who tend to vote loyally for their party's candidates in most elections" is the textbook's definition of

a. split-ticket voters.

b. straight-ticket voters.

*c. base voters.

d. loyalists.

70) Which type of voting would be most likely to lead to a divided government?

*a. split-ticket voting

b. straight-ticket voting

c. base voting

d. loyalist voting

71) How do people around the world view the two major parties in the United States?

a. Very different, with the Republicans much more likely to support Israel.

*b. Pretty much alike.

c. Both as left of the world center.

d. Very different, with the Democrats much more likely to support Israel.

72) Over the past twenty-five years, approximately what percentage of Democrats have tended to support stronger environmental regulations?

a. 51

b. 67

*c. 93

d. 100

73) Which of the following has NOT been identified as a probable cause of individual party identification?

a. personality

b. parental influence

*c. careful study of political issues

d. political context

74) In which decade were political scientists guessing that political parties might be losing importance?

a. 1940s

b. 1950s

*c. 1960s

d. 1990s

75) The three presidential elections from 1996 to 2004 featured the most intense party competition since the

*a. 1880s.

b. 1920s.

c. 1940s.

d. 1960s.

76) A meeting of all Democrats and Republicans in either the House of Representatives or the Senate is commonly known as a

a. party manifesto.

*b. party caucus.

c. party platform.

d. party grouping.

77) Differences *within* each of the two major parties in Congress have

*a. all but disappeared.

b. intensified dramatically in recent years.

c. intensified dramatically in the 1990s and waned a little since.

d. become more common.

78) People who are worried about bitter partisanship suggest

a. it was the Founders' intention.

b. it is based on constitutional principles.

*c. it leads to bad policy.

d. it leads to entertaining drama.

79) What is the term that signifies at least one house of Congress is controlled by a party different from the party in control of the White House?

a. checks and balances

*b. divided government

c. separation of powers

d. party division

80) Which statement is true as it relates to major party competition in the United States today?

a. The parties are more unified today than they were in the 1960s.

*b. The parties are more divided today than they were at any time in the recent past.

c. The parties are more unified today than they were in the 1930s.

d. The parties are more divided today than they were in the 1960s but more unified than they were in the 1950s.

81) How many single-member districts are used to elect members of the House of Representatives?

a. 500

b. 270

c. 50

*d. 435

82) In the United States, how many people are elected to the House of Representatives from each district?

*a. 1

b. 2

c. 15

d. 100

83) What do the initials "PR" normally stand for as they relate to electoral systems?

a. plurality rule

b. proportional return

c. poorly represented

*d. proportional representation

84) Which of the following arguments is made by individuals who advocate for PR elections?

*a. It would lead to better policy by ensuring that a wider spectrum of policy options are considered.

b. It would help ensure that only the most educated are allowed to vote.

c. It would prevent third parties from confusing electoral options.

d. It would lead to better policy by limiting the number of voices that are heard in Congress.

85) Which of the following arguments is made by individuals who advocate for PR elections?

*a. It would increase representation of women and minorities.

b. It would help to prevent coalition governments.

c. It would prevent multiparty democracy.

d. It would increase the influence of elites and the most educated.

86) Which of the following is an example of how third political parties are discouraged by the US electoral system?

a. They are disadvantaged by proportional representation election laws.

b. They are disadvantaged by multimember districts.

c. They are outlawed in many states.

*d. They are rarely allowed to participate in debates.

87) A proportional representation system provides minor parties with representation equivalent to their

*a. electoral support

b. money contributed

c. registered party members

d. strength of leadership

88) A report arrives on a Congressional officer's desk just as it is need, who likely wrote the report

a. secretary

*b. lobbyist

c. presidential staff

d. reporter

89) What percentage of independent voters had a favorable view of political parties?

a. 42 percent

b. 38 percent

*c. 8 percent

d. 2 percent

90) The first president to warn about political parties was?

a. James Madison

b. Thomas Jefferson

c. John Adams

*d. George Washington

91) Bogging down the government with interest groups is referred to as

*a. hyperpluralism

b. pluralism

c. multipluralism

d. demipluralism

92) When a group of lobbyists organize a series of meeting for out-of-town clients they refer to this as a

a. Gucci Gulch

*b. Fly-in

c. Revolving door

d. Third House

93) When lobbyists make it rain they are referring to

a. weather

b. politicians flying in

*c. raising funds

d. lobbyist meetings

94) The biggest lobbyist client, according to amount spent, is

a. Blue Cross/Blue Shield

b. Boeing Co

c. Governor's Coalition

*d. US Chamber of Commerce

95) How many members of the Senate were neither Democrats or Republicans in 2019?

*a. 2

b. 4

c. 6

d. 8

96) The third party president who go the highest number of electoral votes in history was

a. Ross Perot

*b. Theodore Roosevelt

c. Eugene Debs

d. Strom Thurmond

97) The only state to elect a third-party candidate governor was

a. Texas

b. Maine

*c. Minnesota

d. Montana

98) The presidential candidate who won two elections without campaigning was

a. Barack Obama

b. Ronald Reagan

c. Abraham Lincoln

*d. George Washington

99) The first party change in the presidency occurred when

*a. Jefferson defeated Adams

b. Kennedy defeated Nixon

c. Clinton defeated Bush

d. Bush defeated Gore

100) Which party supported leaving the slavery issue to the states and territories?

a. Republicans

*b. Democrats

c. Whigs

d. No party

Chapter 10

Congress

1) A congressional caucus convenes regularly to discuss common interests and consists of which of the following?

   a. House members

   b. Senate members

   *c. both House and Senate members

   d. only House leadership

2) The conference committee is critical because

   *a. it allows the House and Senate to work out a compromise on a particular piece of legislation.

   b. it is the first step in the bill process.

   c. it is where the filibuster occurs.

   d. it is a permanent collection of House and Senate members.

3) All of the following congressional powers could be found in article 1, section 8, except

   a. legal.

   b. financial.

   *c. administrative.

   d. national defense.

4) A president needs congressional cooperation primarily to

   *a. advance executive policies.

   b. debate public policy.

   c. use the veto process.

   d. limit executive decision making.

5) A House member represents a district of about

a. 300,000 people.

b. 100,000 people.

c. 1 million people.

*d.730,000 people.

6) Mark Twain's comment that "every senator is a little king" suggests

a. senators have unlimited power.

b. most senators have life terms.

*c. senators possess a remarkable degree of autonomy in comparison to House members.

d. senators are generally viewed as demagogues.

7) A filibuster is a power unique to the

a. House.

*b. Senate.

c. House and Senate.

d. president.

8) A filibuster can only be stopped by a process called

a. logrolling.

b. franking.

*c. cloture.

d. pork barreling.

9) Congress went from most powerful to increasingly deferential to the White House in the

*a. middle of the twentieth century

b. early twentieth century

c. late twentieth century

d. twenty-first century

10) Today, diversity is more represented in

a. the House and Senate.

*b. the House.

c. the Senate.

d. none of the above

11) The idea of diverse representation can be clearly seen with

a. the diverse number of House members.

*b. the emergence of the Congressional Black Caucus in the House.

c. the number of women represented in the Senate.

d. the number of minorities represented in the Senate.

12) The idea of diverse representation is important because

a. it most closely addresses the challenges of popular preference.

b. it allows various constituent interests to be represented.

c. it tempers the idea of one group dominating all other interests.

*d. all of the above

13) Congressional members must address various levels of representation that include all of the following except

a. geographic representation.

b. descriptive representation.

c. substantive legislation.

*d. procedural legislation.

14) Besides enacting legislation, one would expect members of Congress to spend a significant amount of time

a. meeting with constituents.

b. attending ceremonial events.

c. attending conventions.

*d. both a and b

15) A Congressional caucus shares

a. political outlook

b. race

c. gender

*d. all of the above

16) The first woman elected to the House was in

a. 1914

*b. 1916

c. 1918

d. 1920

17) The reason that congressional members should return frequently to their districts is the need to

*a. win elections.

b. take advantage of their franking privileges.

c. promote the president's agenda.

d. seek new challengers.

18) When we hear the term *City on the Hill* it most likely refers to the idea that

a. Congress is built on a hill.

*b. Capital building is also the heart of a small city

c. legislation is difficult to pass.

d. congressional salaries are equal to most CEO salaries.

19) Today, a congressional salary is approximately

a. $90,000.

b. equal to the that of the president.

c. equal to that of the average NBA player.

*d.$174,000.

20) The idea that particular funding goes to particular districts is often known on Capitol Hill as

*a. a Christmas tree project.

b. lucky funding.

c. logrolling.

d. gerrymandering.

21) Someone hoping to enact landmark legislation would most likely be referred to as a

a. demagogue.

*b. whale.

c. minnow.

d. shark.

22) A member of Congress who lacks the capacity to promote significant reform would most likely be referred to as a

a. bass.

*b. minnow.

c. darter.

d. none of the above

23) What crime can the House impeach the president for

a. theft

b. perjury

*c. high crimes and misdemeanors

d. murder

24) After the president is impeached the trial is held in the

a. White House

*b. Senate

c. Supreme Court

d. House of Representatives

25) A central function of the Speaker of the House is to

a. settle all debates.

*b. lead the majority party.

c. compromise on key issues.

d. make sure all proposed legislation goes to the president.

26) The second in command in the House is known as the

a. minority leader.

*b. majority leader.

c. majority whip.

d. minority whip.

27) Party discipline would most likely be achieved by

a. the Speaker of the House.

b. the majority leader.

*c. the majority party whip.

d. the minority leader.

28) The Senate position with the longest experience is known as

a. the vice president.

*b. the president pro tempore.

c. the majority leader.

d. the minority leader.

29) The only person who can break a tie in the Senate is the

*a. vice president.

b. president pro tempore.

c. minority leader.

d. whip.

30) The greatest concern about proposed legislation is that

a. it will pass.

*b. it will die in a committee.

c. it will develop into an entirely different piece of legislation.

d. it will not be debated.

31) The ________ committee is a permanent committee in Congress.

a. select

*b. standing

c. conference

d. social

32) Special committees are often referred to as ________ committees.

*a. select

b. standing

c. investigative

d. social

33) A committee comprising both House and Senate members is often referred to as a ________ committee.

a. reserved

*b. joint

c. ways and means

d. investigative

34) Committees are central to Congress because

a. they create more jobs for staffers.

*b. they allow congressional members to specialize on a particular issue.

c. they were mandated by Congress.

d. they allow for easier passage of legislation.

35) The Ways and Means Committee is a permanent committee located in the

*a. House.

b. Senate.

c. House and Senate.

d. executive branch.

36) If you were a House member, one of your goals would be to secure which of the following?

*a. earmarks

b. more franking privileges

c. greater authority

d. more meetings with the Speaker

37) There are ________ members in Congress.

*a. 435

b. 535

c. more than 1,000

d. 270

38) The main responsibility of Congress is which of the following?

*a. enact legislation

b. promote new hiring

c. check the president

d. allow for greater spending

39) Who can introduce legislation?

a. only House members

b. only Senate members

*c. both House and Senate members

d. only senior House and Senate members

40) How many sponsors are needed for a bill?

a. 12

b. 3

*c. 1

d. 7

41) The more cosponsors a bill has the

*a. higher likelihood of passage

b. more time allowed for debate

c. better the committee

d. higher the placement on the floor

42) Major rewrites of a bill occur in the

a. conference committee.

b. subcommittee.

*c. markup sessions.

d. Judiciary Committee.

43) Most proposed legislation

a. becomes law.

*b. does not become law.

c. is debated endlessly in the House.

d. is debated endlessly in the Senate.

44) A key legislative reform of the 1970s mandated that

a. all proposed legislation be passed.

*b. all committees keep full records of important votes.

c. all critical legislation be censured.

d. all legislation move to the conference committee.

45) In order for a bill to reach the Senate floor, it must achieve

a. good public backing.

*b. unanimous consent.

c. the president's approval.

d. the Speaker's approval.

46) How many senate votes does it take to put a bill on hold?

a. bills cannot be put on hold

*b. 1

c. 3

d. 5

47) The Senate seeks to lift a legislative hold through the process of

a. logrolling.

b. gerrymandering.

c. franking.

*d. cloture.

48) On noncontroversial issues, legislation will conclude with a

*a. voice vote.

b. conference vote.

c. roll call vote.

d. cloture vote.

49) On more controversial issues, a ________ is required.

a. voice vote

*b. roll call vote

c. committee vote

d. conference vote

50) There are ________ nonvoting delegates in Congress.

a. 4

b. 3

c. 0

*d. 6

51) All nonvoting delegates serve ________-year terms.

a. 1

*b. 2

c. 3

d. 4

52) Congress is like a small city because there are

a. 541 members.

b. 25,000 staff.

c. numerous lobbyists.

*d. all of the above

53) Congressional committees aid and ________ the legislative process.

a. improve

*b. fragment

c. redirect

d. enhance

54) What percentage of bills made it to law?

*a. 3 percent

b. 12 percent

c. 17 percent

d. 48 percent

55) House-Senate conferences hopefully yield a

*a. single version of a bill

b. bill the president will sign

c. annotated bill

d. cheaper version of the bill

56) The House-Senate conference committee bill must be ________ before it goes to the president.

a. similar

*b. identical

c. different

d. complex

57) A bill most likely will falter after the conference committee because

*a. the president could veto.

b. the president could cloture the bill.

c. A Senate member could still filibuster.

d. unanimous votes are required.

58) To overcome a presidential veto, Congress needs

a. two-thirds approval of the House.

b. three-quarters approval of the Senate.

*c. two-thirds approval of House and Senate.

d. four-fifths approval of House and Senate.

59) How many Senators does it take to override a veto?

a. 57

*b. 67

c. 77

d. 87

60) All budget measures must begin in the

a. conference committee.

*b. House.

c. Senate.

d. House or Senate.

61) Impeachment proceedings begin in the

*a. House.

b. Senate.

c. subcommittee.

d. standing committee.

62) Prior to 1913 the ________ was elected directly by the public.

a. Senate

*b. House

c. President

d. Supreme Court

63) A system to remove public officials because of high crimes and misdemeanors is known as

a. an indictment.

*b. an impeachment.

c. an arraignment.

d. an oversight.

64) To approve a treaty the Senate must reach a ________ decision.

a. one-quarter

b. one-half plus one

*c. two-thirds

d. unanimous

65) Other Senate responsibilities include all of the following except

a. ratifying treaties.

b. reviewing presidential appointees.

*c. introducing monetary measures.

d. use of the filibuster.

66) It can be inferred that House and Senate power is

*a. roughly equal.

b. diminishing in recent years.

c. more tilted toward the Senate.

d. more tilted toward the House.

67) The Senate has sole power to review

a. budget legislation

*b. presidential nominations

c. infrastructure laws

d. health care concerns

68) Senate terms last ________ years.

a. 4

b. 2

c. 3

*d. 6

69) The nation looks to the ________ to pursue policy objectives.

a. House of Representatives

*b. President

c. Senate

d. Majority Party

70) The power to pass legislation remains with the

a. President

*b. Congress

c. House of Representatives only

d. Senate only

71) A bill goes to the floor for

*a. the final debate

b. signatures

c. filibuster

d. printing

72) A senator who dislikes the president's actions can place a legislative ________ on all legislation the president supports.

a. veto

*b. hold

c. enjoinder

d. clarification

73) The "People's Branch" is otherwise referred to as

a. the House.

b. the Senate.

*c. Congress.

d. the courts.

74) The Constitution places which branch of government at the center of American government?

*a. Congress

b. Executive

c. Judicial

d. Bureaucracy

75) Reasons for lack of congressional approval center around

a. their salaries.

b. work commitment.

*c. partisan fighting and gridlock.

d. lack of diversity.

76) During the 1950s and 1960s the Senate was mostly controlled by the

*a. Democrats.

b. Republicans.

c. Libertarians.

d. Socialists.

77) The percentage of each party's House and Senate members who vote with the party majority is referred to as

*a. party cohesion.

b. bureaucratic politics.

c. central decision making.

d. legislative control.

78) Since 1990, congressional members have voted ________ along party lines.

a. 75 percent

b. 65 percent

*c. 90 percent

d. 100 percent

79) The idea that the two chambers of Congress and the presidency are controlled by different parties is referred to as

*a. a divided government.

b. a subdued government.

c. an open government.

d. a bifurcated government.

80) The accounting of legislative organization and authority is found in Article

*a. one

b. two

c. three

d. four

81) The power to tax is part of the ________ role of Congress.

*a. financial

b. economic

c. administrative

d. institutional

82) According to the Constitution who is responsible for regulating trade and commerce among the states?

a. State Legislatures

*b. US Congress

c. President

d. Governors

83) According to the textbook, Congress has become more

*a. partisan.

b. cooperative.

c. trustworthy.

d. effective.

84) According to James Madison, it is ________ that groups will pursue their own interests.

*a. likely

b. unlikely

c. doubtful

d. none of the above

85) Madison argued that the best way to control factions was to ________ one against the other.

a. subjugate

*b. balance

c. discredit

d. credit

86) One of the major reform challenges relating to Congress addresses the concern of

a. the military.

b. senior leadership.

*c. lobbyists.

d. the intricate relationship between Congress and the presidency.

87) Lobbyists are problematic because they can ________ the political agenda.

a. destroy

b. reduce

*c. overly influence

d. minimize

88) Congressional reelection rates are so high because

a. there are no challengers.

*b. direct constituent service is superb.

c. Congress members pass vast quantities of legislation.

d. overall congressional public approval ratings are high.

89) One would find a constituent in a

a. state.

b. district.

c. borough.

*d. all of the above

90) Most congressional power is found in

a. article 1, section 9.

*b. article 1, section 8.

c. article 2, section 3.

d. article 2, section 1.

91) Setting up federal courts is part of the _______ job of Congress.

a. national defense

*b. institutional

c. administrative

d. legal

92) The power to establish U.S. citizenship laws lies with the

a. President

*b. Congress

c. Supreme Court

d. states

93) Geographic representation assures that members of Congress live in

a. Washington D.C.

*b. state or district they represent

c. United States

d. biggest city in their state

94) The first woman elected to the House was from

a. Wyoming

*b. Montana

c. New York

d. Virginia

95) "I take my voting instructions directly from my constituents" would likely be said by what type of legislator?

a. Trustee

*b. Delegate

c. incumbent

d. retiring

96) U.S. House members spend most of their time

*a. meeting with staff

b. floor action

c. office work

d. caucus meetings

97) Most congressional members work in Washington

a. Monday thru Friday

b. Wednesday only

*c. Tuesday thru Thursday

d. Seven days a week

98) Which is the only building allowed to be taller than the Capitol building?

a. White House

b. Lincoln Memorial

c. Smithsonian Museum

*d. Washington Memorial

99) In what year did Senators begin having staff?

*a. 1891

b. 1893

c. 1895

d. 1897

100) Who handles most constituent requests?

a. Chief of Staff

b. legislative director

*c. legislative correspondent

Chapter 11

The Presidency

1) The branch of federal government that has changed the most is the

*a. Executive

b. Legislative

c. Judicial

d. all are about the same

2) In 1829 when someone wanted to see President Jackson they would

a. make an appointment

b. send a letter

*c. walk right into the White House

d. send an email

3) Presidential power is vaguely defined in

a. Article 1 of the Constitution

*b. Article 2 of the Constitution

c. Article 3 of the Constitution

d. Article 4 of the Constitution

4) The shortest presidency, in months was that of

a. George Washington

b. Andrew Jackson

*c. William Henry Harrison

d. Franklin D. Roosevelt

5) The longest presidency, in months was that of

a. George Washington

b. Andrew Jackson

c. William Henry Harrison

*d. Franklin D. Roosevelt

6) Which president held a patent?

a. Thomas Jefferson

*b. Abraham Lincoln

c. John Kennedy

d. Donald Trump

7) Originally the president would serve a four-year term, which could be renewed

*a. indefinitely.

b. two times.

c. three times.

d. four times.

8) The only president who has served more than two terms was

a. Ronald Reagan.

b. James Madison.

*c. Franklin Roosevelt.

d. Thomas Jefferson.

9) Which amendment bars a president from serving a third term?

*a. the Twenty-second

b. the Twenty-third

c. the Twenty-fourth

d. the Nineteenth

10) The agreed-on way to elect the president is

a. by Congress.

*b. through the Electoral College.

c. by the courts.

d. by the political parties.

11) In the Electoral College, each state's number of votes is _______ its congressional delegation.

a. greater than

b. less than

*c. equal to

d. significantly less than

12) Who determines how electors to the Electoral College are chosen?

*a. states

b. Congress

c. President

d. Political Parties

13) In order to win the presidency, one must win

a. the Electoral College and popular vote.

b. the popular vote.

*c. the Electoral College.

d. a simple plurality in the Electoral College.

14) Executive expressed powers include all of the following except

a. commander in chief.

*b. power to declare war.

c. power to make treaties.

d. power to grant pardons.

15) Treaty ratification can only occur with

a. House approval.

b. judicial approval.

*c. Senate approval.

d. bureaucratic approval.

16) Senatorial approval of a treaty requires

a. one-third support

*b. two-thirds support

c. three-quarters support

d. unanimous support

17) The idea that the executive branch can issue a rule on congressional legislation is known as

a. proscribed powers.

b. legislative power.

*c. delegated powers.

d. enumerated powers.

18) The three forms of presidential powers are

a. expressed, reserved, and formal.

b. expressed, delegated, and reserved.

*c. expressed, delegated, and inherent.

d. inherent, reserved, and delegated.

19) Powers that are vaguely reflected in article 2 of the Constitution are known as

a. reserved powers.

b. expressed powers.

*c. inherent powers.

d. de facto powers.

20) Holding enemy combatants without a hearing can be traced to which executive power?

a. reserved

*b. inherent

c. delegated

d. expressed

21) The _______ can determine whether the president exceeded the scope of inherent powers.

*a. Supreme Court

b. House

c. Senate

d. bureaucracy

22) Many parliamentary systems grant their executives which of the following?

a. right to use emergency powers

b. right to use partial line-item vetoes

c. right to introduce budgets

*d. all of the above

23) Presidents are elected ________ via the Electoral College.

*a. indirectly

b. directly

c. by plurality

d. by national popular vote

24) Executive power generally ________ during crises.

a. diminishes

*b. expands

c. stays the same

d. completely changes

25) The Alien and Sedition Acts can be traced to which presidency?

*a. John Adams

b. George Washington

c. Thomas Jefferson

d. James Madison

26) The Alien and Sedition Acts were considered controversial because they punished false and scandalous speech, but they also could be viewed as an attack on which amendment?

*a. First

b. Second

c. Third

d. Fourth

27) The idea that no other branch can check the president is known as the

a. supremacy theory.

*b. unitary executive theory.

c. imperial theory.

d. take care clause.

28) The idea that the president could demand swift and even secretive action is supported by

*a. unitary executive theory.

b. legislative theory.

c. inherent theory.

d. pluralist theory.

29) The unitary executive theory can be viewed as

*a. a threat to the system of checks and balances.

b. an important way to change governmental roles.

c. a way for the president to serve more than two terms.

d. a way for Congress to override the president.

30) The idea that an executive could possibly change a republic into an empire is directly related to which of the following theories?

a. legislative

*b. imperial

c. pluralist

d. majoritarian

31) Republicans accused ________ of embodying the imperial presidency.

*a. Barak Obama

b. Lyndon Johnson

c. Bill Clinton.

d. Jimmy Carter

32) Presidents are extremely vulnerable in relation to

a. foreign affairs.

*b. domestic issues.

c. legislative issues.

d. judicial issues.

33) The president presides over the world's largest fighting force and is otherwise known as the

*a. commander in chief.

b. chief legislator.

c. chief diplomat.

d. chief executive.

34) Free trade agreements, global warming concerns, and Middle East concerns all require the use of

a. force.

b. economic sanctions.

*c. diplomacy.

d. boycotts.

35) The president can act as a ________ and recommend and veto measures from Congress.

*a. chief legislator

b. chief diplomat

c. chief custodian

d. commander in chief

36) Prior to World War II what type of standing army did the United States have?

a. large

*b. small

c. strong

d. weak

37) After World War II what type of standing army did the United States have?

a. small

*b. large

c. weak

d. all male

38) An annual event where the president addresses the nation is called

a. the annual talk.

*b. the State of the Union address.

c. the Executive Talk.

d. the State of Affairs Talk.

39) Which of the following can formally propose a law?

a. President

*b. Congress

c. the Supreme Court

d. both a and b

40) _______ is the presidential power to block an act of Congress by refusing to sign it.

a. Executive power

b. Legislative power

*c. Veto power

d. Take care clause power

41) Congress can override a presidential veto with a _______ vote in both chambers.

a. three-quarters

b. two-fifths

*c. two-thirds

d. four-fifths

42) How often has Congress been able to override presidential vetoes?

a. most of the time

b. all the time

c. never

*d. rarely

43) Written declarations commenting on a bill that is signed into law is known as

*a. a signing statement.

b. an executive decree.

c. an executive declaration.

d. a public declaration.

44) The executive branch includes _______ departments.

a. nine

b. eight

*c. fifteen

d. ten

45) Today, the federal government has approximately _______ employees.

*a. 2.7 million

b. 27 million

c. 100,000

d. 10 million

46) Individuals appointed by the president to top positions in executive agencies are known as

*a. political appointees.

b. executive appointees.

c. command appointees.

d. diplomatic appointees.

47) Executive orders are unique because

a. they require congressional approval.

*b. they do not require congressional approval.

c. the president rarely uses them.

d. the president always uses them.

48) Members of the bureaucracy who keep their positions regardless of presidential changes are the

a. political appointees

*b. civil servants

c. cabinet secretaries

d. speechwriters

49) Which of the following has been implemented via executive order

a. regulatory rollbacks.

b. bans on entry from selected countries

c. stripping funds from sanctuary cities

*d. all of the above

50) If Congress blocks an executive initiative, the president could issue an _______ to get around Congress.

*a. executive order

b. executive initiative

c. executive line-item veto

d. executive pardon

51) One area where the president is not granted authority is with

a. national security concerns.

*b. economic authority.

c. civil rights.

d. civil liberties.

52) In the United States, the title of head of state is

a. ceremonial only.

*b. ceremonial and policy oriented.

c. policy oriented only.

d. none of the above

53) George Washington was _______ political parties.

a. supportive of

*b. against

c. neutral about

d. ambivalent about

54) Party leader became a role for the president during the presidency of

a. John Adams

b. Andrew Jackson

*c. George Washington

d. Franklin Roosevelt

55) The statement "ask not what your country can do for you, ask what you can do for your country" comes from which administration?

*a. Kennedy

b. Reagan

c. Taft

d. Obama

56) A successful president uses the power to

*a. persuade.

b. argue.

c. debate.

d. enforce.

57) A president who is able to make key military decisions uses the position of

a. chief diplomat.

*b. commander in chief.

c. chief legislator.

d. chief executive.

58) Presidential power has ________ since the founding of the country.

a. diminished

*b. increased

c. stayed the same

d. usurped the role of the courts

59) Presidential oversight of all executive agencies reflects presidential power as

a. chief diplomat.

*b. chief bureaucrat.

c. chief legislator.

d. commander in chief.

60) ________ is important because it allows presidents to win support for themselves or their ideas.

*a. Going public

b. Debating Congress

c. Withholding sensitive national security information

d. Vetoing Congress

61) The first live televised press conference occurred during which administration?

*a. Kennedy

b. Taft

c. Wilson

d. McKinley

62) Which of the following is a way for the president to connect with the American public?

a. call town hall meetings

b. give speeches before large crowds

c. speak directly to the camera from the Oval Office

*d. all of the above

63) A successful president must

a. constantly debate Congress.

*b. manage their image in the public eye.

c. make bold and secretive decisions.

d. force Congress to accept executive legislation.

64) Which of the following is true?

a. Most presidents have consistently high public approval ratings.

*b. No president stays above 50 percent approval rating for an entire term.

c. Most presidents have had 90 percent approval ratings.

d. Economic performance is not important in approval ratings.

65) The end of the first Gulf War saw public approval of George H. W. Bush

a. decline.

b. increase slightly.

*c. increase dramatically.

d. decrease slightly.

66) George W. Bush's approval ratings right after the 9/11 attacks

a. diminished greatly.

*b. increased dramatically.

c. decreased slightly.

d. increased slightly.

67) According to a panel of historians, who was the top-ranking president?

a. Franklin Roosevelt

b. Harry Truman

*c. Abraham Lincoln

d. Ronald Reagan

68) What year was the first live televised presidential press conference?

a. 1945

*b. 1961

c. 1972

d, 1921

69) George Washington has been extolled as a great president because of his ability to

a. end slavery.

*b. define the presidency and the nation.

c. defeat France.

d. promote the Alien and Sedition Acts.

70) Franklin Roosevelt was considered a very strong president because of his ability to

a. balance the budget.

b. declare war on Japan.

*c. rethink the presidency and the federal government's role in national life.

d. create the Federal Reserve.

71) According to presidential historian Stephen Skowronek, each president must address the rise and fall of

*a. political orders.

b. inflation.

c. recession.

d. turbulent wars.

72) According to Skowronek, a political order develops as follows:

*a. new order, order refreshed, and old order crumbles.

b. order refreshed, old order crumbles, and new order.

c. new order develops, old order crumbles, and order refreshed.

d. new order emerges from older orders.

73) A new order could mean which of the following?

*a. A president introduces a fresh philosophy of government.

b. A president uses the veto often.

c. A president seeks to avoid Congress.

d. A president refuses to address critical social issues.

74) A new order president is

a. Jimmy Carter

*b. Ronald Reagan

c. Herbert Hoover

d. John Adams

75) Presidential approval ratings usually start above

*a. 60 percent

b. 65 percent

c. 70 percent

d. 90 percent

76) An example of an "old order crumbles" situation can be linked to which administration?

*a. Hoover

b. Fillmore

c. Taft

d. Carter

77) Presidents would like their approval rating to be around ________ for reelection.

a. 70 percent

b. 60 percent

*c. 50 percent

d. 40 percent

78) Nixon's ability to negotiate with both China and Russia would be an example of a

a. chief legislator.

*b. chief diplomat.

c. commander in chief.

d. chief custodian.

79) The set of institutions, interests, and ideas that shape a political era is the

a. political times

b. political zone

*c. political order

d. executive times

80) How may administrative assistants did Herbert Hoover have?

*a. 4

b. 6

c. 8

d. over 100

81) Herbert Hoover's presidential staff was how large?

a. 100

b. 70

*c. 40

d. 15

82) Power in the executive branch is measured by

*a. proximity to the Oval Office

b. number of years in the job

c. age of the person

d. number of meetings with the president

83) The shortest presidency was

a. John Adams

b. Harry Truman

*c. William Henry Harrison

d. George W. Bush

84) The longest presidency was

a. George Washington

*b. Franklin Roosevelt

c. Ronald Reagan

d. Abraham Lincoln

85) The last president without a college education was

a. Franklin Roosevelt

*b. Harry Truman

c. John Kennedy

d. Jimmy Carter

86) The first election in which a woman ran for president was

*a. 1872

b. 1900

c. 1920

d. 1964

87) How many presidents have there been in the last 85 years?

a. 12

*b. 14

c. 16

d. 18

88) Vice presidents have taken over after presidential death ________ times.

a. five

b. nine

*c. eight

d. two

89) The vice president's role has ________ during the latter part of the twentieth and early part of the twenty-first century.

*a. greatly increased

b. greatly decreased

c. stayed the same

d. slightly increased

90) Vice presidents preside over the

a. House.

*b. Senate.

c. bureaucracy.

d. Central Intelligence Agency.

91) Vice presidents vote in the Senate

*a. when there is a tie.

b. during close votes.

c. on controversial issues.

d. when they have the chance.

92) The president's official advisors are called

a. advisors.

*b. the cabinet.

c. the bureaucracy.

d. executive aides.

93) The central gatekeeper for the president is called the

a. gatekeeper.

*b. chief of staff.

c. head cabinet officer.

d. press secretary.

94) The president's office manager is the

a. gatekeeper.

*b. chief of staff.

c. head cabinet officer.

d. press secretary.

95) Democrats have generally organized their White House office in a manner referred to as

*a. creative chaos

b. military precision

c. personality driven

d. organized chaos

96) Republicans have generally organized their White House office in a manner referred to as

a. creativity chaos

b. organized chaos

*c. military precision

d. personality driven

97) Going against tradition the Obama White House was organized in _______ style.

a. chaotic

b. Democratic

c. creative

*d. Republican

98) How did George H.W. Bush demonstrate the new order to his speechwriting team?

*a. stripped of White House Mess privileges

b. paid them less

c. central office

d. moved them out of the White House

99) EOP staffers are

a. subject to Senate confirmation

*b. not subject to Senate confirmation

c. subject to House confirmation

d. must be approved by the Cabinet

100) The first lady who was the first to have an office in the West Wing was

a. Lady Bird Johnson

b. Jacqueline Kennedy

*c. Nancy Reagan

d. Hilary Clinton

Chapter 12

Bureaucracy

1) Most Americans hold

a. a very high opinion of the federal government.

*b. a very low opinion of the federal government.

c. a high opinion of the French government and a low opinion of the American federal government.

d. no opinion about the federal government.

2) What makes the government run?

*a. the bureaucracy

b. the president

c. Congress

d. Donald Trump

3) Approximately how many people are on the American government payroll?

a. 2 million

b. 5 million

*c. 23 million

d. 50 million

4) The bureaucracy, compared to Congress,

a. is older.

b. is younger.

*c. is much more diverse.

d. is more educated.

5) The practice by which political winners reward their supporters with government jobs and contracts is known as

*a. the spoils system.

b. pandering.

c. pay-for-play.

d. the nepotism system.

6) Bureaucracies are characterized by all of the following, *except*

a. hierarchy.

b. division of labor.

*c. flexible goals.

d. fixed routines.

7) The act of Congress requiring the federal government to hire well-qualified public servants in 1883 was

a. the Hatch.

b. the Hire Qualified Government Workers Act of 1883.

c. the McCain-Feingold Act.

*d. the Pendleton Civil Service Act.

8) A clear chain of command, in which all employees know who their supervisors are as well as who reports to them, is an example of a

*a. hierarchy.

b. merit-based system.

c. spoils system.

d. patronage.

9) The ultimate purpose of creating a professional merit-based civil service system is to

a. give jobs to friends

*b. hire well-qualified individuals

c. win elections

d. hire party members

10) The single biggest historical event responsible for the large bureaucracy we have today was

a. WWI.

b. passage of the Pendleton Act.

*c. WWII.

d. the Spanish-American War of 1898.

11) The effort to outlaw all liquor under Prohibition created a new law enforcement agency in the

a. Church of Jesus Christ of Latter-day Saints.

b. Department of the Interior.

c. Federal Bureau of Investigation.

*d. Department of the Treasury.

12) The Federal Reserve was created

*a. to stabilize banking.

b. to save money.

c. to prepare for World War I.

d. to build Fort Knox.

13) The primary source of power for a member of a bureaucracy is

a. job security.

*b. expertise.

c. ties to politicians.

d. presidential connections.

14) In many policy areas, multiple agencies have overlapping responsibilities, leading to

*a. turf wars.

b. imperialism.

c. clientelism.

d. iron triangles.

15) When one agency does not communicate with another, to the detriment of citizens,

a. it is suffering from clientelism.

*b. there is a lack of coordination.

c. there is a surfeit of coordination.

d. there is a need for a budgetary increase.

16) According to the text, bureaucracies run on

a. money.

b. paperwork.

*c. expertise.

d. political spoils.

17) Laws written by Congress are typically

a. very precise.

b. consensual.

c. detailed.

*d. vague.

18) There are two steps to the bureaucratic process of putting a law into practice:

*a. rulemaking and implementation.

b. rulemaking and adjudication.

c. agenda setting and evaluation.

d. printing and dissemination.

19) After an agency has devised a rule, it sends the rule to the ________ for approval.

a. Office of Rule Enforcement

b. General Accounting Office

c. Federal Register

*d. Office of Management and Budget

20) The daily journal of the federal government is

*a. the Federal Register.

b. the *New York Times.*

c. the *Journal of Rules.*

d. the *Hill.*

21) The rule that stipulates how a government program will actually operate is known as

a. the Federal Rule.

b. the Complete Rule.

*c. the Final Rule.

d. the Federal Register Rule.

22) Because bureaucracies are so rule based, they

a. make decisions that usually only serve public employees.

b. make poor decisions.

c. make conflicting and confusing decisions.

*d. make decisions with accountability and equality, but also with a lot of bureaucratic red tape.

23) Bureaucracies exist

*a. in both the private and public sector.

b. only in government.

c. at the federal level.

d. in Europe, for the most part.

24) Debates over how laws will work take place

a. among elected officials in committee meetings.

*b. deep in the shadows where only experts have an idea of what is going on.

c. in the glare of the media spotlight.

d. in private meetings at the White House.

25) The last step in the long bureaucratic process of creating a law is

a. problem definition.

b. presidential signature.

*c. implementation.

d. formulation.

26) The final rule is published in the

a. *Federal Rule Book*

b. *Federal Guidelines*

c. *Federal Bureaucracy Guidelines*

*d. Federal Register

27) Bureaucracies touch

*a. every aspect of our lives.

b. very little of our day-to-day existence.

c. the economy, mainly.

d. social issues, mainly.

28) Bureaucratic officials participate in which steps in the policy-making process?

a. none of them

*b. all of them

c. the agenda-setting stage

d. the implementation stage

29) Civil servants speak

a. Latin.

b. legalese.

*c. bureaucratese.

d. French, the language of bureaucrats.

30) Which of the following is an example of a federal agency designed to serve a clientele group?

a. State Department

b. Department of Justice

c. Homeland Security

*d. Agriculture

31) President George Washington's administration had all of the following cabinet departments *except*

*a. Interior.

b. War.

c. State.

d. Treasury.

32) All of the following are events that led to growth in the federal bureaucracy *except*

a. 9/11.

*b. the Emancipation Proclamation.

c. WWII.

d. the Great Depression.

33) The cabinet secretary who sits farthest away from the president at cabinet meetings is

a. Secretary of Defense.

b. Secretary of Treasury.

*c. Secretary of Homeland Security.

d. Secretary of State.

34) The cabinet department with the most employees is

a. the Department of Education.

b. the Department of Veterans Affairs.

c. the Department of Labor.

*d. the Department of Defense.

35) All of the following institutions can bottleneck a presidential nominee *except*

*a. the EPA.

b. the FBI.

c. the White House.

d. Congress.

36) In recent years the confirmation process for presidential appointees has become

a. easier.

*b. more difficult.

c. tied to campaign contributions.

d. less deferential to governors' preferences.

37) The Constitution bars members of Congress from taking

a. tax breaks.

b. campaign contributions.

*c. any civil office.

d. trips to their district while Congress is in session.

38) The average length of time a presidential appointee serves is

a. the length of time the president is in office.

b. eight years.

c. under one year.

*d. three years.

39) The bureaucracy is discussed in which article of the Constitution?

*a. The bureaucracy is not mentioned in the Constitution.

b. Article 1

c. Article 2

d. Article 3

40) Which of the following is NOT an organization in the federal bureaucracy?

a. independent agencies

b. government corporations

*c. citizen advisory councils

d. cabinet-level departments

41) How many cabinet departments are there today?

a. 4

b. 7

c. 11

*d. 15

42) How many cabinet departments did George Washington have?

*a. 4

b. 7

c. 11

d. 15

43) What percentage of the federal bureaucracy is active-duty military?

a. 15 percent

b. 23 percent

*c 34 percent

d. 56 percent

44) How many women have headed cabinet-level departments?

a. 15

b. 23

c. 31

*d. 36

45) The cabinet agency charged with supervising Indian affairs is

*a. the Department of the Interior.

b. the US Geological Survey.

c. the Environmental Protection Agency.

d. the Department of Energy.

46) All of the following are independent executive agencies *except*

a. the CIA.

*b. the State Department.

c. NASA.

d. the US Postal Service.

47) Bureaus of the federal government that regulate business are dubbed

a. cabinets.

b. government corporations.

*c. independent regulatory commissions.

d. market watchers.

48) Deregulation is a result of

a. farming subsidies

b. railroad freight expense

c. space travel

*d. regulatory capture

49) When a regulatory agency does the bidding of the industry it is supposed to be regulating, political scientists call this phenomenon

*a. regulatory capture.

b. interest group acquisition.

c. going native.

d. moral hazard.

50) Created in 1887, the ________ was the first independent regulatory agency.

a. Equal Employment Opportunity Commission

*b. Interstate Commerce Commission

c. National Labor Relations Board

d. Federal Election Commission

51) An example of a central service agency is

a. the Environmental Protection Agency.

b. the Executive Office of the President.

c. the Food and Drug Administration.

*d. Office of Personnel Management

52) An example of a central service agency is

a. the Environmental Protection Agency.

b. the Executive Office of the President.

c. the Food and Drug Administration.

*d. the General Services Administration.

53) Abolished in 1985, which agency regulated competition in the airline industry?

*a. the Civil Aeronautics Board

b. the Interstate Commerce Commission

c. the Civilian Air patrol

d. ENRON

54) One of the principal arguments for contracting out government services to private companies is that

a. private companies are less efficient than government agencies.

*b. private companies are more efficient than government agencies.

c. private company personnel have less expertise and will therefore do less damage.

d. private companies are more concerned about the public good than government agencies.

55) The logic driving presidential appointees to head government agencies

a. is neutral competence.

b. is a remnant of the responsible party model.

*c. is to provide political direction to bureaucracies.

d. is to ensure agency independence.

56) A key challenge for a smoothly run federal bureaucracy is

a. the civil service system based on merit and neutral competence.

b. the lifetime tenure requirement for bureaucrats.

c. the lack of citizen demand for government services.

*d. the time—more than a year—that it takes a new administration to get its leadership team in place.

57) In theory, who controls the bureaucracy?

*a. the president

b. Congress

c. the people

d. the interest group universe

58) Congress controls the bureaucracy by all of the following *except*

a. funding.

*b. personal contributions.

c. oversight.

d. authorization.

59) The details of how policymakers control those working for them, despite the knowledge difference is

a. micromanagement

b. macromanagement

*c. principal-agent theory

d. oversight.

60) While agency leaders frequently lobby Congress on behalf of their agency, they also frequently complain about congressional

a. load shedding.

b. pork barreling.

c. integrity.

*d. micromanagement.

61) In the relationship between Congress and the bureaucracy, bureaucrats often have more, and better, information than the politicians who pass laws. This imbalance is called

*a. information asymmetry.

b. moral hazard.

c. rent seeking.

d. the market model.

62) Public officials who deal directly with the public are called

a. grunts.

*b. street-level bureaucrats.

c. political appointees.

d. policy entrepreneurs.

63) The ability for street-level bureaucrats to decide who is more, or less, deserving of some government service or benefit is called

a. issue advocacy.

b. groupthink.

*c. bureaucratic discretion.

d. issue entrepreneurialism.

64) All of the following exert some control over the bureaucracy *except*

a. the president.

b. the Congress.

c. interest groups.

*d. nonvoters.

65) While bureaucracies have multiple principals who monitor their actions and create policies, bureaucrats still

*a. operate with considerable autonomy.

b. must face the voters.

c. have to be recertified every three years.

d. are required to justify their entire budgets every year.

66) A federal worker who reports corruption or fraud is known as a

a. bureaucrat.

*b. whistle-blower.

c. fraudster.

d. congressional aide.

67) The officials who actually run programs are

a. secretaries

b. aides

*c. street-level bureaucrats

d. appointees

68) As a total proportion of America's gross national product over the last forty years, the cost of the federal bureaucracy has

a. shrunk dramatically.

b. increased dramatically.

*c. remained generally steady.

d. grown exponentially.

69) Why do NASA flights always take off from Florida?

a. Florida has 29 votes in the Electoral College.

b. Florida has an exclusive government contract from NASA.

c. Florida is at sea level.

*d. An obscure 1950s rule prohibited the flight of test aircraft west of the Mississippi River.

70) Civil service pay scales have inched up since

*a. 2010.

b. 2008.

c. 2001.

d. 1989.

71) What decade saw the public's faith in government tumble?

a. late 1930s

b. late 1940s

c. late 1950s

*d. late 1960s

72) Politicians from ________ routinely bash the bureaucracy.

a. the Republican Party

b. the Democratic Party

*c. both political parties

d. the civil service unions

73) The primary effect of sunshine laws has been to open up the

*a. policy-making process to the public.

b. White House decision process to outside review.

c. federal judiciary's closed-conference proceedings to the people.

d. political appointment process to outside influence.

74) The 1966 ________ facilitates full or partial disclosure of government documents and information.

*a. Freedom of Information Act

b. Full Disclosure Act

c. Campaign Finance Reform Act

d. Civil Rights Act

75) In the early 1990s Vice President Al Gore spearheaded the "reinventing government" project, designed to

a. eliminate wasteful bureaucratic agencies.

*b. cut bureaucratic delays.

c. deregulate the financial sector.

d. deregulate the airline industry.

76) Bureaucratic agencies have

a. little reason to perform efficiently.

b. no incentive to serve the public.

*c. multiple constituencies with multiple goals.

d. a strong incentive to please their shareholders.

77) A critical dimension to making privatization of government services work is

a. codes of ethics.

b. noncompetitive bidding.

c. cheap labor.

*d. careful oversight.

78) The bureaucracy

a. is unnecessary in the twenty-first century.

*b. performs many jobs we need and value in our society.

c. has no checks or balances.

d. has no ties to our elected branches of government.

79) How have health outcomes changed in Bootheel since the bureaucracy stepped in?

*a. improved

b. remain the same

c. gotten worse

d. changed

80) Senator Ted Cruz compared bureaucracy to a

a. group villains

*b. plague of locusts

c. army of armadillos

d. bus of Spring Break students

81) In the nineteenth century U.S. jobs were considered

a. earned by merit

b. for professionals only

*c. political prizes

d. bought

82) A government running according to transparent rules with impartially applied is using

a. commercial politics

b. business politics

c. spoils system

*d. universalistic politics

83) The presidential assassination that led to civil service reform was

*a. James Garfield

b. Abraham Lincoln

c. John Kennedy

d. Ronald Reagan

84) After the Pendleton Civil Service Act how did civil servants get their job?

a. spoils system

*b. exams

c. payoffs

d. appointment

85) Those who wanted reform of the civil service had an advantage which was?

a. more money

b. support of the president

*c. jobs needed done

d. computers were being used

86) During World War I the number of civilian employees

a. stayed constant

b. quadrupled

c. tripled

*d. doubled

87) The problems that develop in bureaucratic systems are known as

*a. bureaucratic pathologies

b. bureaucratic issues

c. government problems

d. government pathologies

88) How many intelligence agencies are there in the federal government?

a. 17

*b.19

c. 21

d. 23

89) Which of the following is NOT a characteristic of bureaucracy?

a. hierarchy

b. division of labor

*c. varied routines

d. equal rules for all

90) When Congress appropriates funds for Social Security checks the bureaucratic workers then

a. decide which programs the money goes to

b. buy bonds to increase the money

c. determine where to send the money

*d. issue checks

91) Bureaucratic steps are

*a. always carried out the same way

b. variable

c. open to discussion

d. just a suggestion

92) Who can comment on a proposed rule in the *Federal Register*?

a. only relevant business leaders

*b. any interested party

c. only federal employees

d. only members of the relevant bureaucracy

93) A draft of an administrative regulation is known as a

a. new rule

b. final rule

*c. proposed rule

d. temporary rule

94) When is the analysis of the likely impact of the new rule published?

a. with the proposed rule

b. when the debates on the rule are published

c. never

*d. with the final rule

95) Where does rule making take place?

*a. far from the public eye

b. in public hearings

c. in Congressional hearings

d. during Presidential press conferences

96) After all the rules are in place who implements the new policies?

a. Congress

*b. Bureaucracy

c. President

d. States

97) The Bureau of Alcohol, Tobacco, Firearms and Explosives is likely to make connections with

a. anti-gun advocates

b. Supreme Court Justices

*c. Congressional members who care about guns

d. Military leaders

98) Appointed agency leaders are tasked with steering their agencies in the direction

a. they think best

b. the workers want to go

c. charted by Congress

*d. charted by the President

99) How many civil servants work their jobs regardless of the party in the White House?

*a. 2.5 million

b. 3.4 million

c. 4.2 million

d. 5.7 million

100) What does a bureaucrat really mean when they say, "We need to syndicate this decision?"

a. You should have protected me from myself.

*b. We need to spread the blame if it backfires.

c. I want to be able to blame you for my mistakes.

d. Expensive

Chapter 13

The Judicial Branch

1) Appellate courts hear cases from the

a. Supreme Court.

*b. lower courts.

c. courts of dual jurisdiction.

d. courts of upper jurisdiction.

2) According to Alexander Hamilton, the weakest of the three branches of government was

a. Congress.

b. the presidency.

*c. the judiciary

d. the bureaucracy.

3) The annual US criminal caseload is ________ million cases.

a. 25

*b. 35–40

c. 200–300

d. 10

4) Federal cases equal about what percentage of the volume in state courts?

*a. 1

b. 5

c. 50

d. 75

5) Most industrial nations rely on mediation in

a. criminal cases.

b. nonlegal cases.

*c. noncriminal cases.

d. foreign policy cases.

6) The use of a third party to solve a legal dispute most likely refers to the process called

a. litigation.

*b. mediation.

c. civic relations.

d. adjudication.

7) Today there are more than ________ lawyers in the United States.

a. 5 million

b. 10 million

*c. 1.1 million

d. 12 million

8) Since Alexis de Tocqueville's study of America in the 1830s, the prestige of lawyers and courts has

*a. decreased.

b. increased.

c. stayed the same.

d. slightly increased.

9) Which of the following cases has contributed to the decline of Supreme Court prestige?

*a. Bush v. Gore

b. *Brown v. Board*

c. *McCullough v. Maryland*

d. *Mendez v. Westminster*

10) The original Supreme Court had how many justices?

*a. 5

b. 7

c. 9

d. 11

11) One of the unusual things about the courts is that

a. there have always been nine Supreme Court justices.

*b. the Constitution never specified the number of Supreme Court justices.

c. Congress has very little role in shaping the courts.

d. the president has very little role influencing who is on the courts.

12) The concept of *judicial federalism* means

a. that the US has one main court system.

b. that the courts should be judicious in making relevant decisions.

*c. that there is both a federal and a state court system in the United States.

d. that state courts are stronger than federal courts.

13) The ultimate arbiter of all cases is the

a. trial court.

b. superior court.

*c. US Supreme Court.

d. federal court.

14) Today the Supreme Court hears about ________ cases a year.

a. 200

*b. 80

c. 1,000

d. 10,000

15) In what year was the Supreme Court set at 9 justices?

a. 1797

b. 1812

*c. 1869

d. 1962

16) The high-profile cases *Bush v. Gore* and *Roe v. Wade* were similar in that

a. they both addressed welfare concerns.

*b. they both began in state courts.

c. they both addressed social security concerns.

d. they both were focused on the right of privacy.

17) Most state judges

a. are appointed for life.

b. are selected by state legislatures.

*c. are elected by the public.

d. have terms that are not renewable.

18) The main ways to select a judge are

a. by public vote.

b. by governor's appointment.

c. by merit committees.

*d. all of the above

19) Acts of terror, insider trading, and immigration would be heard by

a. state trial courts.

*b. federal trial courts.

c. state appeals court.

d. state supreme court.

20) A district court is a

a. state appellate court.

b. state trial court.

*c. federal trial court.

d. state supreme court.

21) Today there are ________ district courts.

a. 5

b. 10

*c. 94

d. 200

22) Texas and California have ________ than other states.

a. fewer district courts

*b. more district courts

c. more powerful district courts

d. weaker district courts

23) District court judges are appointed by the

a. people.

b. governor.

*c. president.

d. state legislature.

24) The role of the circuit courts is to

*a. review the trial record of cases decided in district court.

b. review the trial record of cases decided in state trial courts.

c. review the trial record of cases decided in state appellate courts.

d. review the record of cases decided in mediation.

25) There are ________ federal appellate courts.

a. 94

b. 10

*c. 13

d. 75

26) The main difference between the federal appellate court and federal district court is that

a. there are more federal appellate courts.

b. federal appellate courts use juries.

*c. federal appellate courts do not use juries or cross-examination.

d. federal district courts do not allow cross-examination.

27) Circuit courts review cases decided in

a. Supreme Court

*b. District Courts

c. Bankruptcy Courts

d. Military Courts

28) Specialized courts hear cases on

a. immigration.

*b. tax disputes.

c. treason.

d. civil rights.

29) Specialized court judges differ from regular federal judges in that

a. they are older than federal judges.

*b. they are not appointed for life.

c. they do not require Senate confirmation.

d. they must be appointed by the governor.

30) If there was a breach of justice by a member of the military, that case would be heard by

a. a district court judge.

*b. a military judge.

c. an appellate court.

d. a state judge.

31) Specialized courts are often referred to as the

a. first judiciary.

b. second judiciary.

*c. third judiciary.

d. gang of four.

32) Which of the following is true?

a. There is great diversity amongst federal judges.

*b. More than three-quarters of federal judges are white.

c. Federal judges must be natural-born citizens.

d. Federal judges are overwhelmingly female.

33) The longest-serving chief justice in US history was

a. John Jay.

b. John Marshall Harlan.

*c. John Marshall.

d. Earl Warren.

34) The principle that enables the courts to check the other two branches of government is known as

a. legal authority.

b. judicial autonomy.

*c. judicial review.

d. statutory relief.

35) The principle of judicial review is traced back to the case of

a. *McCullough v. Maryland.*

b. *Gibbons v. Ogden.*

*c. Marbury v. Madison.

d. *Plessy v. Ferguson.*

36) Judicial review allows the courts to

a. check only Congress, if it has exceeded constitutional authority.

*b. check the executive and legislative branches, if they have exceeded constitutional authority.

c. check only the executive branch, if it has exceeded constitutional authority.

d. check the military.

37) Judicial review is ________ in the Constitution.

a. clearly mentioned

b. vaguely mentioned

*c. not mentioned

d. reflected through the Judiciary Act of 1789

38) The statement "When there is doubt about what the Constitution holds or implies, the Supreme Court makes the call" refers to the principle of

a. stare decisis.

*b. judicial review.

c. certiorari.

d. senatorial courtesy.

39) After *Marbury v. Madison,* which of the following occurred?

a. The Court frequently invalidated acts of Congress.

b. The Court frequently invalidated executive decisions.

*c. The Court did not overrule an act of Congress until the Missouri Compromise in 1854.

d. The Court supported African American rights in the *Dred Scott* decision.

40) The issue of whether enemy combatants could get a fair trial was decided by

a. the president.

*b. the Supreme Court.

c. Congress.

d. state court.

41) The fact that the Supreme Court has struck down statutes that supported segregation policy is a form of

*a. judicial activism.

b. legal rationalism.

c. judicial restraint.

d. strict constructionism.

42) The idea that the Supreme Court can take a vigorous or active approach when reviewing the other governmental branches is a form of

*a. judicial activism.

b. judicial restraint.

c. legal activism.

d. common law practice.

43) The idea that the court should overturn the elected branches of government reluctantly is called

a. judicial reproach.

*b. judicial restraint.

c. judicial activism.

d. loose constructionism.

44) The early English legal system was known as

a. majority rules.

b. the Magna Carte.

*c. common law.

d. common precedent.

45) Judicial cases today may be important tomorrow because they establish the concept of

a. judicial review.

*b. precedent.

c. legal formation.

d. civil law.

46) A judge that makes a legal decision on a case today may look at past case law and follow the concept of

*a. precedent.

b. civil law.

c. criminal law.

d. home rule.

47) A person charged with theft will face the rules and consequences under

*a. criminal law.

b. civil law.

c. humanitarian law.

d. common law.

48) The person bringing the suit in a civil case is called the

a. prosecutor.

b. litigator.

c. defendant.

*d. plaintiff.

49) The person being sued in a civil case is known as the

a. respondent.

b. plaintiff.

*c. defendant.

d. petitioner.

50) The chief justice during the *Brown v. Board of Education* case was

a. Oliver Wendell Holmes.

b. Louis Brandeis.

c. Hugo Black.

*d. Earl Warren.

51) Federal courts differ from the executive and legislative branches of government because they

a. are above politics.

b. serve longer periods.

c. are all from one political party.

*d. do not have an electoral base.

52) Supreme Court justices are in session

a. all year round.

*b. for 9 months.

c. for 6 months.

d. for 11 months.

53) A brief submitted by a person or group that is not a direct party to the case is called

*a. amicus curiae.

b. third-party brief.

c. legal extension.

d. case law.

54) The Supreme Court process of selecting a case is known as

a. the gang of four.

*b. rule of four.

c. the process of advise and consent.

d. rule of twelve.

55) Which of the following is essential for having a case heard by the Supreme Court?

a. standing

b. legitimate controversy

c. no moot cases

*d. all of the above

56) Someone adversely affected or suffering imminent harm would be able to satisfy the concept of

a. due process.

*b. standing.

c. amicus curiae.

d. justiciability.

57) Supreme Court clerks are usually

a. first year law students

b. lawyers between firms

*c. recent law school graduates

d. Harvard Law professors

58) The official statement of the Court is known as

a. the dissent.

*b. the majority opinion.

c. the concurrent opinion.

d. the remand.

59) A justice that agrees with the majority opinion but for different reasons is known as

a. an opposite opinion.

*b. a concurrent opinion.

c. a dissenting opinion.

d. a circulatory opinion.

60) A statement on behalf of the justices voting in the minority is called the

*a. dissent.

b. concurrent opinion.

c. differing opinion.

d. legal treatise.

61) Justices are guided by the concept of ________ in making legal decisions.

a. common law.

*b. stare decisis.

c. devolution.

d. rule of four.

62) "Stand by the things decided" is the definition for which Latin term?

a. writ of certiorari

b. writ of mandum

c. writ of habeas corpus

*d. stare decisis

63) Political scientists have generally found that justices' decisions are most closely tied to

*a. their political ideologies.

b. the case at hand.

c. the political nature of the case.

d. the role of big business.

64) A judge who observes a living and changing Constitution is known as a

a. theorist.

*b. pragmatist.

c. rationalist.

d. legalist.

65) A judge who interprets the Constitution literally is known as a(n)

a. legalist.

b. loose constructionist.

*c. originalist.

d. pragmatist.

66) The idea that judges are influenced by their peers in making legal decisions reflects the principle of

a. originalism.

b. pragmatism.

*c. collegiality.

d. legalism.

67) The case of *Marbury v. Madison* and the principle of judicial review was set forth by which Supreme Court justice?

a. Robert Taney

*b. John Marshall

c. Hugo Black

d. John Marshall Harlan

68) *McCulloch v. Maryland* was important to court development because

a. it allowed the federal government to tax a state.

b. it evoked the principle of the good faith and credit clause.

*c. it evoked the necessary and proper clause to block the state of Maryland from taxing the bank of the United States.

d. it allowed states to create complex interstate compacts.

69) The outcome of *McCulloch v. Maryland* affirmed the principle that

*a. the federal government is superior to state governments.

b. states are superior to the federal government in most instances.

c. state and federal power is equal.

d. states can use state mandates to trump federal power.

70) The court ruled in *Santa Clara Co. v. southern Pacific Railroad* that a corporations

*a. were entitled to Fourteenth Amendment protection

b. should be taxed differently than persons

c. are not separate entities from the stockholders

d. must pay income tax

71) The famous case that denied civil rights to former slaves was known as

a. *Plessy v. Ferguson.*

*b. Dred Scott v. Sandford.

c. *Marbury v. Madison.*

d. *Guinn v. United States.*

72) A key principle in the Dred Scott case was that slaves could not sue because

a. they did not have enough money.

*b. they lacked standing to sue.

c. their cases were only common law concerns.

d. their cases were not federal.

73) *Santa Clara Co. v. Southern Pacific Railroad* was significant because

a. it was the first case about the rights of the transcontinental railroad.

*b. the courts treated corporations as legal persons.

c. the state of California wanted to tax the federal railroad.

d. the state of Nevada wanted to tax California's railroad.

74) The idea that a corporation was viewed as a legal person meant

a. that corporations did not have to pay federal taxes.

b. that corporations were protected under the equal protection clause of the Thirteenth Amendment.

*c. that corporations were protected under the equal protection clause of the Fourteenth Amendment.

d. that corporations could use their own lawyers during trial.

75) Black equality was promoted through which amendments?

a. Seven, Eight, and Nine

*b. Thirteen, Fourteen, and Fifteen

c. One, Two, and Three

d. Five, Eight, and Nine

76) *Plessy v. Ferguson* dissenting justice stated that the Constitution was

a. not applicable in this case

*b. color blind

c. for all people

d. silent on separation issues

77) The outcome of *Plessy v. Ferguson* was

a. fair and equal treatment for all people.

b. the promotion of desegregation with all deliberate speed.

*c. the separate but equal policy.

d. the development of a color-blind society.

78) The sole dissenting voice in *Plessy v. Ferguson* was

a. John Marshall.

*b. John Marshall Harlan.

c. Oliver Wendell Holmes.

d. Robert Taney.

79) *Lochner v. New York* addressed the concern over

a. immigration.

*b. workers' rights.

c. health care.

d. national security.

80) The Lochner era (1905-1937) was an era in which the courts

a. promoted workers' rights.

b. addressed civil rights.

c. denied individual economic liberty.

*d. denied workers' rights.

81) *Muller v. Oregon* was a case that

*a. addressed the number of hours women could work.

b. addressed the rights of former slaves.

c. addressed the rights of farm workers.

d. addressed the concerns of corporations.

82) The outcome of *Schenck v. United States* was

a. the equal protection clause.

*b. the clear and present danger test.

c. the due process clause.

d. the grave and probable danger test.

83) *National Labor Relations Board v. Jones and Laughlin Steel Corporation* differed from the Lochner case because the Court supported

a. the corporation.

*b. workers' rights.

c. women's rights.

d. immigrant rights.

84) The case that forced Japanese Americans into internment camps during World War II was

*a. Korematsu v. US.

b. *Schenck v. US.*

c. *Gitlow v. New York.*

d. *Plessy v. Ferguson.*

85) The Korematsu case was significant because it was

*a. one of the first cases to use the strict scrutiny test.

b. one of the first cases to use the clear and present danger test.

c. one of the first cases to use the grave and probable danger test.

d. one of the first cases to use the bad tendency rule.

86) *Town of Greece v. Galloway* was a case that addressed the

a. full exercise clause.

b. free exercise clause.

*c. establishment clause.

d. full faith and credit clause.

87) The case that overturned *Plessy v. Ferguson* was

a. *Gitlow v. New York.*

b. *Guinn v. United States.*

c. *Korematsu v. United States.*

*d. Brown v. Board

88) The court in *Brown v. Board* stated that

*a. separate schools are inherently unequal.

b. separate facilities are inherently unequal.

c. separate movie theaters are inherently unequal.

d. separate restrooms are inherently unequal.

89) *Mapp v. Ohio* addressed concerns over the

a. Eighth Amendment.

*b. Fourth Amendment.

c. Third Amendment.

d. Sixth Amendment.

90) *Gideon v. Wainwright* was one of the first in a series of landmark judicial decisions addressing

a. the right to bear arms.

b. the right of free speech.

*c. the rights of defendants in criminal proceedings.

d. the rights of immigrant workers.

91) The case that struck down a Texas law outlawing abortion was

*a. Roe v. Wade.

b. *Mapp v. Ohio.*

c. *Gideon v. Wainwright.*

d. *Miranda v. Arizona.*

92) The case that addressed the right of the president to use executive privilege was

a. *Roe v. Wade.*

*b. US v. Nixon.

c. *US v. Ford.*

d. *Bush v. Gore.*

93) The idea that the president can withhold sensitive national security information from Congress or the courts is known as an

a. executive order.

b. executive pardon.

*c. executive privilege.

d. executive agreement.

94) The famous case that denied a Florida recount in the 2000 presidential election was

a. *Gore v. Bush.*

*b. Bush v. Gore.

c. *Kerry v. Bush.*

d. *Clinton v. Gore.*

95) The outcome of *National Federation of Independent Business v. Sebelius* was that

a. President Obama's health plan was repealed.

*b. Congress had the power to tax, which upheld the Obama reform.

c. people did not have to pay for health care.

d. Congress had the power to tax under the interstate commerce clause.

96) *National Federation of Independent Business v. Sebelius* took on controversial features of

a. Union law

b. Taxation law

*c. Health Reform law

d. Bankruptcy law

97) The important question in *National Federation of Independent Business v. Sebelius* was if Americans had to

a. pay union dues

b. work overtime

c. buy car insurance

*d. buy health insurance

98) The Court rule din 2010 that Congress could not change the rules of ________ and require states to expand programs.

*a. Medicaid

b. Medicare

c. Higher Education

d. Highway Systems

99) *Obergefell v. Hodges* brought ________ to the Supreme Court.

a. tax evasion

*b. same sex marriage

c. health benefits

d. death rights

100) The Court used the ________ amendment in deciding *Obergefell v. Hodges.*

a. 1st

b. 11th

*c. 14th

d. 22nd

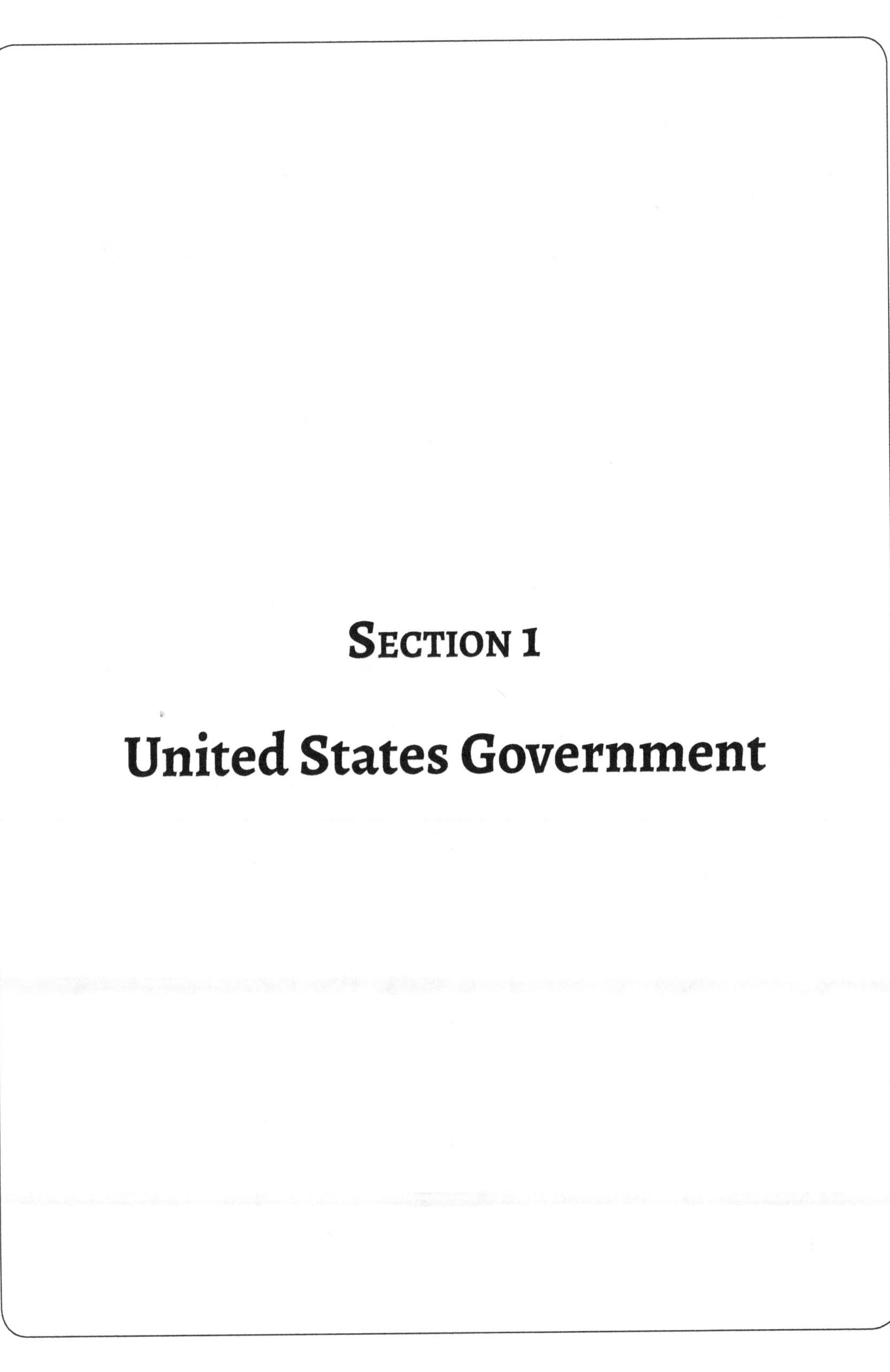

SECTION 1

United States Government

Chapter 1

Ideas That Shape American Politics

In this chapter, you will:

- Learn about the four questions that guide this book
- Explore the seven key ideas that shape American politics
- Investigate the essential questions: How do ideas affect

The Spirit of American Politics

- Who Governs?
  - Republic: government in which citizens rule indirectly and make government decisions through their elected representatives
  - Pluralist Theory: people influence government
  - Elite Theory: power rests in the hands of wealthy and powerful individuals
  - Bureaucratic Theory: control lies with the workers of modern government
  - Social Movement Theory: citizens wield power when they organize and rise up in protest

The Spirit of American Politics

- How Does American Politics Work?
  - Who gets what, when, and how?
  - Politics is how a society makes its collective decisions
  - Four "Is": ideas, institutions, interests and individuals
  - Ideas
    - Seven essential ideas
    - Liberty, democracy (self-rule), individualism, limited government, American Dream, equality, faith in God

- Institutions
  - Organizations norms and rules that structure political action
  - Organize behavior
- Interests
  - Interest groups
  - Individuals
    - » Rational Choice Theory: individuals maximize their own self-interest
  - Public interest
- Individuals
  - Ordinary people influencing politics and changing their world

- What Does Government Do?
  - "Establish justice, ensure domestic tranquility, provide for the common defense, promote the general welfare, and secure the blessings of liberty"
  - Priorities seen in the budget
- Who Are We?

A Nation of Ideas

- American Exceptionalism
  - View that the United States is uniquely characterized by a distinct set of ideas such as equality, self-rule and limited government
- Seven Key Ideas
  - Liberty
  - Self-rule (democracy)
  - Limited government
  - Individualism
  - American Dream
  - Equality
  - Faith in God
- Liberty
  - "The Land of the Free"
    - Freedom: ability to pursue one's own desires without interference from others

- The Two Sides of Liberty
  - Negative Liberty: freedom is the absence of constraints
    - » More familiar
    - » Society responsibility to make sure others do not interfere with individuals
    - » Limits government action
  - Positive Liberty: freedom to pursue one's goals
    - » Individuals cannot really be free if they lack the basic necessities of life
    - » Every citizen should have food, shelter, healthcare and educational opportunities
- The Idea of Freedom is Always Changing
- Self-Rule
  - Legitimate government flows from the people
  - One Side of Self-Rule: Democracy
    - » Government in which citizens rule directly and make government decisions for themselves
    - » Referendum: election in which citizens vote directly on an issue
    - » Initiative: process in which citizens propose new laws or amendments to the state constitution
  - Another Side of Self-Rule: A Republic
    - » Government in which citizens rule indirectly and permit elected representatives to make decisions
    - » People rule indirectly through elected representatives
  - A Mixed System
    - » U.S. democratic republic
    - » Includes elements of a democracy and a republic
  - American Exceptionalism
    - » View that the United States is uniquely characterized by a distinct set of ideas such as equality, self-rule and limited government

- Seven Key Ideas
  - Liberty
  - Self-rule (democracy)
  - Limited government
  - Individualism

- American Dream
- Equality
- Faith in God

– Liberty
  - "The Land of the Free"
    – Freedom: ability to pursue one's own desires without interference from others
  - The Two Sides of Liberty
    – Negative Liberty: freedom is the absence of constraints
      » More familiar
      » Society responsibility to make sure others do not interfere with individuals
      » Limits government action
    – Positive Liberty: freedom to pursue one's goals
      » Individuals cannot really be free if they lack the basic necessities of life
      » Every citizen should have food, shelter, healthcare and educational opportunities
  - The Idea of Freedom is Always Changing

Self-Rule

– Legitimate government flows from the people
– One Side of Self-Rule: Democracy
  - Government in which citizens rule directly and make government decisions for themselves
  - Referendum: election in which citizens vote directly on an issue
  - Initiative: process in which citizens propose new laws or amendments to the state constitution
– Another Side of Self-Rule: A Republic
  - Government in which citizens rule indirectly and permit elected representatives to make decisions
  - People rule indirectly through elected representatives
– A Mixed System
  - U.S. democratic republic
  - Includes elements of a democracy and a republic

Limited Government

- The Origins of Limited Government
  - Americans distrust centralized leadership
  - Seek to limit leadership power
- And Yet . . . The United States Has a Big Government
  - Conservatives: Americans who believe in reduced government spending, personal responsibility, traditional moral values, and a strong national defense
  - Liberals: Americans who value cultural diversity, government programs for the needy, public intervention int eh economy, and individuals' right to a lifestyle based on their own social and moral positions
- Limits on Government Action
  - Americans say they do not like government and then demand government action
- When Ideas Clash: Self-Rule and Limited Government
  - Self-rule says that the winning party should be able to put their policies into place, in a democracy, the majority should rule
  - Government should not meddle in private lives, so designed to be difficult for elected officials to follow through on promises

Individualism

- Individuals,notthesociety,areresponsiblefortheirownwell- being
- Community Versus Individualism
  - Social democracies emphasize community
    - Members of society are responsible for one another
    - Government a source of mutual assistance
    - Based on solidarity
  - Individualism: People and their families are responsible for their own welfare
- The Roots of American Individualism: Opportunity and Discord
  - Golden Opportunity
    - Endless land and opportunity
    - Hard work and a little luck anyone could earn a decent living
  - Social Conflict
    - Enormous differences within society
    - Country big and population too diverse to develop sense of solidarity

- Who Are We:Individualism and Solidarity?
  - Individualism and solidarity always compete in American politics
  - Individualism more robust, sense of solidarity also unites

American Dream

- If you are talented and work hard, you can achieve personal success
- Spreading the Dream
  - Legacy of Revolutionary War was the spread of the American dream to all classes
  - Common people as the basis of government
- What Do You Think? Individualism Versus Solidarity
- Challenging the Dream
  - Is the System Tilted Toward the Wealthy?
    - Top 1% of house holdsen joy more of the nation's wealth
    - Gap between richest and poorest widens
  - Does the American dream Promote the Wrong Values?
    - Chaseforwealth

Equality

- Every citizen enjoys the same privileges, status, and rights before the laws
- Three Kinds of Equality
  - Social equality
    - All individuals have same status in society
    - No fixed social classes
  - Political equality
    - All citizens have the same political rights and opportunities
    - Right to vote
  - Economic equality
    - Only small differences in wealth between citizens
    - Today the nation has changed toward inequality
- Opportunity or Outcome?
  - Equal opportunity: every American has the same chance to influence politics and achieve economic success
  - Equal outcome: idea that citizens should have roughly equal economic circumstances

- United States aims for equal opportunity
- United States has gone from most equal society in the world to one that is considerably less equal than other wealthy nations
- Politics emphasizes other ideas
  - Negative liberty
  - Individualism
  - American dream of getting ahead

Religion

- Still A Religious Country
  - Religion plays enduring role in American politics
  - Americans maintain high levels of religiosity despite becoming wealthier
- So Many Religions
  - Americans have a lot of religions to choose from
  - Many other nations have a single faith, often supported by the government
  - Colonies began with distinct religious affiliations •
- The Politics of Religion
  - What does the Constitution forbid
  - Religious faith often inspires people to throw themselves into political issues
  - Religious fervor sometimes fosters a missionary sense in American politics
    - Manifest Destiny: Goad gave an entire continent to his chosen people
    - Cold War: invoked God to contrast with communist nations

How Do Ideas Affect Politics

- Ideas in American Culture
  - Political Culture: attitudes, beliefs and assumptions that give order and meaning to public life
  - Culture develops slowly over time, shaped by history and experience
  - Perpetual work in progress
- The Ideas in Political Institutions
  - Institutions are key to political action
  - Government would operate smoothly even if citizens greedy and leaders corrupt
  - Institution would shape popular behavior

Chapter 2

The Constitution

In this chapter, you will:

- Discover the roots of the Constitution in colonial and revolutionary America.
- See why Americans declared independence from England and learn about the first constitution, the Articles of Confederation.
- Follow the arguments that shaped the Constitution and get an overview of the final document.
- Read about the great national debate over whether to adopt it.
- Learn how Americans have changed the Constitution—and how the Constitution has changed America.

The Colonial Roots of the Constitution

- Salutary neglect
    - King and army three thousand miles away
    - Paid little attention to colonies
- Every colony elected its own legislature
    - First: Virginia House of Burgesses 1620
    - Colonists had experience with representation
- Plentiful land
    - Created opportunities for ordinary people
    - Economic conditions helped foster a republic
- Compacts or Covenants
    - Some colonies began with mutual agreements
    - First: Mayflower Compact 1620

- Religion
  - Colonists came to practice religion in peace
  - New idea: individual freedom without government interference
- Border areas violent
  - Pushed the Americans to adopt strong central government

Why the Colonists Revolted

- The Colonial Complaint: Representation
  - Americans used to making their own decisions through elected assemblies
  - English violated the idea of self-rule
  - Delegate Representation: do what the voters want
  - Trustee Representation: do what is best for voters
- The Conflict Begins with Blood on the Frontier
  - French and Indian War
  - Settlers poured westward
  - Native Americans fought back
  - England closed the border and prohibited settlers from moving westward
  - Mercantilism: government restrains imports and promotes exports to maintain national power
- The Stamp Tax and the First Hints of Independence
  - Parliament ignored colonial assemblies and announced new taxes
  - Colonists began working together
- The Townshend Acts Worsen the Conflict
  - Stamp Tax lifted but followed up with new taxes
  - American Board of Customs created to collect taxes
  - Bureaucracy denying colonists self-governance
  - Legislatures dissolved
  - Boston Massacre
- The Boston Tea Party
  - Taxes repealed except tax on tea
  - Fifty men dumped tea from ships into Boston Harbor

Why the Colonies Revolted

- Revolution!
  - Intolerable Acts
    - Boston Harbor closed
    - Abolished town meetings
    - Quarter troops in homes
    - Massachusetts under military control
  - First Continental Congress 1774
    - Petitioned to end Intolerable Acts
    - Boycott British goods
    - Asserted colonial rights
  - April 1775 British looking for guns met armed colonists

The Declaration of Independence

- Second Continental Congress 1775
  - Declare independence
  - Mobilize army
  - Organize government
  - Adopted Declaration of Independence
    - Statement to world of America's purpose
    - Two parts: statement of principles, list of grievances
- The Principle: "We Hold These Truths . . ."
  - All people are equal
  - Their creator endowed them with rights that cannot be taken away
  - These rights include life, liberty, and the pursuit of happiness
  - People form governments to protect those rights
  - Governments derive their just powers form the consent of the governed
- Grievances
  - Violations of the right of representation
  - Standing army not under civilian control
  - Loss of an independent court

The First American Government The Articles of Confederation

- The National Government
  - National government weak
  - States strong
  - Congress selected and paid for by the states
  - No chief executive
  - No central authority to tax
  - No central power to muster an army
  - Each state had single vote in Congress
  - Changes required agreement of all thirteen states
- Some Success . . .
  - Northwest Ordinance of 1787
    - Process for buying western lands
    - Process for becoming a state
- . . . And Some Problems
  - Congress could not raise taxes and had no money of its own
  - Impossible to amend the articles due to unanimity rule
  - State governments dominated by their legislatures
  - Weak national government had a difficult time standing up to a foreign power
- Secrecy
  - Constitutional Convention
  - All agreed deliberations would be secret

Constitutional Convention

- How Much Power to the People?
  - Government answers to the people
  - Too much power to the people leads to chaos
  - Filtration or indirect elections
    - Public votes for those who would vote for public officials
    - Public less involved in government
    - People would vote for only one federal office: House of Representatives
- National Government Versus State Government

    - Most authority granted to national level
    - Compromise on a system that included both national and state power
    - Federal government had function
    - States had functions
- Big States Versus Small States
    - Virginia Plan
        - Bicameral legislature, representation by population
        - Citizens vote for House of Representatives
        - Congress would elect the President
        - National courts established
        - Congress legislate in cases where the states were incompetent
    - New Jersey Plan
        - Unicameral legislature, each state would have one vote
        - Congressional acts law of the land
        - Congress would elect executive committee
        - Executive committee would select a supreme court
        - National government could tax
    - Connecticut Compromise
        - Bicameral Congress
            - » House of Representatives: based on population
            - » Senate: two representatives from each state
            - » All finance bills introduced first in House
- The President
    - An Individual
    - Four year term
    - Electoral college would elect the president
- Separation of Powers
    - Each branch has a job to do
    - Legislative power in Congress
    - Executive power in the president
    - Judicial power in the courts
    - Checks and Balances

    - Each power is balance by a countervailing power in another branch
    - Each branch involved in the others' business
    - Most distinctive feature of American Constitution
- "A Principle of Which We Were Ashamed"
  - Slavery
  - Delegates wanted strong union more than they hated slavery
  - Three-fifths Compromise: slaves counted as three-fifths of free population
  - Slave Trade continued for twenty years
  - Fugitive Slave: rest of nation would assist in returning runaway slaves

An Overview of the Constitution

- Preamble
  - Authority rests on "we the people"
  - Six goals for the new government
    - Form a strong union
    - Establish equal justice for all
    - Insure domestic tranquility
    - Provide for the common defense
    - Promote the general welfare
    - Secure liberty for ourselves and our posterity
- Article 1: Congress
- Article 2: The President
- Article 3: The Courts
- Article 4: Relations Between the States
- Article 5: Amendments
- Article 6: The Law of the Land
- Article 7: Ratification

Ratification

- The Anti-Federalists
  - Argued against ratification
  - Classical Republicanism
  - Republics small and local, maximum popular participation

- Four major criticisms
  - Stripped political control from citizens, place in powerful national government
  - President looked like a king
  - Standing armies and navies were a threat to peace and liberty
  - Missing a Bill of Rights
- The Federalists
  - James Madison, Alexander Hamilton, John Jay wrote the arguments
  - *Federalist Papers*
    - Pro-Constitution editorial
    - Guide to thinking that guided the Constitution
    - Theoretical essays about politics and government
    - Federalist 10 argues large national government can protect liberty more than small local governments
    - Factions: groups that pursue their self-interest at the expense of others
    - Federalist 51: popular government must be organized to protect minorities from majorities
    - Have many factions to keep any one from dominating
- Two Strong Arguments
  - Anti-Federalist: local government that responds directly to the people
  - Federalists: national government could protect people's rights
- A Very Close Vote
  - Small states ratified quickly and unanimously
  - Larger states were slower
  - If 3 percent of delegates across Virginia, Massachusetts, New York had changed vote would not have been ratified

Changing the Constitution

- The Bill of Rights
  - First ten amendments
  - Rights and liberties that every citizen is guaranteed
  - Applied only to Federal government until Fourteenth Amendment
  - Incorporated to states using Fourteenth Amendment

- One right at a time
- Most recent second amendment in 2010

- The Seventeen Amendments
  - After Bill of Rights amendments rare
  - Seventeen since 1791
  - Amendments do one of four things
    - Extend rights
    - Adjust election rules
    - Change government operations
    - Affect governmental powers over individuals
- The Constitution Today
  - Americans disagree about how to read the Constitution
  - Originalism: relies on the original meaning of those who wrote the Constitution
  - Pragmatism: living, breathing, changing Constitution speaks to each generation differently

Chapter 3

Federalism and Nationalism

In this chapter, you will:

- Learn what federalism is
- Explore the strengths of federal and state governments
- Examine how federalism works—how it has evolved
- Review the contemporary conflicts that surround federalism
- Explore American nationalism, the force that binds and shapes our federalist polity

Forging Federalism

- Unitary Government
  - National polity governed as a single unit, with the central government exercising all or most political authority
  - Most nations in the 1780s
  - National government makes policy for the nation
  - Local government is an administrative extension of national government
- Confederation
  - Group of independent states or nations that yield some of their powers to a national government, although each state retains a degree of sovereign authority
  - Most power in the states or provinces
  - Weak central authority for common defense or economic benefits
  - Americans tried under Articles of Confederation
- Constitutional Convention delegates devised an innovative hybrid: federal system in which power is divided and shared between national and state governments
  - Constitution gives some decisions to national government and others to the states

- Conflict is built into the system
- Also have independent local governments
  - Derive authority from state government

Who Holds Government Authority?

- Most important issue in federalism is who decides what
- Advantages of State-Level Policy
  - Proponents of state action argue that state officials are more responsive to citizens
  - States sometimes offer more protection for individual rights
  - Federalism fosters political innovation
    - States can experiment with new programs
    - Try new programs out on local and state level before they go to the national level
      - » Diffusion: spreading of policy form one city or state to others; a process typical of U.S. federalism
  - Federalism gives people more choices
- Advantages of National Policy
  - More fair
    - Can lead to a race to the bottom
    - Bidding war occurs in which each state tries to cut programs more than neighboring states to attract middle-class people
  - Equalize resources across the nation
  - Standardize best practices
    - National policy can ensure minimum standards
    - No state chooses inadequate health or education policies
  - Leaving authority in state hands introduces problems of coordination
    - Federal, state and local agencies address similar problems
    - Patchwork of rules and regulations across states can leave citizens and national companies bewildered about which rules apply where
    - Sets up continual dispute about who is in charge
- Federalism gives advocates on both sides many different political venues in which to address problems, challenge policies, and assert rights

How Federalism Works

- Federalism offers endless opportunities for confusion and discord as different layers of government tussle over who has responsibility for what
- Rules hammered that enable federalist system to function pretty well
- Constitution Sets the Ground Rules
  - Constitution empowers national authority
    - Delegated powers
      - » Express or enumerated powers
      - » National government powers listed explicitly in the Constitution
    - Commerce Clause: empowers Congress to regulate commerce with foreign nations, between states, and with Indian tribes
    - Necessary and Proper Clause: constitutional declaration that defines Congress's authority to exercise the necessary and proper powers to carry out its designated function
      - » Elastic clause
        - ➢ Stretches national government authority to include anything implied in the Constitution's text
        - ➢ Implied Powers: national government powers implied by, but not specifically named in, Constitution
    - Supremacy Clause
      - » Buttresses the delegated and implied powers
      - » National government's authority prevails over any conflicting state or local government's claims
    - Inherent Powers
      - » Powers not specified or implied by the Constitution but necessary for the President or Congress to fulfil their duties
  - Constitution Protects State Authority
    - States have authority guaranteed by the Tenth Amendment
    - Reserves to the states all powers not specifically granted to the national branches
    - Reserved Powers; Constitutional guarantee that the states retain government authority not explicitly granted to national government

    - Constitution Authorize Shared Power
        - States and national authorities share many responsibilities
        - Concurrent powers: governmental authority shared by national and state governments
    - Full faith and credit: constitutional requirement that each state recognize and uphold laws passed by any other state
    - Constitution empowers and limits both the national and the state governments
- Dual Federalism (1789-1933)
    - Clear division of governing authority between national and state governments
    - State and national governments had relatively clear responsibilities
    - State government wielded at least as much authority as the federal government
    - "Layer cake" federalism: separate layers of government
    - National government in charge of three major areas
        - International relations
        - Internal improvements
        - Regulated relations and commerce between the states
    - States retained control over almost everything having to do with individual citizens
- Cooperative Federalism (1933-1981)
    - Mingled governing authority, with functions overlapping across national and state governments
    - Congress responded to Great Depression by passing policies that strengthened national government's role
    - More active federal government and blurred lines of authority
    - Marble Cake: different government functions swirled together
    - Funds through grants-in-aid: national government funding provided to state and local governments, along with specific instructions about how the funds may be used
- New Federalism
    - Version of cooperative federalism, but with less oversight by the federal government (which still provided funds) and more control on the state and local level
    - Reagan presidency (1981-1989) ushered in

    - Power away from national officials with more authority by state and local officials
    - Block grants: national government funding provided to state and local governments, with relatively few restrictions or requirements on spending
- Progressive Federalism
    - Modern federalism variant in which the national government sets broad goals for a program and relies on state innovations to achieve them
    - Obama administration building on the George W. Bush administration introduced in 2009
    - National government sets program goals and relies on state innovations to achieve them
    - State and federal government are partners, constantly negotiating
    - Programs are defined through the intricate back and forth between federal and state officials
- Federalism Today
    - Trump administration trying to go back to new federalism
        - Fewer federal dollars
        - Fewer federal regulations
    - Battlefield in partisan conflict

Issues in Federalism

- Perpetually shifting nature of government power and accountability
- Unfunded Mandates
    - Obligation imposed on state or local government officials by federal legislation, without sufficient funding support to cover the costs
- Drowned in the Bathtub? Reducing the Federal Government
    - Devolution: transfer of authority from national to state or local government level
    - Preemption: invalidation of a U.S. state law that conflicts with a federal law
- Federalism in the Courts
    - Explanation for major historical shifts: party in power
    - Courts offer another chart to the tides of federalism, Judges play a balancing role

Nationalism, American Style

- American public's sense of identity as Americans
- Helps maintain federal balance by instilling loyalty to nation, state, and locality
- The Rise of American Nationalism
    - Constitution a touchstone for Americans' shared sense of belonging
    - Double-edges sword
        - Strong sense of national identity fosters mutual support and loyalty
        - Most enthusiastic nationalists are those most likely to draw strict boundaries around who counts as an American
- America's Weak National Government
    - Passionate nationalist sense linked to relatively weak governing institution
    - Strength of central governments measured by three principles: size, authority and independence
    - Size
        - American national government smaller than other nations
        - Grew after World War I
        - U.S. government still spends less than most other wealthy nations
    - Authority
        - Most developed nations had powerful and efficient national bureaucracies, American government engaged citizens without bureaucracy
        - Civic voluntarism: citizens voluntarily participating in public life without government involvement
            - » Projected robust nationalist feeling
            - » Widespread individual efforts for the common good
            - » Lived on for generations
            - » U.S. emphasizes community participation over centralized administration
        - Independence
            - » Americans separate and divide governing power more than any other wealthy country
            - » Federalism operates along a vertical dimension
            - » Power is shared among different levels of government

Chapter 4

Civil Liberties

In this chapter, you will learn:

- The rise of civil liberties.
- The right to privacy—a controversial liberty that is not mentioned in the Constitution and involves abortion and same-sex marriage.
- The freedom of religion.
- The right to free speech and its special status.
- The right to bear arms.
- The rights of the accused.
- The difficult balance between fighting terrorism and protecting civil liberties

The Rise of Civil Liberties

- Civil Rights and Civil Liberties
  - Civil liberties are the limits on government so that individuals can exercise their personal freedoms
  - Civil rights: freedom to participate int eh full life of the community—to vote, use public facilities, and exercise equal economic opportunity
  - The battle for civil rights led to more robust civil liberties
- Purpose of Civil Liberties
  - "The very purpose of a Bill of Rights was to withdraw certain subjects from the vicissitudes of political controversy, to place them beyond the reach of majorities and officials" Supreme Court 1943
- The slow rise of civil liberties
  - Bill of Rights originally applied only to the national government

- Fourteenth Amendment
    - *No state shall. . .deprive any person of life, liberty, or property, without due process of law; nor deny any person within its jurisdiction the equal protection of the laws.*
    - *Selective incorporation* is extending protections from the Bill of Rights to the state governments, one right at a time.

Privacy

- Penumbras and Emanations
    - Penumbras: the shadows of the amendments give people a right to make their own choices free from government interference
    - Emanations: things that flow out from other amendments were designed to protect privacy
    - Ninth amendment declares that other rights exist besides the ones mentioned in the Constitution that are retained by the people
    - The Griswold case was one of the first privacy cases
- *Roe v. Wade*
    - The Roe case drew on the right to privacy and struck down a Texas law banning abortion within the first three months of pregnancy
- *Planned Parenthood v. Casey*
    - The Roe case also brought forth two new ideas:
        - Judicial Rule: hared-and-fast boundaries between what is lawful and what is not
        - Judicial Standards: guiding principles that help governments make judgment calls
- Sex Between Consenting Adults
    - Right to privacy extended to same-sex couples
    - *Lawrence v. Texas*
- Clashing Principles

Freedom of Religion

- *Congress shall make no law respecting an establishment of religion, or prohibiting the free exercise thereof*
- There are two primary clauses relating to freedom of religion: the establishment clause and the free practice (exercise) clause.

- Establishment Clause
  - Congress shall make no law establishing or favoring one religion over another, or religion over no religion.
  - Strict separation calls for the Lemon principles to be applied in judging whether a law establishes a religion
    - Secular purpose
    - Neither advance nor inhibit religion
    - Must not excessively entangle government in religion
  - Two Perspectives
    - Strict separation: strict principles articulated in the Lemon test for judging whether a law establishes a religion
    - Accommodation: government does not violate the establishment clause as long as it does not confer an advantage to some religions over others
- Free Exercise of Religion
  - Sherbert or Balancing Test
    - Government cannot impose a significant burden on an individual's ability to exercise his or her faith
    - Did the government have a compelling interest for imposing the burden
  - *Employment Division v. Smith*
    - Neutrality Test
    - Is law applied to everyone and does not target a religious group the Court will permit it
  - Religious Freedom Restoration Act of 1993 (RFRA)
    - Required federal and state government so use Sherbert balancing test
    - Court ruled Congress lacked constitutional authority to order balancing test
    - New Congressional Act passed and all reverted to Sherbert Balancing test

Freedom of Speech

- Preferred Position
  - Of all civil liberties, free speech holds a preferred position
  - When another right conflicts with the right to free speech, generally the right to free speech will be protected
- Political speech
  - Clear and Present Danger

    - Charles Schenck guilty of violating Espionage Act
    - Pamphlets urged men not to enlist for World War I
    - Court doctrine that permits restrictions of free speech if officials believe that the speech will lead to a prohibited action such as violence or terrorism
  - The clear and present danger test stood for over 50 years and was rewritten in 1969 saying that a state may not interfere with speech unless the speech "incites imminent lawless action" and is likely to actually produce such action.
- Symbolic speech
  - Act, rather than actual speech, used to demonstrate a point of view
  - May not intimidate others
- Limits to Free Speech: Fighting Words
  - "personally abusive epithets which, when addressed to the ordinary citizen, are, as a matter of common knowledge, inherently likely to provoke violent reaction"
  - Expressions inherently likely to provoke violent reactions and not necessarily protected by the First Amendment
- Limited Protections: Student Speech
  - Students "do not shed their constitutional right to freedom of speech or expression at the schoolhouse gate"
  - Balance student rights with the schools' education mission
  - Students less protection than adults

Freedom of the Press

- Freedom of the press follows most of the rules as freedom of speech
- Shares "preferred position" enjoyed by speech
- Prior restraint
  - Legal effort to stop speech before it occurs
  - Increasing media outlets online both within and outside the US, enforcement of Court decisions is increasingly difficult.
- Obscenity
  - Obscenity is not a form of protected speech, although its interpretation is often criticized as being somewhat subjective.
  - The Miller test for obscenity holds that speech is not protected if it has all three of the following characteristics:
    - » "The average person, applying contemporary community standards, would find that the work, taken as a whole, appeals to the prurient interest."

    - » "It depicts sexual conduct in a patently offensive way."
    - » "The work lacks serious literary, artistic, political, or scientific value."
  - Court flatly forbids child pornography
- Libel
  - Publishing falsehoods about a person, is not protected, and neither is slander, which is speaking falsehoods about a person. Proving libel or slander against public officials requires showing malicious intent, or a "reckless disregard for the truth."
  - The burden of proof of libel in the US is on the official seeking to demonstrate libel against him/herself, whereas the burden of proof under English law is on the writers to prove the truth about the speech.

Right to Bear Arms

- The right to bear arms is found in the Second Amendment to the Constitution
- A well-regulated militia, being necessary to the security of a free state, the right of the people to keep and bear arms shall not be infringed
- One hand: amendment simply protects colonial-era militias, On another: guarantees the right to own weapons
- Relic of the Revolution
  - Protected militias
  - Citizens volunteered for service in local militias that defended nation
  - Forbids national government from disarming local militias
- Palladium of all Liberties
  - Many see as the most important right of all
  - The one right that allows rights to exist at all
  - Supreme Court moving to defend gun rights
  - Second Amendment incorporated in 2010

Right of the Accused

- The rights that protect people accused of crimes are found in the Fourth, Fifth, Sixth, and Eighth Amendments
- Thirty-one different rights for those who face criminal charges
- Fourth Amendment—search and seizure
  - "the right to be left alone"

- This amendment protects citizens from unlawful searches and obtaining of evidence. There must be probable cause, typically demonstrated through a warrant, for a search to occur.
- The exclusionary rule is based in the *Mapp v. Ohio* decision
- Exclusionary Rule: ruling that evidence obtained in an illegal search may not be introduced in a trial

– The Fifth Amendment—rights at trials
- Grand Jury: a jury that does not decide on guilt or innocence but only on whether there is enough evidence for the case to go to trial
- Double Jeopardy: an individual cannot be tried twice for the same offense
- Miranda Warnings: set of rights that police officers are required to inform suspects of, including the right to remain silent

– The Sixth Amendment—right to counsel
- This amendment guarantees a speedy and public trial by an impartial jury
- Lawyers must be provided for those who cannot afford them

– The Eighth Amendment: The Death Penalty
- 101 nations have abolished the death penalty, violation of human rights
- Proponents argue that some crimes are so terrible that justice demands capital punishment
- Opponents respond that killing people is immoral and that no government should be given the power to "play God"

Terrorism, Non-Citizens, and Civil Liberties

– USA Patriot Act: legislation that sought to enhance national security, passed in the aftermath of September 11, 2001, terrorist attacks

– Contacts with Forbidden Groups: rules enhanced that bar Americans from offering aid to terrorist organizations

– Surveillance
- Domestic surveillance requires a warrant
- International surveillance does not require a warrant

– Rights of Non-Citizens
- Most rights extended to non-citizens
- Immigration law applies to non-citizens, rights more restricted

Chapter 5

The Struggle for Civil Rights

In this chapter, you will:

- Explore the seven steps to winning civil rights.
- Review the African American experience that set the pattern for civil rights.
- Assess women's quest for economic and political rights.
- Examine the political experience of Hispanics and Asians.
- Consider the rights of other groups, including disabled people and same-sex partners.

Struggle for Civil Rights

- Civil Rights: freedom to participate in the full life of the community
    - Vote
    - Use public facilities
    - Exercise equal economic opportunity
- Discrimination occurs when people denied rights and opportunities
- Once citizens win rights, public attention shifts to protecting them
- Battle to win civil rights is most powerful story in American history
- History can be viewed two ways
    - Steady march toward a deeper and richer equality
    - Sometimes rights expand, sometimes they contract

Winning Rights: The Political Process

- Seven Steps to Political Equality
    - Group defines itself

- Group challenges society
- Stories change
- Federalism comes into play
- Executive branch often breaks the ice
- Congress legislates a blockbuster
- It all ends up in court

– How the Courts Review Cases
  - Judicial framework important
  - Three categories for determining whether acts violate "equal protection of the laws" guaranteed by Fourteenth Amendment
    - – Suspect Categories
      - » Strict scrutiny
        - ➢ Strike down any law that singles our race, ethnicity or religion
        - ➢ Compelling government interest
    - – Quasi-Suspect Categories
      - » Special category for gender cases
      - » Rest on important state purpose
    - – Nonsuspect Categories
      - » Rational connection between legislation and legitimate government purpose
      - » Weakest test

Race and Civil Rights: Revolt Against Slavery

– African Americans developed the tactics that other groups would use in their own battles for civil rights

– Opened the door to civil rights across society

– The Clash over Slavery
  - Slaves permitted churches
  - Dream of freedom became a kind of religious faith
  - Three forces precipitates national crisis over slavery
    - – Moral crusade for abolition
    - – Economic interests
    - – Political calculations

- Abolition
  - Nineteenth century movement demanding an immediate and unconditional end to slavery
  - Abolitionists diverse for the time

- The Clash over Slavery (cont)
  - Economics
    - Every new settlement: slave or free?
    - Slavery opposed for moral and economic reasons
  - Politics
    - Political balance between slave states and free states in Congress
    - Slaves gave southerners an additional thirty-six seats in the House of Representatives
    - Missouri Compromise 1820 drew a line through the Louisiana Territory
      - » North of line free, except Missouri
      - » South of line slavery
    - Compromise of 1850
      - » Decision of free or slave turned over to residents of new territories
  - Abolition
    - Nineteenth century movement demanding an immediate and unconditional end to slavery
    - Abolitionists diverse for the time
  - Economics
    - Every new settlement: slave or free?
    - Slavery opposed for moral and economic reasons
  - Politics
    - Political balance between slave states and free states in Congress
    - Slaves gave southerners an additional thirty-six seats in the House of Representatives
    - Missouri Compromise 1820 drew a line through the Louisiana Territory
      - » North of line free, except Missouri
      - » South of line slavery
    - Compromise of 1850
      - » Decision of free or slave turned over to residents of new territories

- *Dred Scott v. Sandford*
  - 1857 Supreme Court decision
  - Slave, Dred Scott, sued for freedom
  - Supreme Court ruled not free because territories nor federal government had power to limit slavery or give black man rights
  - Missouri Compromise unconstitutional
  - Popular sovereignty unconstitutional
  - No territory could restrict slavery or elevate blacks to citizenship
- The Second American Founding: A New Birth of Freedom?
- Gettysburg address announced "a new birth of freedom"
- "government of the people, by the people, for the people" rewrote the idea of freedom
- Innovation institutionalized in four documents
  - Emancipation Proclamation
    - Freed the slaves in areas rebelling
    - No power to enforce his decree
  - Civil War Amendments
    - Full legal force to Lincoln's new birth of freedom
    - Thirteenth Amendment: abolished slavery
    - Fourteenth Amendment: anyone born in the United States a U.S. citizen
      - » No state shall "deprive any person of life, liberty or property without due process of law" or equal protection of the law
      - » Applied Bill of Rights to the states
      - » Equal protection of the law: requires equal treatment for all citizens
    - Fifteenth Amendment: guarantees voting rights
  - Reconstruction
    - Failed effort, pursued by Northerners and Southerners, to rebuild the South and establish racial equality after the Civil War
    - Rebuild South over sense of racial justice
    - Organized *Freedmen's Bureau* to assist former slaves
    - Civil Rights Act of 1866 guaranteed African Americans same property rights as white Americans
    - Civil Rights Act of 1875 limited private racial discrimination

- Dreams of racial equality slipped away
    - » North withdrew army from the South
    - » Congress repealed laws that implemented Civil War amendments, no national mechanism left to enforce
- Civil Rights Cases of 1883 Supreme Court struck down the Civil rights Act of 1875
- State governments gutted Fifteenth Amendment 1890s
    - » Grandfather clause: if grandfather had not voted could not vote
    - » Poll taxes
    - » Literacy tests: requirement that voters be literate
- Jim Crow
    - » System of racial segregation in the U.S. South 1890-1965, violently enforced
- Supreme Court ruled in 1896 nothing inherently discriminatory in separate but equal facilities (*Plessy v. Ferguson*)
- Segregation held in place by brutality of lynching

The Fight for Racial Equality

- Great Migration: vast movement of African Americans from rural South to the urban North between 1910 and 1960s
- Two Kinds of Discrimination
    - De jure: involves laws that explicitly deny civil rights
    - De facto: more subtle forms of discrimination that exist without a legal basis
- The Modern Civil Rights Campaign Begins
    - National Association for the Advancement of Colored People (NAACP formed 1909)
    - President Roosevelt created Fair Employment Practices Committee 1941
    - President Truman desegregated the armed forces 1948
- The Courts
    - NAACP went to court and chipped away at Jim Crow laws
    - President Roosevelt appointed a court sympathetic to civil rights
    - Supreme Court struck down all-white Democratic primary 1944
    - *Brown v. Board of Education* 1954 ruled that segregated schools violated equal protection clause

- Nothing changed
- Court did not impose timetable or implementation plan
- National officials did not support
- States opposed

- The Civil Rights Movement
  - Ordinary American people rose up and defeated segregation
  - Movement began in Montgomery, Alabama 1955
  - Court opened legal door, Protestors protested, Change Won
  - Freedom Riders 1961: black and white activists who rode buses together to protest segregation on interstate bus lines
  - Kennedy administration submitted strong civil rights legislation to Congress
- Congress and the Civil Rights Act
  - Congress blocked civil rights legislation
  - March on Washington 1963 marked high point of peaceful protest movement
  - Civil Rights Act of 1964
    - Forbade state and local governments from denying access to public facilities on the basis of race, color, or national origin
    - Employers could not discriminate
    - Private business could not discriminate
    - Led to rapid integration of southern schools
  - Voting Rights Act 1965
    - Protected voting rights
    - Secured Fifteenth Amendment

The Post Civil Rights Era

- Affirmative Action in the Workplace
  - Affirmative Action: direct, positive steps to increase the representation of groups that have faced discrimination in the past
  - Disproportionate impact: effects some policies have in creating discrimination even if discrimination is not consciously intended
    - Developed by Supreme Court 1971
    - Companies could not hire or promote employees in a way that created "built-in headwinds"

    - Affirmative action raises difficult issues
        - Equality of opportunity is goal
        - Equality of outcome is product
- Affirmative Action in Education
    - School busing: an effort to integrate public schools by mixing students from different neighborhoods
    - Achieve racial integration
    - Declined 1980s

Women's Rights

- Suffrage
    - Intertwined with the fight for racial equality
    - Women in abolition movement grew frustrated by their own barriers
    - Seneca Falls Convention 1848: first convention dedicated to women's rights
    - Women's Christian Temperance Union 1870s
        - Attacked alcohol
        - Championed voluntary motherhood
        - Suffrage for women
        - Decent wages
    - Nineteenth Amendment gave women the vote 1920
- The Civil Rights Act of 1964
    - Designed to bar racial discrimination
    - "sex" added to bill as a joke
    - Opened the door to gender change
    - Officials ignored gender provision
    - National Organization for Women (NOW) began demonstrations, rallies, lobbying and litigation
    - Congress passed Federal Education Amendments 1972: required equal athletic opportunities for men and women
- Equal Rights Amendment
    - Introduced in Congress every year between 1924 and 1972
    - Three states short of ratification when reframed: women want to be a wife, mother and homemaker

    - Stopped ERA
- The Courts
    - Women targeted the courts
    - Challenged discriminatory state laws, case by case
    - Gender was a non-suspect category: upheld as long as it had some rational connection to legitimate state purpose
    - Court lifted gender into category of heightened scrutiny 1976
    - Recent court decisions have made it more difficult to sue for discrimination

Hispanics

- Largest minority group
- Challenging Discrimination
    - League of United Latin American Citizens (LULAC) 1929
        - Fought segregation through lawsuits
        - Latino school segregation struck down 1947
    - Turned to activism 1960s
        - Fight more aggressively against discrimination
        - Challenged immigration policies
        - Chicanismo: defiant movement expressing pride in Latino origins and culture in the face of discrimination
        - United Farm Workers organized migrant workers, another symbol of Latino mobilization
- The Politics of Immigration
    - Hispanic politics wrapped up with immigration
    - Ancient Fears
        - Immigrants trigger fears that are repeated for every new group
        - President Trump has made limits on immigration one of his signature issues
    - Three Categories of Immigrants
        - Born in United States or have become American citizens
        - Resident Aliens
        - Not legally authorized to be residents
    - Undocumented individuals
        - People not legally authorized to be in the United States

  - Debate especially intense
  - Racial profiling: law enforcement practice of singling out people on the basis of physical features such as race or ethnicity
- Language Controversy: Speak English!
- Political Mobilization

Asian Americans

- Third largest minority in the United States
- Do not share a common language
- Do not share a common historical experience
- Highest education level
- Chinese Exclusion Act 1882 barred Chinese immigrants
- California Alien Land Law of 1913 forbade Asian immigrants from owning land
- After Japanese attack on Pearl Harbor 1941 Japanese Americans placed in internment camps
- Schools segregated
- "Model Minority"

Native Americans

- The Lost Way of Life
  - Dark side of American expansion was "Indian removal"
  - Settlers moved west Indian tribes forced from homelands
  - Indians not passive, at time forced white settlers to retreat
  - Federal government forced most Native American populations into reservations
  - Tribes were pushed to adapt European lifestyles
  - Dawes Act of 1887
    - Divided lands into individual parcels
    - Destroyed traditional ownership customs and encourage farming
    - Boarding schools for children
- Indians and the Federal Government
  - Supreme Court ruled 1831 Indian tribes were "domestic dependent nations"
    - Separate people
    - Without the rights of an independent nation

    - Not considered citizens, not protected by the Constitution
    - Indian Citizenship Act 1924, Indians citizens with rights
    - Reservations subject to federal but not state governments
    - Bureau of Indian Affairs responsible for Native American issues
- Social Problems and Politics
  - Poverty rates almost double the national rates
  - Life on reservation difficult
  - Two Camps
    - Ethnic minority: argues Indians should engage American democracy and mobilize for rights and equality
    - Tribal movement: withdraw from American politics and society, revitalize Native American culture and traditions
  - Civil rights protest of 1960s included Native American activists

Groups without Special Protection

- People with Disabilities
  - Before 1970 people with disabilities lived outside mainstream society
  - Section 504 of the 1973 Rehabilitation Act: no handicapped person denied access to any program
  - Section 504 gave activists a political focus
  - Government action provided new legal rights; the group then organized and demanded further change
  - Went from requesting welfare benefits to demanding civil rights
  - Americans with Disabilities Act 1990 forbade companies form discriminating against handicapped people, make reasonable accommodations
- Sexual Orientation and gender identity
  - Movement for same-sex rights began with a riot 1969 when police raided a gay bar
  - Moment LGBT community affirmed its identity
  - American Psychiatric Association removed homosexuality from its list of mental disorders 1973
  - Early 1980s AIDS pushed gay groups into local politics
  - Supreme Court enshrined same sex marriage as a national civil right 2015
  - LGBTQ individuals still face formidable barriers to full civil rights

The Fight for Civil Rights Goes On

- Voting Rights Today
  - 22 states debated bills to make voting more difficult 2018
  - Supreme Court made restricting the vote easier 2013
    - Stuck down the central requirement in the Voting Rights Act of 1965
    - States no longer required to clear voting rights changes with the federal Justice Department
- Economic and Social Rights Today
  - Health: life expectancy getting closer
  - Income: Black poverty rate remained roughly three times white poverty rate
  - Incarceration: African American men are seven times as likely to be in jail as whites
    - New Jim Crow: idea that mass incarceration of African Americans has effects comparable to legal segregation

Chapter 6

Public Opinion and Political Participation

In this chapter, you will:

- The sources of our opinions about public issues.
- How public opinion is measured
- The role of public opinion in a democracy.
- Different forms of political participation across U.S. history
- Examine why people participate
- The benefits and drawbacks of an emerging "clickocracy," as political engagement moves online

Sources of Public Opinion

- Sum of individual beliefs and opinions
- Political Socialization
    - Process by which individuals acquire their political values and outlooks
    - Parents and Friends
    - Education
        - Graduate degree likely to lean left
        - College Professors more likely to identify as liberals
    - Race
        - African Americans more Democratic
        - Hispanics trend Democratic
        - White Americans lean Republican
    - Religion

    - White Evangelicals vote strongly Republican
    - Catholic voters tend to split
    - Black Protestants, Latino Catholics, Jews, Muslims trend Democratic
  - Life Events
- Party
  - Strong predictor of individual opinion
  - Most politically active aligned with Democrats or Republicans
- Self-Interest: Voting our Pocketbooks
  - Economic self-interest matters most
  - People with more money will vote for lower taxes
  - People with less money will vote to expand social programs
  - One factor
  - Poorer Americans likely to affiliate with Democrats
  - Wealthy Americans are divided
- Elite Influence
  - Political elites: individuals who control significant wealth, status, power, or visibility and consequently have significant influence over public debates
  - Elites frame the issue—give it a particular slant
- Wars and Other Focusing Events
  - Americans pull together during crises
  - Produce consensus and spike in government approval rating
  - Often fades quickly

Measuring Public Opinion

- Polling Bloopers
  - *Literary Digest* 1920
  - Presidential Election 2016
- Polling 101
  - Random sample: a sample in which everyone in the population (sampling frame) has an equal probability of being selected
  - Sampling frame: designated group of people from whom a set of poll respondents is randomly selected

- Demographic group: people sharing specific characteristics such as age, ethnicity/race, religion, or country of origin
- Refining the Sample
  - Choose likely voters to more accurately predict the outcome
  - Likely voters: persons identified as probably voters in an upcoming election. Often preferred by polling organizations, but difficult to specify with great accuracy
- Timing
- Wording
  - Framing effects: the influence, on the respondent, of how a polling questions is asked; changes in wording can significantly alter many people's answers
- Lies, Damn Lies, and Polls
  - Push poll: form of negative campaigning that masquerades as a regular opinion survey.
- Technology Error
- Sampling error and response bias
  - Margin of sampling error: degree of inaccuracy in any poll, arising from the fact that surveys involve a sample of respondents from a population, rather than every member
  - Response bias: tendency of poll respondents to misstate their views, frequently to avoid "shameful" opinions such as sexism or racism

- Do Opinion Surveys Influence Us?
  - Bandwagon effect: when people join a cause because it seems popular or support a candidate who is leading in the polls
  - Boomerang effect: discrepancy between candidates' high poll ratings and election performance, caused by supporters' assumption that an easy win means they need not turn out

Public Opinion in a Democracy

- Ignorant Masses
  - Nonattitudes: lack of a stable perspective in response to opinion surveys; answers to questions may be self-contradictory or may display no ideological consistency
- Rational Public

- Information Shortcuts: cues about candidates and policies drawn from everyday life.
- Groupthink: tendency among a small group of decision makers to converge on a shared set of views; can limit creating thinking or solutions to policy problems

– Governing by the People
  - If public opinion is to guide government, three conditions must be met
    - People know what they want
    - Public must clearly communicate its desires to political leaders
    - Political leaders must pay attention to public views—and respond
  - Do the People Know What They Want?
  - How Do the People Communicate Their Desires?
    - Mandate: political authority claimed by an election winner as reflecting the approval of the people
  - Do Leaders Respond to Public Opinion?
    - Approval rating: a measure of public support for a political figure or institution
    - Policy agenda: issues that the media covers, the public considers important, and politicians address. Setting the agenda is the first step in political action.

Getting Involved: Political Participation

– Traditional Participation
  - Engaging in political activities through the formal channels of government and society
  - Voting
  - Electoral Activities
  - Voice

– Civic Volunteerism: citizen participation in public life without government incentives or coercion, such as getting together to build a playground

– Direct Action
  - Participating outside of normal political and social channels through civil disobedience, demonstrations, and even riots
  - Civil disobedience: protesting laws one considers unjust by refusing ot obey them—and accepting the punishment

- Political voice: exercising one's public rights, often through speaking out in protest or in favor of some policy change

- Participation Puzzle
  - American voting rates are low
  - Americans are quick to get involved in direct action

Why Do People Get Involved?

- Five Factors spur individuals to participate
  - Background: Age, Wealth, Education, and Race
    - Age: older people vote more often
    - Wealth: high earners more involved in public life
    - Education: more education, higher voting levcls
    - Race:
  - Friends and Family
  - Community
    - Social capital: relations between people that build closer ties of trust and civic engagement, yielding productive benefits for the larger society
  - Political Mobilization
    - Efforts to encourage people to engage in the public sphere
    - Issue Advocacy: organized effort to advance (or block) a proposed public policy change
  - Government Beneficiaries
  - Historical Context
    - Workers in 1930s
    - Students in 1960s

What Discourages Political Participation?

- Voter turnout: measure of what proportion of eligible voters or voting age voters who cast a ballot in a given election
  - Elections are held on Tuesday
  - U.S. holds more frequent elections
  - U.S. holds primary elections
  - Registering to vote can be burdensome and complicated

- Paradox of voting: for most individuals, the cost of voting (acquiring necessary information, traveling to polling site and waiting in line) outweighs the apparent benefits. Economic theory would predict very low voter turnout, given this analysis
- Alienation
  - Feel powerless, inability to control political fate
  - Alienated people ignore politics
  - Get involved through direct action—intense or violent protest
  - Political establishment focusing on matters that avoid real problems
- Institutional Barriers
  - How difficult is it to register?
  - How long does voting take place?
  - How long are the lines at polling places?
  - Motor Voter Law
    - National Voter Registration Act of 1993
    - Enables prospective voters to register when they receive their driver's license
- Complacency
  - People satisfied with lives do not participate
  - "culture of contentment"
    - Those at the top fight hard to sustain contended way of life
    - Those at bottom discouraged from participating

New Avenues for Participation: The Internet, Social Media and Millennial Participation

- Most wired group in history
- Political participation has expanded to include online activities and social media
- Clicktivism: democratic engagement in an online age
- Scenario 1: Rebooting Democracy
  - Internet sources promote active users
  - People can easily respond
  - Expands the range of commentary
  - Democratize news production
  - Internet offers new ways for politicians and parties to reach out
  - Less involved in political campaigns

  - Do not identify strongly with either political party
- Scenario 2: More Hype and Danger than Democratic Renaissance
  - Central control
  - Sheer volume and variety of information
    - Din: shorthand for the sheer volume of information and noise generated by online sources; can be a disincentive to participate politically
  - Incubates lies, malice, and falsehood
- Does Social Media Increase Political Participation?
  - Social media have become a fact of political life
  - Opportunities for broad participation and policy innovation
  - Social media users more likely to participate in politics
- How the Millennial Generation Participates
  - Vote less than other age groups
  - Less involved in political campaigns
  - Do not identify strongly with either political party

CHAPTER 7

Media, Technology and Government

In this chapter, you will:

- How media coverage of politics is changing
- The democratic promises and pitfalls of mainstream and social media
- How the media is (and is not) biased
- The rules that channel the media into its current forms
- How the U.S. media is distinctive
- How media coverage influences politics, campaigns, and elections

Changes in Issue Campaigns

- Information is cascading faster and faster
- Today's media includes many more voices and formats
- New media permits the public to be much more active

Media and American Democracy

- Providing Information
    - Informs the public
    - Researchers have shown that new information rarely influences people who have strongly held opinions
    - New information reinforces existing opinions, regardless of content
    - Loud signal: media stories with very broad coverage and an unambiguous message
    - News media most likely to influence people who pay the least attention to it
- Watching Political Leaders
    - Public Watchdog

- Media coverage that alerts the public when a problem arises in politics or society

- Shaping the Political Agenda
  - Editors and reporters have influence on what Americans think about
  - Choose one or two stories to headline and a dozen others for second tier
    - Politicians address
    - Congress investigates
    - Talk shows debate
    - People discuss
  - Policy agenda: issues that the media covers, the public considers important, and politicians address. Setting the agenda is the first step in political action
  - Setting agenda is one of most important influences the news media has on politics
  - When the media focuses on an issue its importance generally rises in public perception
    - Priming: affecting public perceptions of political leaders, candidates, or issues by reporting on topics in ways that either enhance or diminish support
    - Framing: the way an issue is defined; every issue has many possible frames, each with a slightly different tilt in describing the problem and highlighting solutions
      - » Defines the nature of the problem
      - » Organizes potential solutions
      - » Wipes out alternative policies

U.S. Media Today Traditional Formats are Declining

- Where People Go for News
  - Fifty years ago: three national TV networks and a daily paper
  - Digital sources replacing traditional media
  - Social media relies on links to traditional news sources, partisan sites and public comments
- Newspapers and Magazine: Rise and Decline
  - First Mass Media: newspapers in 1830s
    - Information and entertainment for broad popular audiences including newspapers, magazines, radio and television

  - Papers reflected the raucous, highly partisan, and often corrupt politics of the era
  - Newspaper influence grew
  - Spanish-American War (1898) known as first media-driven war
  - After more than two centuries at the center of the news media newspaper is waning, with magazine circulation falling as well
- Radio Holds Steady
  - First commercial radio stations began in 1920s
  - President Franklin Roosevelt delivered weekly radio addresses during Great Depression of the 1930s
  - Personal presidency: the idea that the president has a personal link to the public. Made initially possible by twentieth century media
  - Accelerated velocity of news and information
  - Made the nation and the world a smaller place
  - Podcasts have enabled radio to thrive as a news provider in current times
- Television: From News to Infotainment
  - Burst onto American scene in the 1950s
  - President John F. Kennedy gave first live press conference 1961
  - The Rise of Cable
    - Two networks monopolized television news business 1960s and 1970s
    - Technology broke the monopoly
    - Cable stations began in 1970s
    - CNN showed live video of American rockets in Baghdad (1991), showed news all day long, broke the network monopoly of news
    - Today, news cycle never ends
  - Infotainment
    - Line between news and entertainment began to evaporate
    - Late night talk shows got into the political act
- New Media Rising
  - Three concerns about New Media
    - Traditional organizations still do the vast majority of basic reporting
    - Important stories may get lost

  - Traditional media tend to include a variety of viewpoints, new media allows users to inhabit an "echo chamber" of views
- Fake News
  - Stories that are made up or twisted to promote a particular viewpoint
  - On the rise
- Citizen participation
  - Record an event on smartphone and post
  - Trace events, public officials' texts can connect them to scandalous revelations

Is the Media Biased?

- Are Reporters Politically Biased?
  - Media reporters less likely to identify as Republican than the national population
  - Dozens of studies fail to show a systematic bias among mainstream media reporters
  - Deeper bias runs through news media: need to attract a larger audience
- Profits Drive the News Industry
  - Media sells its audience to advertisers
  - Prime directive is to expand the audience
  - Market forces each news source toward the politics of its audience
- Drama delivers audiences
  - Narrative Arc
    - Protagonist
    - Pathos
    - Villain
    - Drama
    - Ending
    - Take-home message
  - "If it bleeds, it leads"
- Investigative "Bias"
  - Series of events transformed media stance toward powerful men and women
    - Civil Rights Movement
    - Press manipulation during Vietnam War
    - Watergate Scandal

» Most significant

How Governments Shape the Media

- How media is organized
  - Government funded
    - Public ownership: media outlets are run by the government and paid for by tax dollars
  - Government can regulate the media to ensure that it operates in the public interest
  - Government can stand aside and let the market guide the media
    - Assumption is that private companies will give the people what they want
- First Amendment Protects Print Media from Regulation
  - Supreme Court has been strict about forbidding government interference with the press
  - Difficult to censor news, convict someone of slander or libel or forbid hate speech
  - Reporters also protect their sources
  - Market forces and audience feedback impose the limits that exist
- Regulating Broadcasters
  - Radio and Television separate category
  - Subject to government regulations from the start
  - Federal Communications Commission (FCC) is the referee of the industry
    - Airwaves belong to the public
    - FCC licenses stations on a given frequency, stations required to be "socially responsible"
    - Fairness Doctrine 1949
      - » Requires all media outlets to devote equal time to opposite perspectives
      - » Repealed 1983
  - Evolves as technology changes
- Protecting Competition
  - Consolidation: media company grows, acquires other companies, threatens to dominate the market
  - Can threaten free speech and fair debate

- Telecommunications Act of 1996: overhaul of communications law that opened door to far more competition by permitting companies to own outlets in multiple media markets and remove or reduce limits on how many outlets one company can own

Media Around the World

- American media is different from other nations
- Strong in US
  - "Watchdog" tradition
  - Near absolute freedom of the press
- Most nations began with government-operated broadcast media
- Government-Owned Stations
  - Most democratic countries introduced public stations owned by the government, funded through taxes
  - Publicly owned BBC largest network in Britain
  - Berlusconi family controls Italian television, Silvio Berlusconi four term prime minister
- Censorship
  - Government controls media in authoritarian nations
  - Government censorship tool of tyrants
  - Democracies can only operate with the free flow of ideas and information
  - New media challenges the ability of authoritarian regimes to control information
  - Link between media and popular government extends beyond the United States
- American Media in the World
  - American media has enormous reach
  - CNN staple in every corner of the world
  - U.S. media model impacts democracies and authoritarian nations

Media in Context War, Terrorism, and U.S. Elections

- Covering Wars and Terrorism
  - Reporters embedded with troops
  - Wars and terrorist attacks have drama
  - Research suggests reporting inadvertently leads to further terrorist acts

- Campaign as Drama
  - Election campaigns involve political rather than armed conflicts
  - Obsessed with who will cross the finish line first
  - Digital media: pace of information even more swift
  - Coverage of campaigns devotes less time to candidates' views
  - Sound bite: brief audio clip; 1968 ran for forty seconds, today runs for under eight seconds
- Candidate Profiles
  - Media sketches a profile of each candidate
  - Image shapes future coverage
  - New media raises the prospect of great changes in campaigning
    - Candidates can speak directly to voters
      - » Facebook
      - » Twitter
    - Sense of belonging
    - Mobilize supporters

Chapter 8

Campaigns and Elections

In this chapter, you will:

- What is unique (and what is not) about American elections.
- To ask how democratic American elections are today.
- To discuss the influence of money in elections.
- To explore presidential and congressional campaigns.
- To identify the keys to a successful campaign for Congress.
- To consider election reforms.

How Democratic Are American Elections?

- Time, place, and manner: constitutional clause that delegates control of elections to the state governments
- Frequent and fixed elections
  - More often than other modern democracies
  - Parliamentary democracies have a five-year ceiling on how long a government can go before calling an election, allowing for politicians to shape political conditions for their advantage.
  - American national elections are on a fixed date
- Over 520,000 Elected Officials
  - Presidents to Municipal Drain Inspectors
  - Thirty-nine states elect judges
- Barriers to Voting
  - Registration requirements
  - Eight states strictly require a photo ID

    - Many states make registration burdensome
    - Some states make it easy
        - Same day registration
        - Vote by mail or vote early
    - Majority party protects itself by adjusting voting rules
- Financing Campaigns: The New Inequality?
    - Too Much Money?
        - Price tag for 2016 presidential and congressional races: $6.5 billion
        - Public officials devote enormous amounts of time and energy to raising money
        - Free speech clause of First Amendment protects groups who wish to support candidates or causes: Supreme Court struck down limits on total donations
    - Democracy for the Rich?
        - Some groups contribute mainly to one party
            - » Labor unions back Democrats
            - » Oil and gas companies support Republicans
            - » Most businesses split their donations between the two major parties
        - Incumbents generally overwhelm their challengers
            - » Sitting senators amassed $9.9 million in 2018, opponents raised $761,000
            - » Reelection rates in 2016 were House 96% and Senate 93%
        - Need to raise funds makes office holders sensitive to their funders
        - Campaign money does not seem to matter in high profile races, but down ballot races is where money seems to count
    - Major Donors: Easier to Give
        - Political Action Committees (PACs)
            - » Organization of at least fifty people, affiliated with an interest group that is permitted to make contributions to candidates for federal office
            - » May legally contribute $10,000 to any one candidate
        - Super PAC
            - » Organizations that raise and spend unlimited amounts of money to promote a candidate or publicize a cause. However, they may not directly contribute to a candidate or coordinate with a campaign
            - » Developed after 2010 *Citizens United v FEC* ruling by Supreme Court

- Bundling
  - A form of fundraising in which an individual persuades others to donate large amounts that are then delivered together to a candidate or campaign
  - Loophole to campaign contribution limits
- 527 Groups
  - Organizations that raise and spend unlimited amounts for "issue advocacy" but are forbidden to coordinate their efforts with any candidate or campaign
  - Forbidden from advocating directly on behalf of any candidate's election
  - Can accept and spend unlimited amounts for "issue advocacy"
  - May not explicitly support or oppose a candidate

Presidential Campaigns and Elections

- Who runs for President?
  - Experienced politicians
  - Senators, vice presidents, and governors
  - Donald Trump first newcomer
- Three phases of Presidential Elections
  - Winning the nomination
    - Invisible Primary (Money Primary)
      - » Build an organization
      - » Compete in debates
      - » Scramble for media attention
    - Iowa caucuses and New Hampshire primary
      - » Caucus: local meeting of voters to select candidates to represent a political party in a general election or to choose delegates who select candidates at a convention
      - » Closed primary: vote cast by party members to select candidates to represent the party in the general election
      - » Open primary: vote cast by any eligible voter to select candidates to represent the party in the general election
    - Super Tuesday: date on the presidential primary calendar when multiple state hold primaries and caucuses
    - State-by-state contests

    » Proportional system—allocation of votes or delegates on the basis of the percentage of the vote received; contrasts with the winner-take-all system
    » Winner-take-all—candidate receiving a simple majority (or, among multiple candidates, a plurality) receives all electoral votes or primary delegates. Sometimes called "first-past-the-post"
  - Organizing the Convention
    - Presents the candidate to the public
    - Electoral bounce: spike in the polls that follows an event such as a party's national convention
  - General election
    - Sprint to November after the conventions with no pause
    - Often feature two or three debates between the candidates; one vice-presidential debate
- Winning presidential elections
  - US economic outlook considered most important
  - Demographics
  - War and foreign policy
  - Domestic issues: set the agenda for the presidency
  - Campaign organization
  - Parties matter
  - The Electoral College and Swing States
  - The Elusive Winning Recipe
- Predicting presidential elections
  - Parts of the prediction model
    - Economy
    - Whether the country is at peace
    - Presidential approval
    - Fatigue with the party in power
    - Trouble dealing with the difficulty of the Electoral College
  - Prediction models are useful tools but not always accurate

Congressional Elections

- Candidates—who runs for Congress?

- Requirements
  - Age—25 for House, 30 for Senate
  - Citizenship—7 years US citizenship for House, 9 years US citizenship for Senate
  - Residence—must live in the state
- Money
  - Winning a House seat costs over $1.7 million in campaign contributions to mount a successful campaign.
  - Winning a Senate seat costs on average $10.5 million in campaign contributions to mount a successful campaign.
  - Despite the wealth needs, relatively few business leaders or celebrities in the US run for Congress, and often those who run lose
  - Money alone rarely swings congressional elections, but big money makes it hard to challenge most incumbents
- Connections
  - Relatives/spouse in Congress
  - Previous seat in state-level government—close to half of nonincumbents in the Senate were political veterans

– Power of incumbency
  - Incumbency advantage: tendency for members of Congress to win reelection in overwhelming numbers
  - Incumbents won more than 90% of the races
  - Members have become skilled at running against Congress: fight the dysfunctional institution (Fenno's paradox)
  - Paradox: people despise Congress but defend their own representatives

– Patterns in Congressional Elections
  - Midterm elections: national elections held between presidential elections, involving all seats in the House of Representatives, one-third of those in the Senate, thirty-six governorships, and other positions
  - Midterm loss: president's party loses Congressional seats during the midterm elections. This has occurred in most midterm elections.
  - Oppositions party usually wins congressional seats in wartime

– Redrawing the lines—gerrymandering

    - Reapportionment: reorganization of the boundaries of the House districts, a process that follows the results of the U.S. census, taken every ten years. District lines are redrawn to ensure rough equality in the number of constituents represented by each House member.
    - Gerrymander: redrawing an election district in a way that gives the advantage to one party
    - Packing: placing all like-minded voters into one district
    - Cracking: spreading out like-minded voters so they form a minority in many districts
- Nonpartisan Districting and Minority Representation
    - Citizens Redistricting Commission
        - California nonpartisan commission to redistrict
        - Compact, contiguous districts faithful to existing geographic communities
    - Preserve communities of interest

How to Run For Congress

- Key 1: Money
    - Money for TV advertising
    - Call lists of potential donors for the candidate to call to make the request
    - Run for an "open seat" without an incumbent (due to death or retirement) to have better chance of spending money effectively to win
- Key 2: Organization
    - Connections with talented staff (speechwriters, fundraisers, get-out-the-vote experts, volunteer coordinators, etc.)
    - Without good organization, political insiders do not consider the campaign "winnable" and will shy away from encouraging donations to the campaign.
    - Candidate-centered elections: system in which individual candidates decide to run, raise their own money, and design their own strategy—as opposed to a party systems in which political parties play these roles
- Key 3: Strategy
    - Building coalitions of supporters—connect with influential leaders of a particular constituency
    - Connecting with voters through the media with high-profile events and paid advertising to raise name recognition

- Name Recognition: an advantage possessed by a well-known political figure, a political celebrity
- Negative campaigning: running for office by attacking the opponent

– Key 4: Message
  - Provide a reason for voters to vote for the candidate.
  - First-time wins can happen by accident, but reelections need a reason for voters to vote.

Reforming American Elections

– Gerrymanders: neutral panels to draw the lines

– Money: forbid anonymous donations, publicly financed elections

– Term limits

CHAPTER 9

Interest Groups and Political Parties

In this chapter, you will:

- Learn what interest groups do—and how they do it.
- Investigate why people identify with one party (or why they don't)
- Analyze a paradox: Americans like their parties and don't like partisanship
- Reflect on whether the U.S. has grown too partisan—and whether interest groups and lobbyists wield too much power

Interest Groups and Political Parties

- K Street: street in downtown Washington, DC that is home to the headquarters for many lobbying firms and advocacy groups
- Interest groups central to American government while receiving lowest approval rating of any professionals
- Political parties also vital in U.S. political system and low-ranked in public esteem
    - Political parties: groups that shares political principles and is organized to win elections and hold power
- Madison warned against interest group
    - Called them factions
    - Solution was to have more of them so none gained too much power
- Special interests: pejorative term often used to designate an interest group whose aims or issue preferences one does not share
- United States is an interest-group society

The Many Roles Interest Groups Play

- Interest groups: organizations whose goal is to influence government

  - Meet regularly to discuss and manage concerns
  - Contact public officials
- Informing Members
  - Inform members what is going on in politics
- Communicating Members' Views
  - Communicate members' views to government officials
  - Lobbyist: person who contacts government officials on behalf of a particular cause or issue
- Mobilizing the Public
  - Encourage groups of people to get politically involved
- What Interest Groups Do for Democracy
  - Debate whether interest-group system represents all (or most) people triggers heated debates
  - Pluralism: open, participatory style of government in which many different interests are represented
  - Hyperpluralism: collective effect of the vast number of interest groups slowing and stalemating American policymaking
  - Power elite theory: view that a small handful of wealthy, influential Americans exercises extensive control over government decisions
- Types of Interest Groups
  - Economic: serve financial interests
  - Citizen or Public Interest: advance the public interest or a particular cause or viewpoint
    - Do not have a built-in constituency the way professional associations do
    - Work hard to retain members
    - Material benefits: swag or other merchandise
    - Expressive benefits: group expresses values members share
    - Solidarity: be a part of the group
  - Intergovernmental: one level or branch of government trying to influence another
    - Public officials form organizations to influence other public officials
    - Reverse lobbying: attempts by government officials to influence interest groups on behalf of their preferred policies

Interest Groups and the Federal Government

- The Multiple Roles of Lobbyists
  - Researchers
  - Witnesses
  - Position Takers
  - Coalition Builders
  - Social Butterflies
- Iron Triangles
  - Cozy relationship in one issue area between interest-group lobbyists, congressional staffers and executive branch agencies
- Rise of the Issue Network
  - Shifting alliances of public and private interest groups, lawmakers, and other stakeholders all focused on the same policy area
  - More diverse patterns of interaction than iron triangles
- Interest Groups and the Courts
  - Lobbying on Judicial Confirmations
  - Filing Amicus Curiae ("Friend of the Court") Briefs
  - Sponsoring Litigation

Interest Groups and Power

- Lobbyists in Washington
  - 11,500 registered congressional lobbyists in 2018, fraction of the total
  - Number likely closer to 100,000
- Interest Groups' Spending
  - Interest groups spend an estimated eight billion dollars each year, inexact figure

Political Parties and U.S. Government

- What Political Parties Do
  - Parties Champion Ideas
  - Parties Select Candidates
  - Parties Mobilize the Voters
  - Parties Organize Governing activity after the election
  - Parties help integrate new groups into the political process

- Two-Party America
  - Democrats and Republicans often take different sides in debates over ideas
  - Republicans see liberty as freedom from government coercion
  - Democrats support government programs that will insure everyone has the basics
  - Winner-take-all electoral rules keep third parties out
  - Most other democracies operate multiparty systems
  - Two-party system advantage: predictable and stable
  - Two-party system less representative
- Third Parties in American Politics
  - Provide a vehicle for people to express alternative views
  - Inject strong and controversial views into American politics
  - When a third-party cause becomes popular, one of the major parties tends to adopt it

America's Party Systems: Origins and Change

- Beginnings: First Party System (1789-1828)
  - Early Americans thought political parties ruined good government
  - By 1800 leaders disagreed on how strong the central government should be and parties developed
    - » Federalist: strong national government
    - » Democratic-Republican: strong states
  - Two main parties contesting elections and building coalitions
- Rise: Second Party System (ca. 1828-1860)
  - Political parties evolved into form recognizable today
    - » Party competition grew fierce
    - » Voting rights expanded to most white males
    - » Party members threw themselves into politics
  - Elected officials dispensed jobs to their followers "spoils of office"
  - Two Main Parties
    - » Democrats: favored small farmers, embraced immigrants, pursued genocidal Indian removal and plunged into war
    - » Whigs: favored business, stronger government, infrastructure projects, limit influence of immigrants

- Neither party could duck the issue of slavery
    - » Democrats: leave to states
    - » Whigs: could not agree, issue destroyed the party
- War and Reconstruction: Third Party System (1860-1896)
    - Republican Party: supported free labor and opposed expansion of slavery
    - After presidential election of 1860 nation entered Civil War
    - After the war Republicans drew on their party to help rebuild the nation
    - Republicans promoted black rights
    - Democrats limited former slaves, restored white dominance
    - 1870s each party had regional identity
        - » Democrats controlled former Confederate states
        - » Republicans dominated Northeast and Midwest
    - Party Machines: hierarchical arrangement of party workers
        - » Immigrants helped by party machines
        - » Party boss: senior figure in a party machine
        - » Notorious for bribery and corruption
- Business and Reform: Fourth Party System (1896-1932)
    - Support for business on one side and pressures for equality on the other
- Depression and New Deal: Fifth Party System (1933-1968)
    - President Franklin Roosevelt helped define, new Democratic coalition into power
    - Great Depression unhinged party politics, crippling Republican Party
    - New Deal: broad series of economic programs and reforms associated with the Franklin Roosevelt administration
    - Democrats hung onto southern majority with both African Americans and southern segregationists
    - As Democrats became the party of civil rights white southern voters shifted to the Grand Old Party (Republican Party)
- Sixth Party System: The Parties at Equal Strength (1972-Present)
    - Republican presidents developed a southern strategy to win middle class white votes
    - Neither party in control, close elections swing party control back and forth
    - Growing partisanship

Who Joins? Party Identification

- Building Party Identification
  - Party Identification: strong attachment to one political party, often established at an early age
  - Often starts with family and demographics
  - Democratic Party
    - Younger, women
    - Multi-cultural identity, urbanites
    - Secular people
    - More open (eager to explore new experiences)
  - Republican Party
    - Male, white identity
    - Suburbanites, rural
    - White evangelicals
    - Mormons
    - Conscientiousness (strong sense of duty, discipline, impulse control)
- The Power of Party Attachment
  - Voting/Participation
    - Strong predictor of voting habits
    - Straight-ticket voters: votes for the same party for all offices on ballot, strong partisans likely to vote straight ticket
    - Voting rates higher among those with strong party identification
    - Key to elections is base voters: party members who tend to vote loyally for their party's candidates
  - Filtering
    - Influence what signals in the media environment people accept or reject
    - "people tend to project favorable characteristics and acceptable issue positions onto the candidates of the party they favor
  - Ideology
    - Parties diverge sharply on many issues
    - Differences have more than doubled in past fifteen years
    - Parties contain multiple factions

- Republican Factions
  - Populists or Trumpists
  - Religious Traditionalists
  - Fiscal Conservatives
  - Libertarians
  - Neoconservatives
  - Moderates
- Democratic Factions
  - Progressives
  - Civil Rights Caucus
  - Organized Labor
  - Centrists

Party Organization

- Party Bureaucracy
  - Raise funds
  - Coordinate election strategies
  - Decide which local races to fund
  - Organize national convention
  - Prepare party platform: party's statement of purpose and its position on issues
  - Issue and enforce the party's rules for primary elections
  - Leaders are party organization: portion of a political party that includes activists, state/local leaders, and affiliated professionals such as fundraisers and public relations experts
- Party in Government
  - Portion of a political party's organization that comprises elected officials and candidates for office
  - Gets the recognition
  - Government officials in each party
- Party in the Electorate
  - Largest (and least organized) component of a political party, drawn from the public at large: registered members and regular supporters
- The Big Tent

- Media focuses on the best-known party leaders
- Unanimity difficult
- Local officials run the party in each state
- Party organizations always make tactical calculations
- Federalism pushes each of the two major parties to adopt a big tent approach
  - Spread themselves wide
  - Embrace divergent views

Party Competition... And Partisanship

- Parties began to lose influence in 1960s
- Interest groups muscled in on territory, mobilized voters, and shaped issue positions
- Americans began to identify with movements and organizations
- Parties Rise Again
  - Revival began even as death declared
  - Campaign finance rules limited contributions to candidates so money went to parties
  - Parties could fund candidates, who became dependent on the parties
- Partisanship Intensifies
  - Parties used to work together
  - Cross-party majorities not unusual, as much difference within party as between parties
  - Today factions remain but parties are far less diverse
  - Strongest divisions between the two parties
  - Partisanship is rising, increasing among the public
    - Americans feel party divisions lead to gridlock
    - Bitter partisanship "breeds bad public policy"
    - Toxic partisan climate is said to drive public officials away from government service
    - Leads to disenchantment, worrying divisiveness and erosion of civil discourse
  - Divided government increasingly yields political paralysis, drives more power to the executive branch

A Political System Ripe For Reform

- Regulate Interest Groups
- Proportional Representation
- Reduce Partisanship in Government

Chapter 10

Congress

In this chapter, you will:

- Learn what Congress does.
- Reflect on how well Congress represents the people.
- Examine the internal workings of Congress.
- Consider the importance of skilled congressional leadership.
- Think about the problems that face Congress—and some possible solutions.

Introducing Congress

- Constitution places Congress at the center of American government
  - Financial (Article 1 Section 8)
    - Raise revenue through taxes and borrowing
    - Pay national debts
    - Regulate trade and commerce
  - Legal (Article 1 Section 8)
    - Establish U.S. citizenship laws
    - Regulate bankruptcy laws
    - Issue U.S. money
    - Punish counterfeiters
    - Establish patent system
    - Fix national weights/measures standards
    - Enact laws to presidential approval
    - Impeach presidents and federal judges

- Institutional (Article 2 Section 2)
  - Organize judicial and executive branches
  - Establish postal system
  - Set up and control national capital
  - Admit new states
  - Control U.S. territories (Article 3 Section 3
  - Alter or amend the time, place, and manner of states' election laws related to congressional elections (Article 1, Section 4)
- National Defense
  - Declare war
  - Regulate rules for prisoners of war
  - Raise and fund defense forces

- Congress ruled for most of American history, middle of twentieth century White House became stronger
- Congress retains powers to introduce, debate and pass legislation
- Presidents need cooperation from House and senate to advance policies
- Two Chambers, Different Styles
  - Bicameral, two houses or chambers
  - House of Representatives
    - 435 members
    - Divided among states based on population size
    - Two-year terms
    - District around 730,000
    - Majority party wields centralized control
    - Speaker of the House control which issues reach the floor
  - Senate
    - 100 members
    - Two from each state
    - Six-year term
    - Senator posses a degree of autonomy
    - Legislative hold: informal way for a senator to object to a bill or other measure reaching the Senate floor. The action effectively halts Senate proceedings on that issue, sometimes for weeks or longer.

- House and Senate Each Have Unique Roles
    - All budget measures must originate int eh House
    - House has power to impeach public officials, including the president
    - Senate has trial and decides to remove official or not
    - Senate approves treaties
    - Senate reviews presidential appointments

Congressional Representation

- Geographic Representation: live in same state or district
- Substantive Representation: share views about political issues
- Descriptive Representation: resemble the people they represent
- Does Congress Reflect America?
    - Half-century ago every senator was white, only two African American members in the House
    - Today, Congress more closely resembles the country—in some respects but still a way to go
- Trustees and Delegates
    - Do the Right Thing
        - Representatives owe their best judgement
        - Do what is best for constituents
        - Trustee view of representation
        - Senators
    - Do What the People Want
        - Faithfully follow popular preferences
        - Take voting instructions directly from constituents
        - Delegate view of representation
        - House members

Getting to Congress And Staying There

- Permanent Campaign
    - Campaigning ongoing
    - House members elected directly by people
    - Senate by state legislatures until 1913, went to people

- Home Style: Back in the District
  - Congress members spend a lot time back in their district or state
  - Spend time back home with constituents
- A Government of Strangers
  - Past: members of Congress lived in Washington, socialized
  - Today: legislators not in Washington long enough to get to know one another

Congress At Work

- The City on the Hill
  - Capital building on a hill with marble dome dominating the Washington skyline
  - No building except the Washington Monument may be taller
  - Small city within a city
  - Congressional staff members major presence, each member has
    - Chief of Staff
    - Legislative Director
    - Press Secretary
    - Scheduler
    - Others
- Minnows and Whales: Congressional Leadership
  - Whales: can influence landmark legislation
  - Minnows followed the others
  - Senate leadership: patient, consensus-minded, manager
  - House leadership: majoritarian principles, tighter central control, more partisan branch
- House Leadership
  - Democrats and Republicans choose party leader from their ranks
  - Majority party votes for Speaker of the House
    - Presides over the chamber on special occasions
    - Rules on procedural issues
    - Chooses members for committees
    - Assigns legislation to committees
    - Maintains order and civility

  - Sets House agenda, determines bill for consideration
  - Negotiate with Senate and executive branch
- House Majority leader is second in command
  - Majority party's floor manager, negotiator, spokesperson
  - Speaker's eyes and ears
- Majority Whip is third in command: responsible for party discipline
- Minority has same leadership with no Speaker

– Senate Leadership
- Vice-President presides over chamber, but rarely shows up
- President Pro Tempore: majority party senator with the longest Senate service, presides on formal occasions
- Normal times: every senator presides in turn serving rotating half-hour stints

– Committees: Workhorses of Congress
- Regular duties play out in committees
  - Draft legislation
  - Sponsor hearings
  - Oversee executive branch
  - Draft the federal budget

– Enduring Power of Committees
- Standing Committees: Permanent bodies, with fixed jurisdiction
- Select (Special) Committees: created to investigate a particular issue, exist for a defined period of time
- Joint Committees: address topics of continuing importance
- Committees enable Congress to devise fairly sophisticated legislative solutions to issues competing for attention

– Leadership and Assignments
- House Speaker key in assigning members and chairs to committees
  - Party votes on members' committee assignments
  - Seniority remains vital factor in determining chairs
- Decisions rests inn majority leader's hands
- Minority party assignments recommended by minority leaders in both chambers

Legislative Policymaking

- Complex process. Difficult to win.
    - Drafting a Bill
        - Only members of the House and Senate have the right to introduce
        - Need at least one primary sponsor: on the first page
        - Can have any number of co-sponsors: more co-sponsors higher likelihood of passage
        - Congressional Research Service helps draft bills
    - Submitting the bill
        - Senate
            - » Page places bill with bill clerk
            - » Clerk writes number on first page
            - » Notes senator's suggestion for committee referral
            - » Places in tray
            - » Printed overnight
        - House
            - » Representative carries bill to rostrum
            - » Hand legislation to clerk or drop in box (hopper)
            - » Delivered to Speaker's office
            - » Assigned a number
            - » Referred to committee
    - Committee Action
        - Committees hold hearings on policy topics
        - Committees prepare legislation for floor consideration
        - Committees also kill legislation
        - Committees exercise oversight
    - Floor Action
        - Getting to the floor
            - » Senate
                - ➢ Placed on business calendar where it will be called up for consideration
                - ➢ Bill must receive unanimous consent to be brought to the floor
            - » House

- ➢ Majority party leaders rewrite legislation
- ➢ House Rules Committee issues directive governing the process for the bill

- » Bills can get stuck on calendar in both chambers

- On the floor
  - » Bill is assigned floor manager: handles amendments and controls time for debate
  - » House manager can extend time for debate, allow multiple votes
  - » Senator may halt all activity by refusing to yield the floor or issuing a hold
- The Vote
  - » Voice vote: congressional vote in which the presiding officer asks those for and against to say "year" or "nay" and announces the result. No record is kept.
  - » Roll-call vote: congressional vote in which each member's vote is recorded, either by roll call (Senate) or electronically (House)
  - » Roll-call votes on major bills most important public act a member of Congress preforms

- Conference Committee
  - Legislation must pass House and Senate in identical form to go to the president
  - Conference committee reconciles differences
  - Can write new bill but sections that were the same cannot be altered
  - Up or down floor vote with no amendments permitted on bill

- Presidential Action: Separated Powers Revisited
  - No bill becomes law until the president takes action, usually by signing
  - Veto: constitutional procedure by which a president can prevent enactment of legislation passed by Congress

Why Is Congress So Unpopular?

- Least popular branch
- Americans re-elect over 90 percent of their representatives year after year
- Constituents like their own representatives and senators, dislikes the partisan fighting and gridlock
- Partisan Polarization in Congress

  - Partisan differences since beginning
  - Parties sorted by ideology, more partisan
  - Republicans pressing partisan fight for their ideals
- Divided Government
  - Each party holds at least one of the three nationally-elected institutions
  - One or both houses of Congress led by a party opposed to the president will result in legislative standoff
  - Slows policymaking process

Some Popular Reforms And Their Limits

- Limit Lobbyists
- Educate the Public

Chapter 11

The Presidency

In this chapter, you will:

- See how the Constitution defines the presidency.
- Focus on presidential power.
- Learn what presidents do.
- Reflect on presidential popularity—and greatness.
- Consider the personal side of the office.
- Tour the executive office of the president and meet the team around a president.

Presidential Overview

- The president personifies America
- The president injects new ideas into American politics
- The president has enormous powers—at least on paper

Defined by Controversy

- Constitutional Convention's delegates
    - Should the United States have a president?
    - How long should a president serve?
    - How should the United States choose its president?
- Presidential Powers (Article 2)
    - Expressed Powers: powers the Constitution explicitly grants to the president
    - Delegated Powers: powers that Congress passes on to the president
    - Inherent Powers: powers assumed by presidents
    - Executive agreements: international agreement made by the president

  - Executive privilege: power claimed by the president to resist request for authority by Congress

An Imperial Presidency

- Authority
  - Unitary Executive Theory
    - Constitution puts the president in charge of executing laws
    - No other branch may limit presidential discretion over executive matters
  - Imperial Presidency
    - American presidency is demonstrating imperial traits
    - Republic is morphing into an empire
  - Paradox: We need powerful leaders; we fear powerful leaders
- A Weak Office?
  - President can appear weak
  - Unable to get basic goals accomplished

What Presidents Do

- Commander in chief
  - Congress declares war
  - President manages it
  - War Powers Act 1973
    - President can send troops
    - Must notify Congress within 48 hours
    - Congress must approve within 60 days
- Top diplomat
  - President has lead role in foreign affairs
  - State Department assists president in foreign affairs
- First Legislator
  - Recommending measures
    - Legislative agenda
    - White House advisors lobby for programs
  - President reports on the state of the Union
    - Annual event

- President declares legislative agenda in speech
- Presidential "Batting Average"
  - Only members of Congress can formally propose a law
  - Congressional liaison team negotiates and cuts deals
  - Legislative success (batting average): successful passage of bills
  - When same party control White House and Congress average higher
- Veto Power
  - Presidential power to block an act of Congress by refusing to sign
  - Returned to Congress with objections
  - Override: process by which Congress can overcome a presidential veto with two-thirds vote in both chambers
- Signing Statements
  - Written presidential declarations commenting on a bill
  - Often includes criticism

- Chief Bureaucrat
  - Appointments
    - Political appointments: top officials in the executive agencies, appointed by the president
    - Civil servants: employed on basis of competitive exams and keep positions with administration change
  - Executive Orders
    - Presidential declaration
    - Force of law
    - Issues instructions to executive branch
    - No congressional approval needed
- Economist in Chief
  - Constitution does not grant president economic authority
  - Role of Council of Economic Advisors
- Head of State
  - Presidential role is both ceremonial and policy oriented
  - Role of dual president
- Party Leader

- Bully Pulpit
  - Role of active president
  - Promote new ideas
- The Impossible Job
  - Presidential authority has grown
  - Role so large no one person can perform every aspect well

Presidential Leadership Success and Failure in the Oval Office

- What is required
  - Managing the public
    - Going public: addressing the public to win support for oneself or one's ideas
    - Presidents constantly try to manage their image in the public eye
  - Approval ratings
    - Polls widely used
    - No president stays above 50% for an entire term
    - Poll Cycle: High at the start, slow decline that bottoms out midway through second year, gradual ascent and peak end of fourth year
- Presidential Greatness
  - Presidents have been ranked, disagreements about what makes a great president
  - Great presidents tell us who we are
- Greatness in Context: The Rise and Fall of Political Orders
  - New Order Rises
  - Order Refreshed
  - Old Order Crumbles
- Burden of the Office
  - Exhausting job
  - Ages presidents

The President's Team A Tour of the White House

- Vice President
  - Wait for a catastrophe
  - Preside over Senate
  - Responsibilities up to the president

- The Cabinet
  - Two roles
    - Run executive branch departments
    - Discuss policy with the president in cabinet meetings
  - Inner Cabinet
    - Secretary of State
    - Secretary of Defense
    - Secretary of Treasury
    - Secretary of Justice
- Executive Office of the President
  - Agencies that help the president manage daily activities
  - Office of Management and Budget
    - Most powerful agency
    - Authority over federal budget
    - Central clearance: OMB's authority to review and clear anything a member of the administration says or does in public
  - Council of Economic Advisors
  - National Security Council
  - Heart of Power: The White House Office
    - Chief of Staff
    - Democrats: traditionally creative chaos
    - Republicans: traditionally clearly defined organization and tasks
- First Spouse
  - Eleanor Roosevelt first active spouse
  - Spouses not involved in policy engagement

CHAPTER 12

Bureaucracy

In this chapter, you will:

- Learn how the bureaucracy developed, how it is meant to work, and why programs and processes sometimes fail.
- See how federal agencies do their job.
- Examine the different kinds of agencies that comprise the public service.
- Consider who—if anyone—controls the bureaucracy.
- Review possible reforms.

How the Bureaucracy Grew

- Birth of the Bureaucracy
- The spoils system: system in which government jobs are given out as political favors
- Universalistic politics: government run according to transparent rules, impartially applied
- The Pendleton Civil Service Act (1883): shifted American government toward a merit-based public service
- Five forces pushed the United States toward a more efficient bureaucracy
  - War
  - Morality
  - Economics
  - Geography
  - Race/Ethnicity
- The bureaucratic model
- Hierarchy

- Division of labor
- Fixed Routines
- Equal Rules for All
- Technical Qualifications
- Bureaucratic pathologies: problems that develop in bureaucratic systems
- Rote
- Imperialism
- Turf wars
- Lack of coordination
- Clientelism

What Bureaucracies Do

- Rule making
- Government rulemaking showcases classic bureaucratic principles in action
- Proposed rule: draft of administrative regulations published in the *Federal Register* for the purpose of gathering comments
- Final rule: the rule that specifies how a program will actually operate
- Implementation
- Street-level bureaucrats: public officials who deal directly with the public

How the Bureaucracy is Organized

- Cabinet departments
- Challenges to governing
- Cabinet meetings
- The rotating bureaucracy
- Cabinet and Diversity
- Other agencies
- Executive agencies
- Independent regulatory commissions
- Central service agencies
- Private contractors

Who Controls the Federal Bureaucracy?

- The People
- The President
- Congress
- Funding
- Oversight
- Authorization
- Reorganization
- Interest Groups
- Bureaucratic Autonomy
- Whistleblower: federal worker who reports corruption or fraud
- Democracy Revisited

Reforming the Bureaucracy

- Critiques
- Costs
- Inertia
- Public mistrust
- Proposed Reforms
- Open up the System
- Freedom of Information Act 1966
- Reinventing government
- Privatization

Chapter 13

The Judicial Branch

In this chapter, you will:

- Consider how the law reflects the American people and our complicated national culture.
- Learn how the judicial system operates.
- Examine the courts'role in American politics.
- Explore the inner workings of the Supreme Court.
- Reflect on how judges decide.
- Review landmark US judicial cases.

Who Are We? A Nation of Laws... and Lawyers

- Embracing the Law—and Lawsuits
  - Litigation: conduct of a lawsuit
  - Mediation: revolving disputes without going to court, a third party helps negotiate a settlement
- Trust in Courts
  - Traditionally, lawyers and courts enjoyed high prestige
  - Today, public approval wanes for courts
  - Controversial cases like *Bush v. Gore*
- Courts in American culture
  - Notable films
  - *To Kill a Mockingbird*
  - *Bridge of Spies*

Organizing the Judicial Branch

- Congress designs federal system
- Divided we Rule
    - Judicial federalism
    - Three layers of courts
    - Lower courts conduct trials
    - Appellate courts hear appeals
    - Supreme Court renders a final verdict
    - National Supreme Court ultimate arbiter for Constitution or Federal cases
- State and Local Courts
    - State trial courts
    - State appellate courts
- Judicial Selection
    - Appointment by governor
    - Selection by state legislature
    - Elect judges
- Federal Courts
    - Crimes that violate federal laws
    - Issues that involve federal treaties
    - Constitution cases
    - Disputes across state lines
    - District Courts
        - First level of federal court
        - Judges appointed by president, subject to approval by Senate
        - Office for life
    - Circuit Courts
- Specialized Courts
    - Military Justice
    - Tax Disputes
    - Terrorism
    - Bankruptcy

- Diversity in the federal judiciary
  - Just below one-third of judges re women
  - Three quarters are white
  - 12.5 percent are African American
  - 9.7 percent are Hispanic
  - 2.9 percent are Asian
  - 1 federal judge is Native American

The Court's Role

- Initially minor role
- Chief Justice John Marshall changed courts role
- Judicial Review
  - *Marbury v. Madison*
  - Supreme Court can overrule act of Congress that violates Constitution
- Activism versus Restraint
  - Judicial restraint: reluctance to interfere with elected branches
  - Judicial activism: vigorous or active approach to reviewing other branches of government
- Judicial Process
  - Common Law: system of law developed by judges in deciding cases
  - Precedent: judicial decisions that offer a guide to similar cases
  - Civil law: cases that involve disputes between two parties
  - Criminal law: cases in which someone is charged with breaking the law
  - Plaintiff: party who brings the action in a lawsuit
  - Defendant: party who is sued in a court case
- Too Much Power?
  - Courts have the power to shape American policy
  - American courts shape our politics
- Or Still the "Least Dangerous" Branch?
  - No electoral base
  - Limited resources
  - Rely on other branches for enforcement

The Supreme Court and How It Operates

- Hearing Cases
  - In session for nine months each year
  - Opens first Monday in October
  - Amicus curiae: brief submitted by a person or group who is not a direct party to the case
- Selecting Cases: Formal Requirements
  - Rule of Four: requirement that at least four Supreme Court judges must agree to hear a case before it comes before the Court
  - Writ of Certiorari issued if justices agree to hear a case
  - Three conditions to be eligible
    - Legitimate controversy
    - Standing
    - Not moot
- Selecting Cases: Informal Factors
  - Two lower courts decide the legal question differently
  - Lower court ruling conflicts with an existing Supreme Court ruling
  - Significance beyond the two parties involved
  - U.S. government a party
- Conference Sessions and Written Decisions
  - Take place on Thursday or Friday
  - Justices only
  - Majority opinion: official statement of the Supreme Court
  - Concurrent opinion: statement that agrees with the majority opinion
  - Dissent: statement on behalf of the justices who voted in the minority
- Supreme Court Clerks
  - Recent law school graduates
  - Help justices write opinions and reach decisions
- Confirmation Battles
  - Significant moment on American political calendar is the appointment of a new justice

- Confirmation hearings are partisan debates engaging wide range of interest groups
- Senate Judiciary Committee holds hearings and recommends to the full Senate

Judicial Decision Making and Reform

- The Role of the Law
  - Theory, justices decide cases on legal facts
  - Abide by precedents set in previous cases
  - Stare decisis: deciding cases on the basis of previous rulings or precedents
- Ideology and Partisanship
  - Beliefs powerful predictor of vote
  - Pragmatists: Constitution as a living, changing document
  - Originalists: interpret document's text literally
  - Conservative: Roberts, Thomas, Alito, Gorsuch
  - Swing: Kennedy
  - Liberal: Ginsburg, Breyer, Sotomayor, Kagan
  - Kavanaugh looks to be a strong conservative vote
- Collegiality and Peer Pressure
  - Justices influence one another
  - Judicial reputation plays an important role in decisions
- Institutional Concerns
  - Justices worry about the standing of the Court
  - *Marbury v. Madison* example of this

Nineteen Cases You Should Know

- *Marbury v. Madison (1803)*
- *McCulloch v. Maryland (1819)*
- *Dred Scott v. Sanford (1857)*
- *Santa Clara Co. v. Southern Pacific Railroad (1886)*
- *Plessy v. Ferguson (1896)*
- *Lochner v. New York (1905)*
- *Muller v. Oregon (1908)*
- *Schenck v. United States (1919)*

- *National Labor Relations Board v. Jones and Laughlin Steel Corporation* (1937)
- *Korematsu v. U.S.* (1944)
- *Brown v. Board of Education* (1954)
- *Mapp v. Ohio* (1961)
- *Gideon v. Wainwright* (1963)
- *Lemon v. Kurtzman* (1971)
- *Roe v. Wade* (1973)
- *U.S. v. Nixon* (1974)
- *Bush v. Gore* (2000)
- *National Federation of Independent Business v. Sebelius* (2012)
- *Obergefell v. Hodges* (2015)
- Nineteen Cases—and the Power of the Court
  - Most cases controversial when decided
  - Judgment calls: not just on the substance of the case but on the scope of the Court's authority

Reforming the Courts

- Ideas for Reform: More Resources
  - Decline in judges pay affects ability to attract judges
  - Small budget
- Term Limits
  - Help address the fear of "unelected judges' overruling elected branches
  - Could move to the appellate bench
  - Judicial term limits may reduce battles that surround judicial appointments
- Share Authority with Congress
  - Authority to modify Court precedents
  - Share power to interpret Constitution

Chapter 14

Domestic and Foreign Policy

In this chapter, you will:

- Trace the five stages of public policymaking
- Review the history of US social policy with attention to "entitlement programs
- Learn how the federal budget process drives much of our policymaking
- The three goals of American foreign policy: security, prosperity, and spreading American value
- Who makes foreign policy and how
- Broadly view American foreign policy over the past hundred years

Public Policy Making in Five (not-so-easy) Stages

- Agenda setting
  - Policy making doesn't begin in earnest until public officials recognize that something is a problem worthy of government attention
  - Focusing event: major happening that attracts widespread media attention to an issue
  - Policy agenda: issues that the media covers, the public considers important, and politicians address
- Framing
  - What are the root causes of the problem?
  - How bad a problem is this?
  - How should public officials respond, if at all?
- Policy Formation
  - Policy analysis involves constructing scientific measures of a proposed policy's costs and benefits

- Cost effectiveness: projected costs of a proposed policy, as revealed by a relatively simple study
- Cost-benefit analysis: more complex study of the projected costs and benefits associated with a proposed policy
- *Ex ante*: before it passes and goes into effect. This is a central feature of contemporary policy making in the United States and other advanced industrial nations
- From cost-benefit analysis to politics: cost-benefit and other *ex ante* evaluations are widely used in policy making, with significant impact on both legislative votes and judicial decisions. They alone, however, do not determine policy.
- Policy window: figurative description of the opportunity to pass a bill a bill in Congress or a state legislature
- Political considerations can trump policy analysis

– Policy Implementation
  - Rule making
  - Top-down delivery
  - Bottom-up delivery

– Policy evaluation and feedback
  - *Ex Post* Policy Evaluation
  - Policy Feedback
  - Path dependence: social-science term for how policymakers' choices are shaped by institutional "paths" that result from policy choices made in the past

U.S. Social Policy

– Old Age Insurance: Social Security
  - Since its 1935 enactment, Social Security has provided Americans 65 and older—provided they have lived in the United States for at least five years—with a monthly living stipend
  - The minimum age was recently raised to 66, and Congress discussed increasing it by another year or two. Social Security payments vary with income
  - Financed through payroll tax

– Unemployment benefits

– Health and Disability: Medicare/Medicaid
  - Medicare

    - A federal program that pays for certain health care expenses for people aged 65 or older
    - Enrolled individuals must pay deductibles and copayments, but much of their medical costs are covered by the program
    - Financed through payroll tax
  - Medicaid
    - Federal health assistance program to help pay medical costs for persons of low income
    - Means tested, benefits provide to those below a certain income level
    - Federal poverty line: annually specified level of income below which people are considered to live in poverty, and eligible for certain federal benefits
  - Entitlement program: government benefit program whose recipients are entitled by law to receive payments
- Health and Disability: Medicare/Medicaid
  - Medicare
    - A federal program that pays for certain health care expenses for people aged 65 or older
    - Enrolled individuals must pay deductibles and copayments, but much of their medical costs are covered by the program
    - Financed through payroll tax
  - Medicaid
    - Federal health assistance program to help pay medical costs for persons of low income
    - Means tested, benefits provide to those below a certain income level
    - Federal poverty line: annually specified level of income below which people are considered to live in poverty, and eligible for certain federal benefits
  - Entitlement program: government benefit program whose recipients are entitled by law to receive payments

Economic Policymaking Fiscal and Monetary Policy

- Fiscal Policy: taxing and spending policies carried out by government in an effort to affect national economic development
- Monetary Policy: actions of central banks designed primarily to maximize employment and moderate inflation

- Federal Reserve Tools
  - Buy Treasury securities
  - Set required dollar reserve levels
  - Influence interest rates
    - Reduce for growth
    - Raise to slow economy

Economic Policymaking The Federal Budget Process

- Federal budget deficit gap between revenues received by the national government and spending on all public programs
- President's budget proposal
  - Since Budget and Accounting Act 1921 presidents first movere in federal budget
  - White House submits proposed budget in early February
  - Office of Management and Budget coordinates
  - Lacks statutory authority
- Congressional budget resolution
  - Budget resolution: joint House-Senate creation that outlines targets for federal spending, revenue levels, and the resultant budget deficit (or surplus) for the coming fiscal year
  - Budget committees in both House and Senate carry out the bulk of the work
  - Senate and House versions are different, worked out in conference committee

Economic Policymaking The Federal Budget Process

- Reign of the Cardinals: Appropriations Committee Action
  - Specify which departments and programs will get how much money
  - Budget in thirteen separate jurisdictions (discretionary spending)
  - Each jurisdiction assigned an Appropriations subcommittee
  - After subcommittee must pass full Appropriations Committee
  - If successful goes to the floor
  - Discretionary programs: non-entitlement program spending, subject to the decision of Congress each year
  - Continuing resolution: congressionally approved act required when no national budget has been passed before the start of a new fiscal year, extends spending at current levels for a prescribed period of time

Making Good Policy

- Three Questions
  - Is the proposed policy feasible?
  - Is the proposed policy fair?
  - Is the proposed policy effective?
- Moral Policies: Justice or Democracy?
  - Public policy should be creating a more just society
    - Equality
    - Individual or group rights
    - Distributive justice
  - Ensure Democratic Outcomes
    - Majority of the people what they want
- Economically Efficient Policies
  - Recommends most efficient system of delivering government services
  - Cost-benefit analysis or similar tool
  - Use free enterprise system to maximize efficiency
  - Rational-choice theory: individual rationality basis for what counts as good public policy
- Capitalism Goes to the Movies
  - Popular culture displays a deep suspicion of free-enterprise system
  - *Avatar*: morality fable about the dangers of corporate greed
  - *Captain America: Civil War*: superheroes refusing to work for restrictive capitalist system
  - *Lego Movie*: ordinary working man turned hero who defeats the evil "Lord Business"
  - Suspicious of big government, but also question benefits of big, unregulated markets

American Foreign-Policy Goal No. 1: Security

- Security means protecting the nation and its values from external threats
- Military Primacy
  - Security through a powerful military

- Primacy: doctrine asserting that the United States should maintain an unrivaled military
- Basis for Primacy: Realism
  - Doctrine holding that nation-states seek to amass power to ensure their self-preservation
  - Emphasize international security threats around the world
  - Expensive military is the price of security
- A Different View: Liberalism
  - Doctrine that views nation-states as benefitting most from mutual cooperation, aided by international organizations
  - Three problems with military primacy
    - Security Trap: musing military force often produces a backlash
    - Cost: more than half a trillion dollars a year
    - Too much emphasis on military power undermines liberty
- Soft Power
  - Influence a nation exerts through culture and commerce; a contrast to attempted influence through force
  - Most administrations rely on hard and soft power
- Foreign Aid and National Security
  - US largest foreign aid donor in the world
  - Less than half a percent of gross national income
  - Liberal view: assisting other nations is an important path to security
  - Others: financial assistance only makes other nations reliant

American Foreign-Policy Goal No. 2: Prosperity

- US is a superpower because of its economy
- National power rests not on armies but on economic engines
- Economic Superpower or Nation in Decline?
  - American dollar international reserve currency
  - English the language of international affairs
  - China catching up
  - Trade deficit: deficit arising when a nation imports more goods from foreign nations than it exports to them

- Free Trade
    - Idea that goods and services should move across international boundaries without government interference
    - Protectionism: efforts to protect local business from foreign competition
    - Free trade helps businesses and consumers in every country
    - Trade agreements
        - Agreements with individual countries or with many nations
        - World Trade Organization (WTO)
        - North American Free Trade Agreement (NAFTA)
- Challenges to Free Trade
    - Cheaper to produce goods in nations that pollute, outlaw unions, reject safety standards, keep wages low
    - Free markets cause social displacement, in the short run
    - As international markets have expanded, they have grown volatile
    - American leaders champion free trade only until they run into powerful interests
- President Trump embraces protectionism
    - Democrats have grown more positive about free international trade
    - Republicans less positive about free international trade
- Energy
    - US consumes almost twenty million barrels of oil a day, fifth of the world total
    - Three major wars in the Middle East, home of oil reserves
- Economic Weapons
    - Boycott: refusing to buy from a country
    - Economic Embargo: restricting the flow of trade into a country
    - Divestment: refusing to invest in another country
    - Freezing assets: seizing bank accounts and other financial assets foreign nationals have in the US
    - Withholding Foreign Aid
    - Need an international coalition for economic weapons
    - Often hurt ordinary people before the rich and powerful

American Foreign-Policy Goal No. 3: Spreading American Ideals

- American Exceptionalism

- United States is unique, marked by a distinct set of ideas such as equality, self-rule, and limited government
- Theory of Democratic Peace: strongly democratic nations are less likely to engage in wars with one another

Who Makes Foreign Policy?

- Congress
  - Constitution balances foreign policy between Congress and the president
  - Congress: declare war, set military budget, ratify treaties
  - Decision clock sped up shifted to the White House
  - Congress last declared war: World War II
  - War Powers Act: legislation passed in 1973 to increase congressional involvement in undeclared wars. Congress required to approve military action by the president within sixty days
- The President
  - Commands military, negotiates treaties, rallies Americans during crises, oversees relations with other nations
  - Decide on foreign intervention
  - Many partners in conducting international affairs
- The State Department
  - First cabinet agency
  - Manage diplomatic relations with other nations
  - Negotiate treaties, distribute foreign assistance, manage daily contact
  - Favor diplomatic solutions
  - Underfunded, can cause neglect
- The Department of Defense
  - Manages the military
  - Largest organization in government, biggest employer
  - Two problems
    - Massive bureaucracy, very slow to change
    - Military is dived between the rivalry between the services
- Intelligence
  - Fifteen different agencies and offices

    - Overlapping jurisdictions and act as rivals
- National Security Council
    - Part of the Executive Office of the President
    - President, Vice President, Secretaries of State, Defense, Homeland Security, Direction of National Intelligence, Head of the Join Chiefs of Staff
- Other Executive Agencies
    - President's economic team
    - Office of U.S. Trade Representative
    - Labor Department
    - Department of Homeland Security
- Interest Groups and the Public
    - Organized groups play an active role
    - More than in most other nations
    - Support for specific countries
    - Lobby for specific causes
    - Public opinion and media can have impact
- Fragmentation or Success?
    - Policies chaotic, messy, unpredictable, open
    - President can break the stalemate
    - U.S. foreign policy has been relatively successful

Grand Strategies in U.S. History

- Grand Strategy: Overarching vision that defines and guides a nation's foreign policy
- Standing Alone (1918-1939)
    - World War I
    - United States would spread democracy to every nation
    - Wilson's League of Nations
    - Congress voted for Isolationism
    - United States intervened only when its own interests threatened
- The Cold War (1945-1991)
    - Japan attacked Pearl Harbor, era of standing alone ended
    - After war only rival was Soviet Union

- United States had to lead the free world against the Soviet Union
- Containment: American Cold War strategy designed to stop the spread of communism
- US joined multilateral organization: international organization of three or more nations organized around a common goal

– The New World Order (1989-2001)
- Fall of Berlin Wall
- Soviet empire collapsed
- US should use military strength to make world peaceful, democratic and secure

– The War on Terror (2001-2009)
- Attacks on 9/11
- Declared act of war, responded with "war on terror"
- Targeted terrorists, nations that harbored terrorists, organizations that assisted terrorists
- Deterrence: build a military so overpowering other nations will be afraid to attack
- Preemptive War: effort to attack hostile powers before they launch attacks, controversial because it sanctions striking first
- Homeland Security Act created Department of Homeland Security
- USA patriot Act: gave police and security personnel latitude to monitor, search, detain suspects abroad and at home

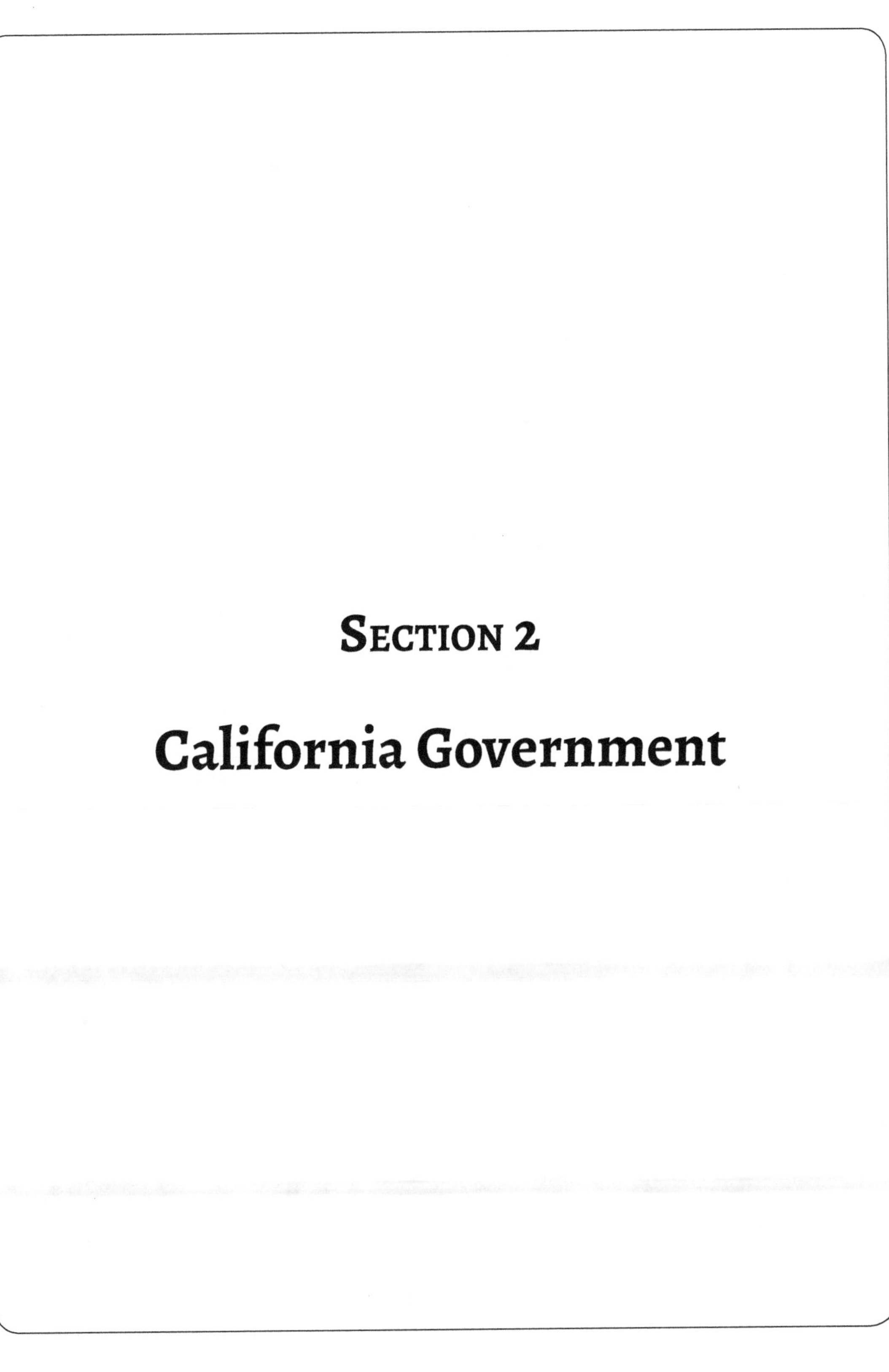

Section 2

California Government

Chapter 1

Introduction and Principles for Understanding Politics

The State Capitol Building: Sacramento, California

Renée B. Van Vechten

Topics to Cover

- A. Overview
  - The Contours of California as a State
    - Distinctive features
- B. Principles for Understanding Politics
  - Definition of politics
  - Five principles: choice, political culture, institutions, collective action, rules, and history

Overview

- Learning Objective:
  - Identify the geographic, economic, social, and political features that make California distinctive.

California

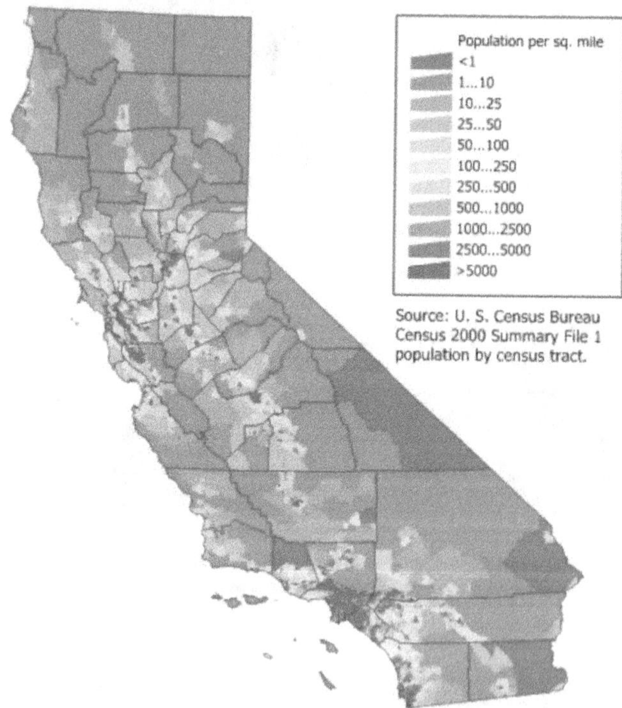

One of the 10 largest "countries" in the world

- *Sixth largest GDP in the world, 2016*

Distinctive Landscape

- Varied geography and topography
  - 770 miles long, 250 miles wide
  - Highest peak in continental United States (Mt. Whitney), lowest point also (Death Valley)
  - 840 miles of coastline
  - Dense ancient forests, dry deserts, and fertile farmlands

Distinctive Economy

- One of the world's 10 largest economies
  - Sixth largest in 2016
  - $2.6 trillion GDP
  - Size of economy rivals that of Brazil, Russia, and France

Gross Domestic Product

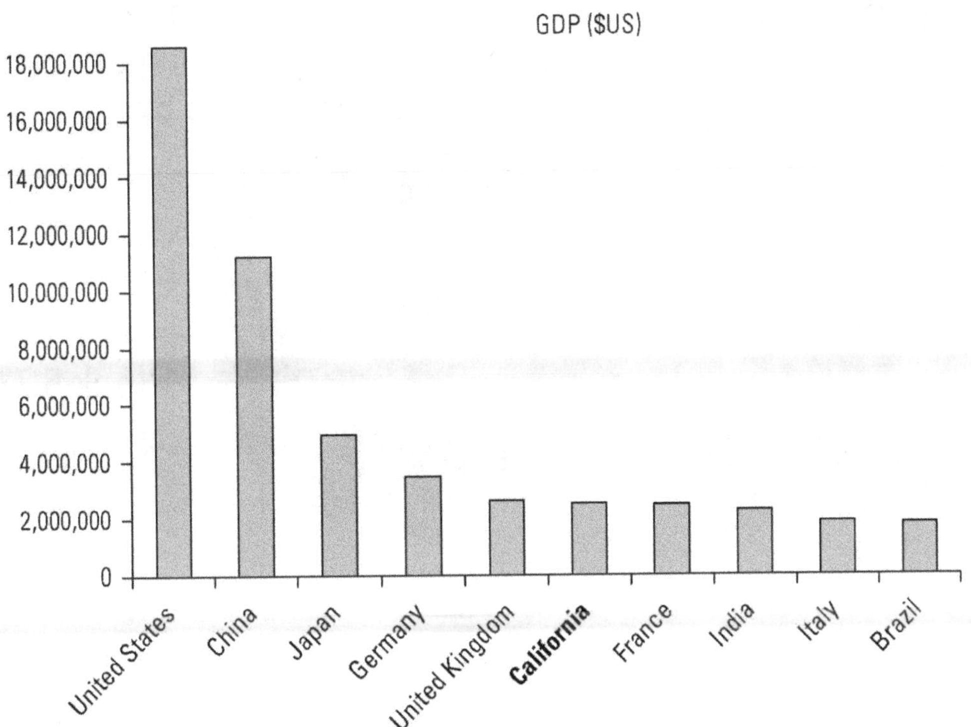

Distinctive Social Features

- One of the world's most diverse societies
  - Almost 39 million people; one of eight Americans live in California
  - One in four (27%) are immigrants
  - Largest city: Los Angeles, 4 million
  - Median household income: $61,818
  - Persons living in poverty: 16.3%

Ethnic Makeup of California

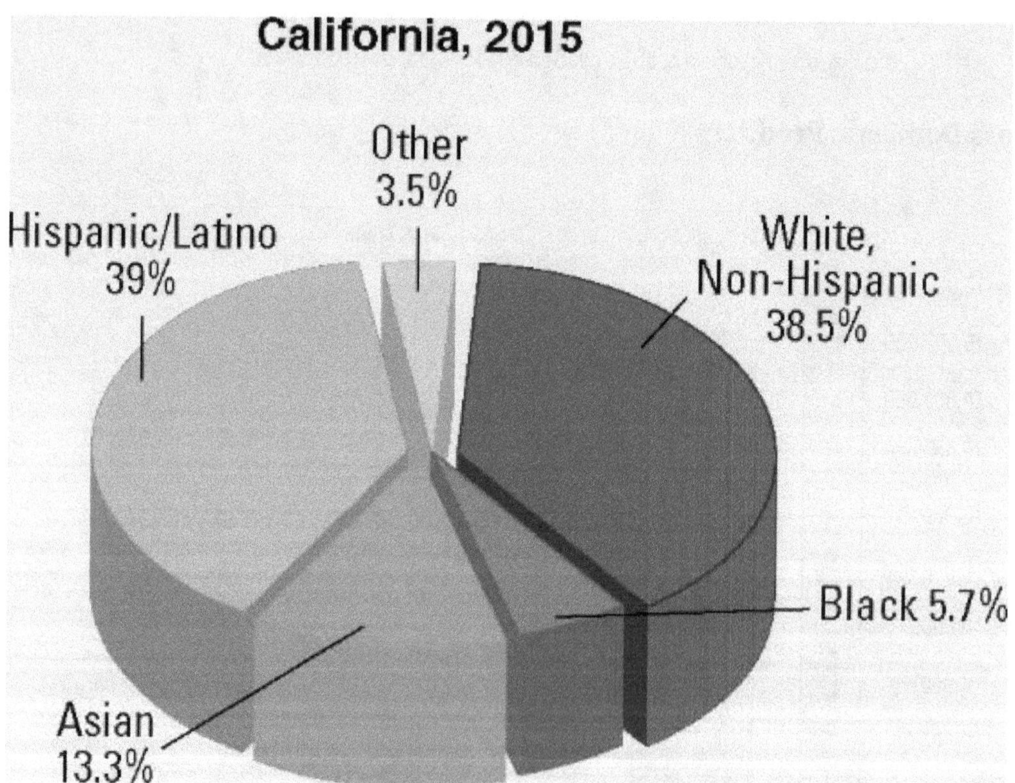

Distinctive Political Features

- "Hybrid" democracy
  - Combines **representative democracy** (citizens elect representatives) with **direct democracy** (citizens can vote directly on laws, called initiatives)
- Political reform is common
  - The people often "tinker" with different parts of government through initiative process
    - Tax reform, term limits for politicians, and new types of primary elections

Distinctive Political Features

- Citizens are generally distrustful of politicians and government
  - Heavy use of initiative process (ranked #1 of states)
    - Initiative process is dominated by big spenders

Distinctive Political Features

- Democrats dominate state elective offices
  - Republicans are a distinct minority
    - Democrats won supermajority status in 2016
    - Democrats dominate executive offices
    - Policies are "progressive" or left-leaning:
      - » Pro-legalization of recreational marijuana
      - » Pro-immigration, protection for "dreamers"
      - » Anti-border wall, against deporting noncriminal undocumented immigrants, "sanctuary" state

Understanding Politics

- Learning Objective:
  - Define the five basic principles for understanding California politics: **choice, political culture, institutions, collective action, rules, and history.**

Politics, Defined

- A **process** through which people with differing goals and ideals try to **manage their conflicts** by **working together** to **allocate goods and values** for society

What Is a Successful Political System?

- A process that narrows **choices** to a **manageable number** and allows **many participants** to **reconcile** their differences as they make choices **together**
  - Facilitates compromises, trade-offs, or bargains that lead to acceptable solutions or alternatives

Principles for Understanding Politics

- Choices
- Political culture
- Institutions
- Collective action
- Rules
- History

The Principle Of Choice

- **Choices** are at the heart of politics

  Examples:
  - *Opting out of elections*
  - *Boycotting or not buying a product because of the process used to make it*
  - *Opting "IN" or "OUT" of the public school system*
  - What other choices are "political"?

The Principle of Political Culture

- **Shared (collective) attitudes and beliefs about the role of government**
  - ...and about people's responsibility toward each other
  - Rooted in history

The Principle of Political Culture

Characteristics of California's political culture:

- Fondness for political reform
- General aversion to politicians
- Distrust of government
- Faith in the initiative process

- Preference for Democratic Party representatives but detachment from parties
- Can you think of others?

The Principle of Institutions

- **Institutions** are organizations and systems that help people solve collective action problems
- Define roles and rules for participants
- Facilitate bargains and compromises

The Principle of Institutions

Examples:

- A constitution
- Legislature
- Elections
- Courts
- Political parties

The Principle of Rules

- Rules matter
  - Codes or regulations defining who has power and how power may be legitimately used
  - Create incentives for action or inaction
- Can be formal
- Can be informal, such as an unwritten expectation (a "norm")

The Principle of Rules

Example:

- Driver's Licenses
  - For those age 16 or 18? For undocumented persons or citizens only? High or low fees? Easy or difficult tests?

The Principle of History

- History matters
  - The past helps set the terms of the present

- Over time, cultural shifts, natural disasters, scandals, economic trends, and other forces condition the **choices** people make
- **Prior choices** and conditions affect **opportunities** and **incentives** for political action

The Principle of History

FOR INSTANCE:

- Property tax rates were rising quickly in the mid-1970s.
- Housing was becoming unaffordable and the legislature did not fix the problem.
- Voters passed Prop 13, capping property tax rates at 1% of a building's sale price.
- Prop 13 also required that all taxes be approved with a two-third vote.
- Funding for schools dropped well below the national average and remains low (to average, depending on calculation).
- Today, voters still distrust politicians and have been unwilling to reform Prop 13.
- California's property taxes remain among the lowest in the United States.

Discussion Questions

What does it take to govern effectively?

At this point in time, how do you think California measures up: Is it governed effectively or ineffectively?

What would it take to enable officials to govern effectively?

Discussion Questions

Is California exceptional in its politics?

What makes California distinctive?

Chapter 2

California's Political History in Brief

Topics to Cover

- History Matters
- Early California
- Progressive Era
- Pre- and Post-War Developments
- Initiative Process Rises
- Current Political Earthquakes

History Matters

- Learning Objective:
  - Recognize how major historical events, economic developments, and prior decisions influence politics today.

Early History Still Evident In Today's Politics

- Independent spirit was fostered by relative isolation
- Vast natural resources fed optimism about the future and promise of a better life
- Reduction and displacement of Native American population
- Marginalization of and discrimination against Asian immigrants and Asian Americans
- Boundaries established; roads, county, and city names reflect Spanish influence

Early California

- Recognize:
  - The enduring influence of Spanish conquest and Mexican rule.

- How the Gold Rush triggered a series of population expansions.
- How the concentration of wealth in the Southern Pacific Railroad and its owners enabled their dominance over state politics.
- How the Transcontinental Railroad was critical in connecting California to the rest of the nation.
- How minority populations were marginalized socially and politically.

Critical Developments

- Spanish conquest, 1542; colonized Mexico (Baja California) first
- First mission established 1769 in Alta California (San Diego)
    - Native populations decimated
        - Social and economic activity centralized in mission complexes located along "El Camino Real"
- Mexican rule (1821–1848)

California's Missions

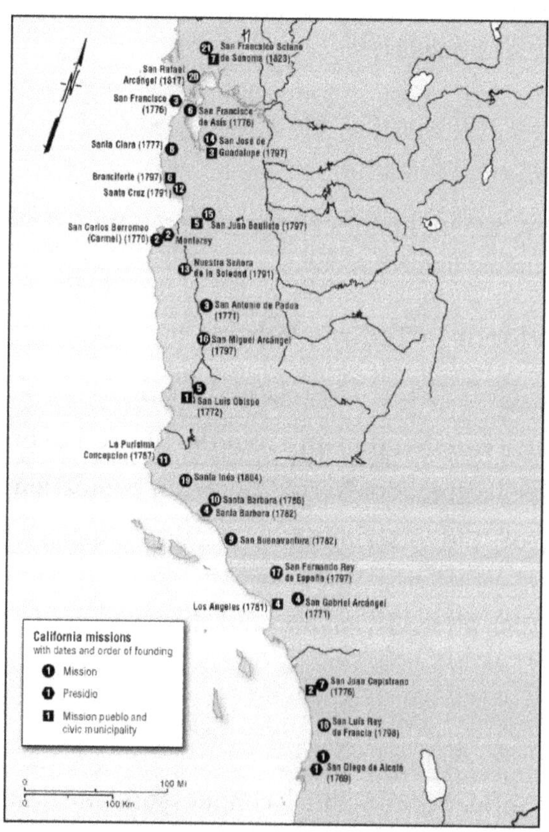

Statehood

- Mexican-American War ends with Treaty of Guadalupe Hidalgo in 1848
- Discovery of Gold leads to Gold Rush
  - Massive influx of gold-seekers
- Statehood granted 1850
  - Isolated from rest of United States by geography

Railroads & Power

- Southern Pacific Railroad (the "SP")
- Owned by the "Big Four": Stanford, Huntington, Hopkins, Crocker
- Built Transcontinental Railroad 1869
  - Connected California to the rest of the country
  - Enabled a long-term population boom
  - Gained vast tracts of land (about 10 million acres)
- "SP" owned or controlled virtually all major industries in California...and politicians

Railroads and Power, cont.

- Minority groups marginalized; denied power
  - Chinese laborers denied citizenship, property rights
  - Exclusionary laws expanded to include all of Asian origin
  - Land and property owned by Mexican settlers appropriated by American pioneers

Progressive Era

- Learning Objectives:
  - Identify the major political reforms established by the Progressives.
  - Recognize the enduring legacy of the Progressives in electoral politics today.

Progressive Party Political Movement

- Movement arose mid-1890s to protest the power of "SP"
  - Branch of the Republican party
  - Committed to reforming the political system
  - Aimed to "restore power to the people," make government more efficient, and obliterate corruption

Progressives in Power

- Politically powerful until about 1918
- Led by Progressive Gov. Hiram Johnson (1911–1918)
- Key, ambitious electoral reforms:
  - **Secret voting**
  - **Direct democracy: initiative, referendum, and recall**
  - **Civil Service** instead of patronage
  - **Direct primary elections**
  - **Nonpartisan elections** for local officials
  - **Cross-filing**
    - Candidates could formally seek nomination of any and all political parties

Pre- and Post-War Developments

- Learning Objectives:
  - Recognize the influence of historical events on the movement of people into California.
  - Explain how political decisions during the post-war era laid the foundation for the politics of today.

Pre–World War II Events

- Great depression
  - Wave of migration from Dust Bowl states
- Socialist journalist Sinclair Lewis's successful nomination for governor
  - 1934 "EPIC" campaign (End Poverty in California)

Post–World War II Developments

- Rapid population and economic expansion
  - Huge investments in infrastructure
    - Transportation, water, and public education
  - Growth of industry
    - Example: agribusiness boomed and relied heavily on foreign workers (Mexican farm workers)

Post-War Politics

- Political parties weakened by progressive reforms
- Special interests empowered
  - Strategy: "select and elect" legislators
    - Amateur legislature: low pay, part-time
- Equalization of political districts
  - "One person, one vote" ruling by U.S. Supreme Court (*Reynolds v. Sims*, 1964)
  - Senate now based on population, not counties
  - Power shifted from rural to urban districts and from north to south
- Constitutional Revision, Prop. 1-A
  - Professionalization of legislature in 1966
    - 3 **s**'s: higher **s**alary, more **s**taff, longer **s**essions
    - Pushed by Assembly Speaker "Big Daddy" Jess Unruh

Initiative Process Rises

- Learning Objectives:
  - Describe the importance of Proposition 13 as a political and historical event.
  - Recognize how the initiative process has fundamentally reconfigured political relationships in the capital and between "the people" and their government.

Propositions 9

- Popular revolt against corruption in government
- Proposition 9 in 1974
  - Campaign finance and regulation of lobbying

Propositions 13

- Proposition 13 in 1978
  - "Grassroots" political response to skyrocketing property values and tax rates
  - Capped property taxes at 1% of a building's sale price, not to rise by more than 2% a year
  - Beginning of "anti-tax" fervor; required two-third vote to raise taxes
  - Renewed use of the initiative process

Recent Impacts of Direct Democracy

- **Term Limitations** imposed on state elected officials,1990
  - Reformed in 2012 (shortened to 12 years total; can serve all in the Assembly and/or the Senate)
- **Recall** of Governor Davis
- **Top-Two primary system**, first used in 2012
- New districts for representatives created by **Citizens Redistricting Commission** (effective 2012)
- Retention of **plastic bag ban** (referendum 2016)
- **Legalization of recreational marijuana** (voted on in 2016)

Current Political Earthquakes

- Learning Objective:
  - Recognize major social, global, economic, and political trends that continue to influence the state's politics.

Democrats in Charge

- Return of Gov. Jerry Brown, 2010–2018
- Democratic Party dominates statewide elected offices (supermajority in legislature in 2012 and 2016; occupy 10 of 12 executive branch seats)
  - Marginalization of Republican legislators
- Budget surpluses since 2013
- Top-two primary elections continue

Social Change

- Continuing growth and diversification of population
  - Waves of **immigrants** from Mexico, Vietnam, China, and Central/South American countries in recent past
  - California is "**hyperdiverse**"
  - **Plurality Latino** in 2014; over half (54%) of all schoolchildren are Latino
  - Asian population expanding faster than other racial/ethnic minority groups
  - The state may be "absolute majority" (over 50%) Latino state by 2050

Conclusion: Political Earthquakes

- Major political earthquakes in early state history: Spanish conquest; Gold Rush/ statehood; opening of Transcontinental Railroad owned by "SP"
- Major earthquakes early to mid-1900s: Progressive reforms such as establishment of direct democracy; Great Depression; post–World War II economic and population booms
- Minor earthquakes caused by direct democracy : Proposition 13 tax reform, term limits, recall of a sitting governor, redistricting, elections (top-two primary)
- "Rolling" earthquakes: population change (continued expansion, growth of Latino, and Asian populations)

Discussion Questions

1. What historical developments have contributed to California's current political culture?
2. How would you characterize California's current political and social climate?
3. Which seem to have had more lasting impact on politics today: political "earthquakes" created by voters, or those that have occurred through historical happenstance?

Chapter 3

Direct Democracy

Topics to Cover

- California's Hybrid Democracy
- Direct Democracy
  - The Statewide Initiative Process
  - Referendum
  - Recall
- Direct Democracy at the Local Level
- Consequences of Direct Democracy

California's Hybrid Political System

- Hybrid democracy: **representative democracy** is combined with **direct democracy**
  - Elected representatives in the legislative and executive branches make laws
  - Citizens also "make" laws at the ballot box
    - Propose and vote on initiatives
  - At state *and* county and city levels

Three Components of Direct Democracy

- Learning Objective:
  - Be able to identify and describe the three components of direct democracy: the initiative process, the referendum, and recall.

Direct Democracy

- **Initiative**

- Citizens may propose laws or constitutional amendments and vote on them
- Appear as "propositions" on the ballot

- Referendum
  - (plural = "referenda")
  - Voters may "second guess" the legislature and governor by voting to reject laws
- Recall
  - Voters may choose to remove an elected official from office

The Initiative Process

- Learning Objective:
  - Identify and describe all four stages of the initiative process.

Initiative Process Generally

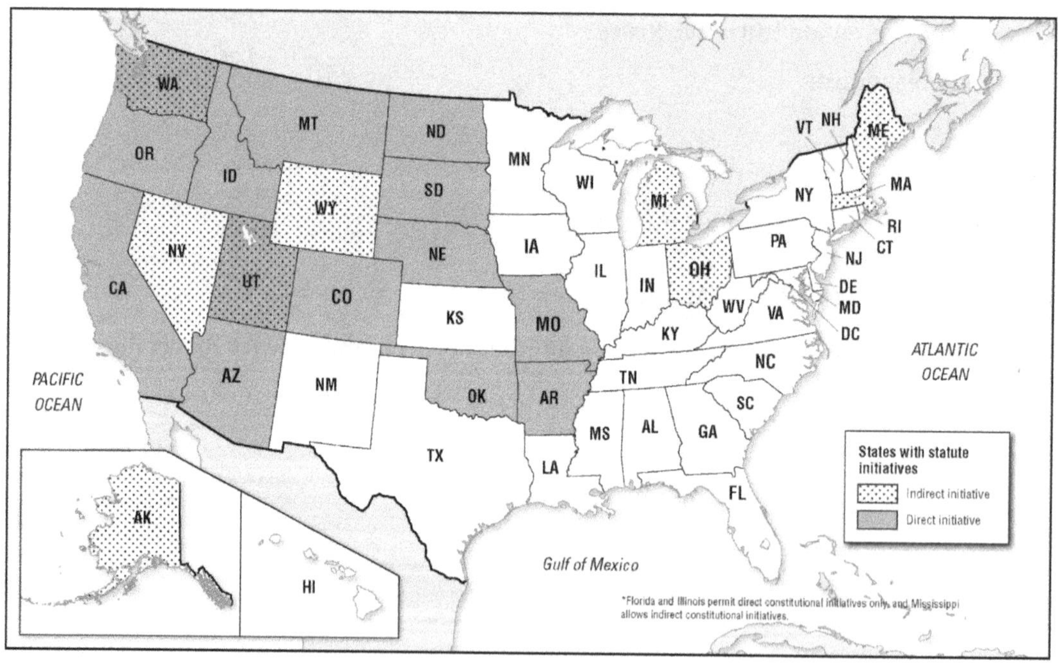

- Established by CA Progressives, 1911 (following states such as Oregon and Wisconsin)
- Californians **use it more than any other state** (but Oregon and Colorado are close rivals)
- **Expensive**: average cost is $3 million to qualify measures

- Costs have dropped because signature requirements are lower as of 2014 (likely to rise in 2018)

- Since 2011: Measures may only appear in general or special election ballots
- **All manner of subjects** covered, but each proposition must only address one issue ("single subject" rule)
  - Government structure and processes
  - Taxation
  - Immigration
  - Social welfare
  - Public morality (drugs; abortion)
  - Criminal justice
  - and so on
- Initiatives are **ballot measures**
- **Initiatives** are referred to by name: "**Proposition** (#)"

Selected Landmark Initiatives, 1966–2016

Number	Description	Year
Proposition 1A	Constitutional reform, legislative professionalization	1966
Proposition 9	"Political Reform Act" (campaign finance reform)	1974
Proposition 13	Property tax limitation	1978
Proposition 98	Minimum annual funding levels for education	1988
Propositions 140, 28	Term limits for state officeholders; 12 years total in either house	1990; 2012
Proposition 184	Three-strikes law	1994
Proposition 187	Ineligibility of illegal aliens for public services	1994
Proposition 215	Medical use of marijuana	1996
Proposition 5	Tribal state gaming compacts, tribal casinos	1998
Proposition 227	Elimination of bilingual education	1998
Propositions 11, 20	Citizens redistricting commission to redraw state and congressional districts	2008, 2010
Proposition 8	Definition of marriage (invalidated by U.S. Supreme Court in 2015)	2009
Proposition 14	Open primary elections (Top-Two Primary)	2010
Proposition 67	Recreational use of marijuana	2016

Stages of the Initiative Process

1. **Preparation Stage:** *Drafting and Titling*
   - Write the initiative and submit to attorney general with $2,000
   - Online for 30 days for public review
   - Authors may change wording in response
   - Attorney General's office assigns it a title and summary
2. **Qualification Stage:** *Gathering Signatures and Signature Verification*
   - 365,880 signatures required for initiative*
   - 585,407 for constitutional amendments*
   - About *double* those numbers are needed to ensure enough signatures are valid
   - Secretary of State verifies signatures and certifies measure for ballot

   *(*These signature requirements are based on 2014 turnout and will change after the 2018 election)*
3. **Qualification Stage:** *Gathering and Verifying Signatures, cont.*
   - Costs about $2–$3 per valid signature; higher closer to deadlines
   - 180 days (6 months) to collect signatures
   - Most fail because of insufficient signatures
   - Secretary of State validates, assigns Prop#
4. **Campaign Stage:** *Persuading Potential Voters*
   - Raise and spend funds to get proposition passed

Proposition	Election year	Subject	Total spent	Spent by proponents	Spent by opponents	Pass/fail (% margin)
87	2006	Oil taxes	$184,340,000	$71,461,000	$112,879,000	F (45/55)
32	2012	Union dues	$145,109,000	$64,174,000	$80,935,000	F (43/57)
30	2012	Taxes for education	$141,350,000	$73,124,000	$68,226,000	P (55/45)
5	1998	Indian gaming	$136,563,000	$97,400,000	$39,163,000	P (62/38)
61	2016	Drug pricing	$128,258,000	$19,152,000	$109,106,000	F (47/53)

5. **Campaign Stage:** *Persuading Potential Voters*
   - Donations to ballot measure campaigns can be unlimited
   - 2000–2012: 98% of all ballot measure campaign donations came from from "big donors"

- Corporations, labor unions, interest groups, wealthy individuals donate huge sums
- Only 2% of all donations are from "small donors" who give $1,000 or less

6. **Post-election Stage:** *Court Challenges and Implementation*
   - Many initiatives are immediately challenged by opponents in court. Those propositions are put "on hold" until a final court decision is made about its constitutionality.
   - A proposition can be challenged in whole or in part and invalidated in whole or in part
7. **Post-election Stage:** *Court Challenges and Implementation, cont.*
   - If two very similar initiatives pass, the one with more votes wins
   - Simple majority (50% + 1) needed to pass
   - Take effect immediately
   - They may only be changed by a future initiative
   - The legislature may not change propositions

The Referendum (*"referenda" = plural*)

- Learning Objectives:
  - Describe how the referendum process works.
  - Recognize the most common forms.

Referenda

- Citizens may **reject all** or **parts of laws** passed by legislature and signed by governor
- Signatures need to be collected and verified to appear on ballot
  - Same requirement as initiatives: 365,880 but need to collect almost double to ensure enough are valid
- Most common are BONDS or "bond measures"
  - Voters must approve state borrowing over $300,000
  - Tend to be in the BILLIONS of dollars to fund large infrastructure projects
    - High speed rail in 2008: $9.9 billion authorized
    - In actuality, bonds cost nearly double their face value after interest is calculated
- Supermajority vote required to pass bond measures:

  - Two-third vote (66.66%) for general obligation bonds
  - 55% for school bonds (locally)

The Recall

- Learning Objective:
  - Describe the recall process and most common types of recall efforts.

Recall

- Voters may remove **local** or **state officials** <u>for any reason</u>
- Voters may also remove **judges**
- Proponents must gather signatures equal to 20% of votes cast in last election for that official's office
- Proponents have 5 months to collect signatures
- Very **rare statewide**: succeeded only once in California (Governor Gray Davis, 2003)
- More **common at local level** (**school board** is most common)

Local Direct Democracy

- Learning Objective:
  - Recognize how state-level and local initiative processes differ.
- Citizens may **propose local laws**
  - For **cities** or municipalities and for **counties**
- Most common local initiatives pertain to:
  - Government and political processes (term limits are popular)
  - Taxation and bonds, especially school bonds
  - Business and labor regulations
  - Land use
- Unlike state initiatives, <u>local</u> officials may avoid a general vote by **adopting** qualified measures first
  - Qualified measures that they do not adopt will be placed on the next ballot

Consequences of Direct Democracy

- Learning Objective:
  - Analyze the outcomes of political reform processes both intended and unintended.

- The process conditions and constrains actions of elected officials
  - Rules affecting them can change through elections, unexpectedly
- Piecemeal reforms target parts of a system rather than the whole
  - Results in fragmented institutions
- Some reforms frustrate compromise
  - An initiative represents one unalterable choice offered to voters
  - Once approved, an initiative can only be changed by the voters
- Wealthy, special interests are empowered
  - Initiative process is costly
- People possess governing power and ultimate "veto" power
  - Citizens have the power to take action on issues the legislature might avoid
    - Example: term limits for representatives
  - Citizens keep elected officials in check between elections
  - Citizens have power to act on issues political parties might be "stalemated" over
    - Example: open primaries and redistricting

Discussion Questions

1. Do voters make more informed decisions than their elected officials?
2. What perceived problems exist with the initiative process, and what reforms have been suggested to remedy them? What are the drawbacks and strengths of each?
3. Which reforms of the initiative process do you believe are most critical and should be implemented?

Chapter 4

The Legislature

State Legislature

- Design, Purpose, and Functions
- Representatives at Work
  - Policymaking and Lawmaking
  - Representation
  - Annual Budgeting
  - Constituency Service and Outreach
  - Executive Branch Oversight
- Leaders

State Capitol, Sacramento Purpose and Design

Purpose and Design

- Learning Objective:
  - Describe structure of the state legislature and articulate the differences between the Senate and Assembly.
- Resembles U.S. Congress in ***form***:
  - **Bicameral** (two houses); **upper vs. lower** houses with different membership **numbers** and **lengths** of terms
- ...and ***in function:***
  - Two chambers designed to "check" each other

Design: Senate

- "Upper house"
- 40 members
  - Represent over 931,000 people
  - 4-year terms
  - Term limited (12 years total in state legislature)
- Democrats are majority
- Leader: President Pro Tem

Senate Floor

Photo: R. Van Vechten

Design: Assembly

- "Lower house"
- 80 members
  - Represent over 465,000 people (***half** the size of Senate districts*)
  - 4-year terms
  - Term limited (12 years total in state legislature)
  - Democrats are majority
  - Leader: Speaker

Assembly Floor

Photo: R. Van Vechten

Side-by-Side Comparison of Two Chambers

SENATE	ASSEMBLY

• 40 members
• **4**-year terms
  – More experienced
• 930,000+ residents per district
• Leader = Senate **President Pro Tem**
• Extra duty: confirm Governor's appointees
	• **80** members
	• **2**-year terms
	  – Higher turnover
	• 465,500+ residents per district
	• Leader = **Speaker**

Design: Term Limits

- Restriction imposed by voters in 1990, modified recently
- Legislators can now serve:
  - Up to 12 years in one house or in both houses
  - Lifetime ban: can't serve as lawmakers again

Design: Districts They Represent

- Boundary lines used to be drawn by legislators themselves
- Under Prop 11, **Citizens Redistricting Commission** draws lines
- **Giant**: state Senate districts contain more people than U.S. House districts

Design: Professionalized

- The Three S's
  - *Staff*: Heavily **staffed**
  - *Session:* Meet year-round, **full-time**
  - *Salary:* **Well paid** (+$107,000 plus per diem)

Profile of Legislature Compared to California Population

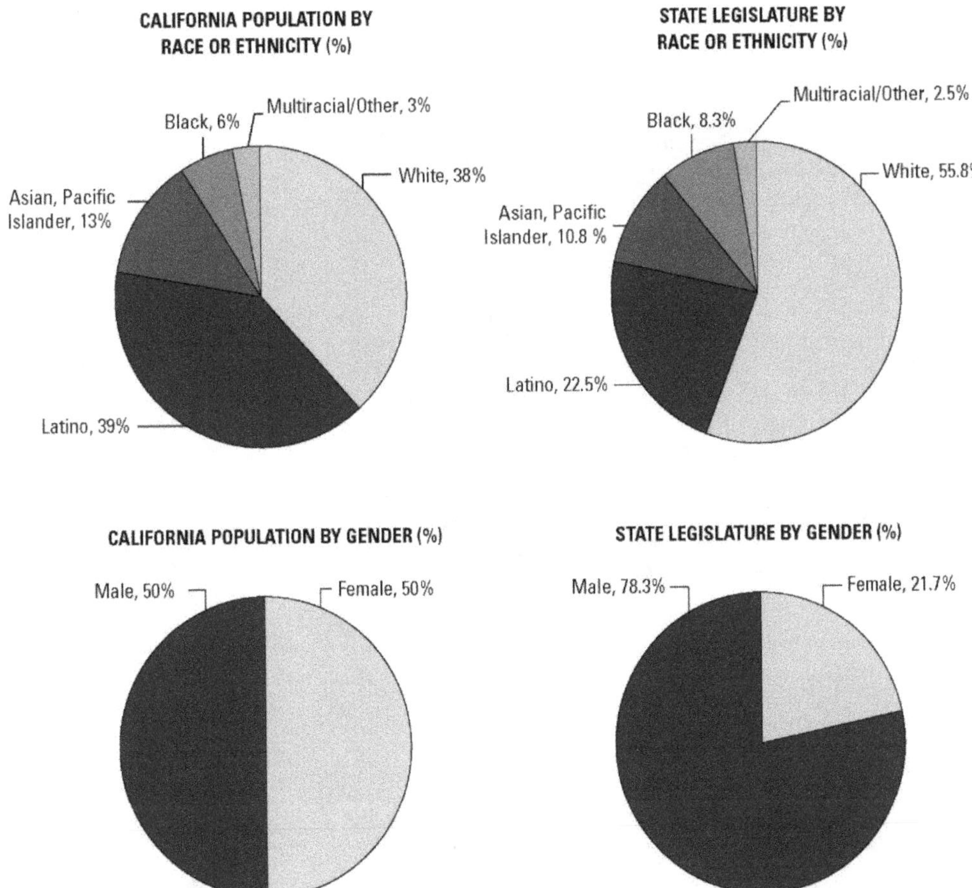

Function: Representatives at Work

- Learning Objective:
- Articulate the roles that Senators and Assembly members fulfill, and the tasks they perform.

Lawmaking

- Lawmakers propose and consider about **5,000** bills in a 2-year session
- Most work occurs in **committees**

Assembly Committee Hearing Photo: R. Van Vechten

Sen. Holly Mitchell asks a question during a committee hearing.

Photo: L. Shelley, Senate Photographer

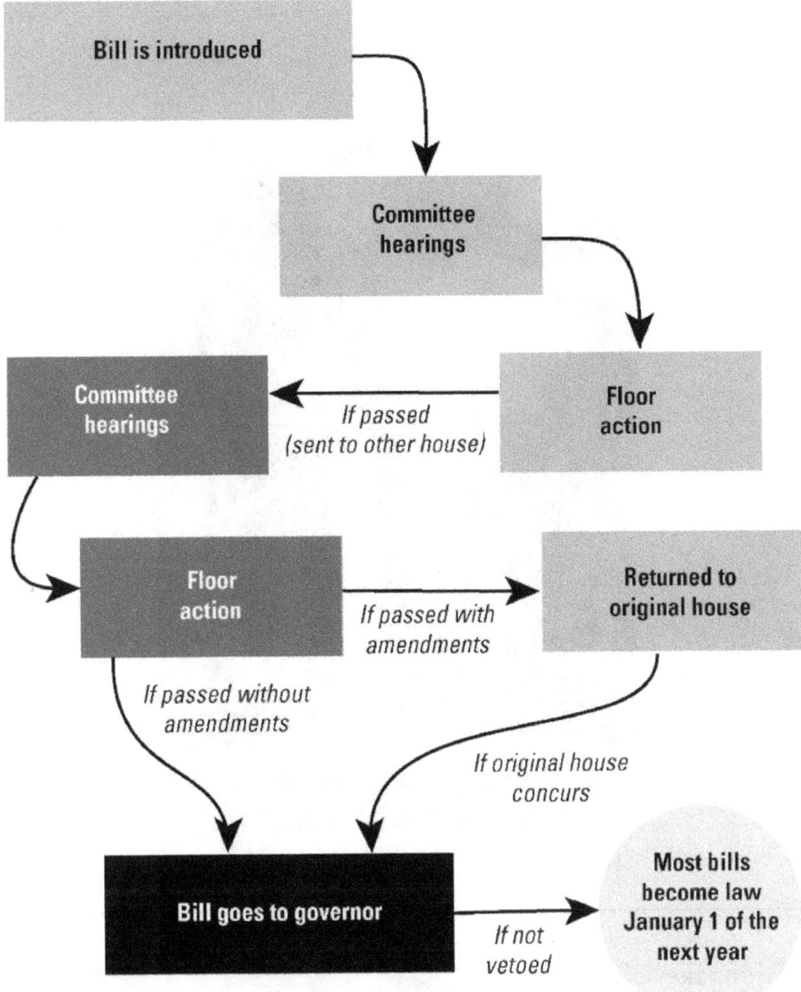

- Many interests fundamentally shape bills:
  - **Lobbyists**, special interest advocates, advocating on behalf of "**stakeholders"** (those affected by a bill)
  - **Staff** (legislative staff, committee staff)
  - **Governor's staff**, **administrators**, **state officials**
  - **Constituents** (people in a representative's district)

Photo: R. Van Vechten

Lobbyists and advocates discuss bills with Assembly members.

- Final action takes place on the "**the floor**" of each chamber
- Both houses must pass bills in same, final form before the governor can sign them

Senate Floor in Session

Photo: R. Van Vechten

Factors That Shape Bills/Laws

- Nature of bill
  - **Costs**
  - **Type:** long term vs. short term, complex or simple, and wide ranging or affects only a few individuals or entities
- Staff **expertise** and assistance
- Rules
  - **Simple majority** for passing bills and budget
  - Supermajority (two thirds) to raise taxes or fees
- Institutional Factors
  - **Party balance** in Assembly and Senate
    - Democrats are majority in both
  - Strength of the majority party
    - How many minority party votes are needed to reach supermajority thresholds?
    - Democrats reached supermajority status in 2012 and 2016
- Governor
  - Persuasiveness, partisanship, and veto threats
- Personal factors
  - Legislators' level of **expertise**, **experience**, and **reputation**
- **Partisanship**
- Interpersonal **relationships**
- **Political environment**
  - Pressure from **lobbyists** who represent important **constituencies**
  - Timing and outside **events** (economy, changing attitudes, etc.)

Representation

- Bringing the concerns, values, and beliefs of constituents to state governance
- ***Substantive*** representation vs. **descriptive** representation
  - Representatives discern their constituents' ***interests***, and collectively are a "**portrait**" of the state based on their outward, personal characteristics
- Representatives must balance:
  - *Statewide* interests and *district* interests

- short-term and long-term concerns
- using one's own judgment or wisdom (as a *trustee*) vs. strictly following public sentiment or opinion (as a *delegate*)

A Day in the Life of Senator Connie Leyva

July 11, 2017
Tuesday

7:45 a.m.	Leave for Capitol
8:30	Senate Public Safety Committee Hearing—Present three bills: AB 90, 1448, and 1528
9:30	Meeting with Senator Portantino, re: SB 328 (bill coming before the Assembly Education committee)
10:00	Briefing by staff for Assembly Higher Education Committee meeting
10:50	Photo with Black Capitol Staff and Members on West Steps of Capitol
11:10	Meeting with California Schools Board Association, re: AB 1220**
11:30	Meeting with Compton Unified School Board members, re: SB 765
11:45	Meet and Greet with Senator Stern, chair of Senate Elections Committee
12:00 p.m.	Noon Democratic Caucus Meeting, lunch provided
*1:30	Higher Education Committee Hearing
*1:30	Senate Human Services Committee—Present AB 1106
*1:30	Senate Natural Resources and Water Committee—Present AB 1323 and special hearing on water stakeholder group
3:30	Meeting re: Campus Climate Select Committee and Anti-Semitism on campuses
*4:00	Meeting with committee chair and stakeholders, re: AB 1220
*4:00	Meeting with committee chair and stakeholders, re: AB 1220
6:00	Phone call with AB 1220 opposition
7:00	Leave Capitol for home; dinner at home
8:00	Calls regarding bill presentations on Wednesday
9:00	Prepare for committee hearing (Assembly Elections and Education)

* Note overlaps. **AB 1220 proposes changes to employment rules for certificated school employees.

Budgeting

- State's annual budget = An economic plan in which ***policy priorities*** are spelled out
- January–June
  - **Budget committees and subcommittees** consider all parts of governor's proposed budget; create **alternative** spending amounts

- Legislative Analyst's Office (LAO) provides analysis
- Must pass by June 15 or legislators lose their pay
- Should be signed by governor by June 30

Constituency Service

- Helping constituents solve state government-related problems
  - Residents seek help to:
    - Locate a check from the state
    - Make appointments at a government agency
    - Obtain a hard-to-get government document
    - and so on
  - Staff assigned to solve each case ("casework")

Outreach

- Contacting constituents to:
  - Gather opinions
  - Get a better sense of district concerns
- Perform "Public relations"
  - Town Hall meetings, newsletters, e-mail contacts

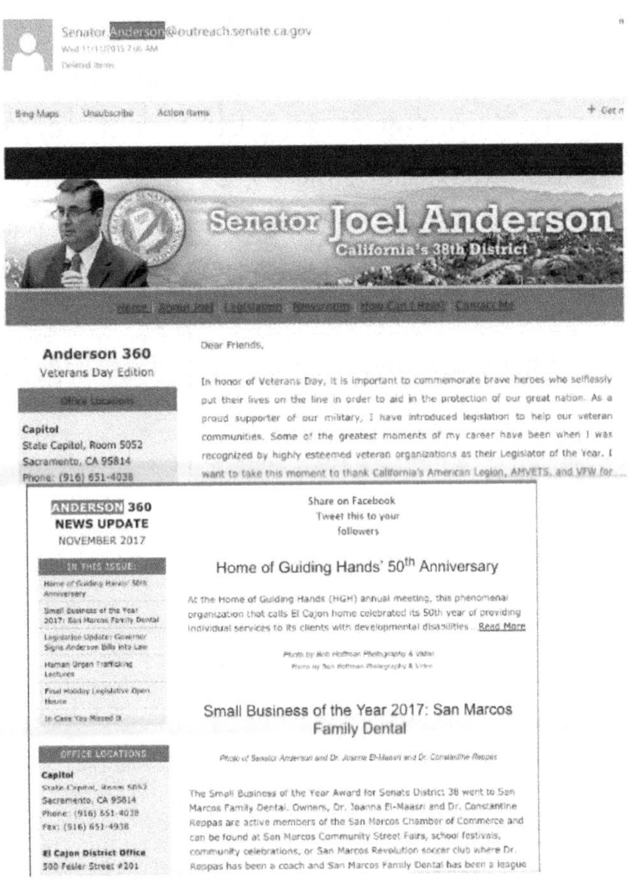

Senator Anderson@outreach.senate.ca.gov

Senator Joel Anderson
California's 38th District

Anderson 360
Veterans Day Edition

Capitol
State Capitol, Room 5052
Sacramento, CA 95814
Phone: (916) 651-4038

Dear Friends,

In honor of Veterans Day, it is important to commemorate brave heroes who selflessly put their lives on the line in order to aid in the protection of our great nation. As a proud supporter of our military, I have introduced legislation to help our veteran communities. Some of the greatest moments of my career have been when I was recognized by highly esteemed veteran organizations as their Legislator of the Year. I want to take this moment to thank California's American Legion, AMVETS, and VFW for...

ANDERSON 360
NEWS UPDATE
NOVEMBER 2017

Share on Facebook
Tweet this to your followers

Home of Guiding Hands' 50th Anniversary

At the Home of Guiding Hands (HGH) annual meeting, this phenomenal organization that calls El Cajon home celebrated its 50th year of providing individual services to its clients with developmental disabilities... Read More

Small Business of the Year 2017: San Marcos Family Dental

The Small Business of the Year Award for Senate District 38 went to San Marcos Family Dental. Owners, Dr. Joanna El-Maasri and Dr. Constantine Reppas are active members of the San Marcos Chamber of Commerce and can be found at San Marcos Community Street Fairs, school festivals, community celebrations, or San Marcos Revolution soccer club where Dr. Reppas has been a coach and San Marcos Family Dental has been a league

OFFICE LOCATIONS

Capitol
Sacramento, CA 95814
Phone: (916) 651-4038
Fax: (916) 651-4938

El Cajon District Office
500 Fesler Street #201

Executive Branch Oversight

- Monitoring activities of administrators
- Questioning whether programs are working as intended
- Can hold hearings and question witnesses from state agencies
  - Can threaten to reduce agency positions or cut funding

Leaders

- Job of a leader: retain or gain majority status
- **Speaker** and Senate **President Pro Tem**
  - Speak for the majority party in their chamber
  - Democrats in both houses
  - Power has equalized under term limits

  + Governor = "Big Three"; often negotiate bills and budget without minority leaders

Discussion Questions

1. What do most legislators spend their time doing?
2. How important is casework or constituency service to the task of governing?
3. How would you define a "good" representative?
4. Does California benefit from having a professionalized legislature?
5. Some have suggested that the legislature return to "amateur" status. What would be the consequences of that change?
6. What people and contributing factors shape laws?

Chapter 5

The Executive Branch

The Executive Branch

- Features of the Plural Executive
- Governor
  - Roles
  - Sources of Power
- Other Constitutional Executive Officers
- Consequences of a Plural Executive
- State Administration

The Plural Executive

- Learning Objectives:
  - Know the nine offices that lead the state executive branch.
  - Identify the roles that each constitutional executive officer fulfills.

Plural Executive, cont.

- Definition: Multiple persons lead the branch
- Rejected by U.S. Founders
  - Regarded as inefficient, competitive, and fractious
  - They opted instead for single executive (a president)
- Plural model adopted with revised California state constitution, 1879

Twelve People in Nine Offices Share Power:

- Governor
- Attorney General
- Lieutenant Gov.
- Secretary of State
- Treasurer
- Controller
- Superintendent of Public Instruction
- Insurance Commissioner
- Board Of Equalization (4)

Plural Executive: Features

- Duty of each: carry into effect state laws, policies, and programs
- **Four-year** terms
- Term limits:
  - **Two terms** or 8 years total
  - **Lifetime ban**: after 8 years in that office, can never serve in it again

Plural Executive: Features

- Incentivized to run for other offices because of term limits
  - "**Musical chairs**": executives often run for other executive positions
    - Example: John Chiang went from Board of Equalization to Controller to Treasurer and is a candidate for governor (2018)
- Do not meet as a group

The Governor

- Learning Objective:
  - Recognize the powers and describe the roles that render the governor "first among equals."

Official portraits of governors are displayed in the Capitol.

- Vested with "**supreme executive power**" by state constitution
- Considered "**first among equals**"
  - Other executives operate independently (governor can't order them to act)
- Has **strongest influence over** state departments, agencies, commissions, and so on, that form the **bureaucracy**

Governor's Roles

- **Head of State**
  - Delivers "**State of the State**" address
  - Receives visiting dignitaries
    - Gov. Brown negotiated a climate agreement with Chinese Pres. Xi Jinping in 2017
  - State's official **liaison** to Washington, D.C.
  - Works with other governors
- Chief Executive
  - Can issue **executive orders** to state employees
  - **Appoints** administrators to key posts
    - Senate confirmation required

  - Fills 300 state **boards and commissions** (about 2,000 positions)
  - Appoints **judges** to the state courts
- Legislative Roles
  - **Monitors** bills; weighs in on important issues
  - Has power to **veto or sign** legislation, including **line-item veto**
  - May **call special sessions** of the legislature to consider pressing issues
  - Can set **special elections**
- Budgeting Power
  - Dept. of Finance (DOF) prepares annual budget
    - Collects financial and demographic information year-round
    - Assembles the budget
    - Explains budgeting rationale to legislators
  - **Prioritizes state spending** in budget
  - Works with legislature to hammer out final budget, **signs** it into law
- Chief of Security
  - **Commander-in-chief** of state's National Guard
    - Controls Army National Guard
    - Air National Guard
    - State Military Reserve
    - Can **commute (lessen) sentences** and **grant pardons**

Sources of Governor's Power

- Institutional Sources
  - State **constitution**
  - Whether **political party** in either house shares the governor's partisanship and cohesiveness of parties
  - Single authority (unlike 120 legislators)
- **Constituency**
  - The entire population of the state
- Personal Sources
  - Power of **persuasion** or **charisma**
  - Ability to **strategically use the media**
    - Gov. Schwarzenegger excelled here

- Perception of having a **mandate**
- Strength of **ideology** and **partisanship**, shared either with the legislative parties or the majority of Californians

- Personal Sources, cont.
  - Personal **characteristics**, such as political **experience**
    - Gov. Jerry Brown has extensive political experience as a former governor, secretary of state, attorney general, party leader, and big city mayor

Other Constitutional Executive Officers

- Learning Objective:
  - Name and describe the duties of each constitutional executive officer.

Other Executive Officers

- **Lieutenant governor** (LG): "governor-in-waiting"
  - Member of state boards, commissions
  - Takes power if governor leaves state, resigns, or dies
- **Attorney General** (AG): chief law-enforcement officer ("Aspiring Governor")
  - Most powerful executive after the governor
  - Prosecutes violators of state law

Gov. Brown testifies at a Senate Rules Committee confirmation hearing for his appointee, Xavier Becerra, as Attorney General. Becerra replaced outgoing AG Kamala Harris, who was elected to the U.S. Senate.

Photo: L. Shelley, Senate Photographer

- **Secretary of State**: chief elections office
  - Runs state and federal elections in California
  - Registers voters
  - Makes lobbying reports available
  - Makes campaign finance info available
  - Archives official records
- **Insurance Commissioner**: regulates insurance
- **Superintendent of Public Instruction**: chief advocate for California's students (the only nonpartisan office)

The "Money" Officers

- **Treasurer**: state's banker, oversees investments, and bond debt
- **Controller**: state's chief financial officer (CFO) authorizes spending
- **Board of Equalization**, 4 members + Controller:
  - Established 1879 to standardize tax systems
  - Gutted in July 2017: most (4,400 of 4,800) employees and tasks transferred to new Dept. of Tax and Fee Administration and operations scaled back to original functions
    - Collect fees and excise taxes

Consequences of a Plural Executive

- Learning Objective:
  - Argue the case for and the case against a plural executive.
- Lack of accountability
  - Difficult to assign blame, except to the governor
- (Possibly) less cohesive state policies
  - Can represent any party, typically a mix of Democrats and Republicans
  - Governor has no power over other executives and their plans/agendas
  - **No centralized planning** mechanism
- **Division of labor** allows for greater expertise to develop
- More accountability than if appointed
- Greater chance for an executive official's specific initiatives to take root
- More **opportunities** for term-limited officials to serve in other capacities

State Administration ("The Bureaucracy")

- Learning Objective:
  - Depict the state's administration as a collection of departments and agencies, recognizing the "superagency" scheme.

State Administration

- Agencies and departments that implement state programs and policies
- Includes **major councils, boards, commissions, and offices**
- Many are nested in seven separate "superagencies"

State Administration: Superagency

- Example: Natural Resources "Superagency" contains 12+ departments, commissions, etc.:

DWR (Dept. Water Resources)	Dept. Forestry and Fire Protection
Dept. of Conservation	Dept. Parks and Recreation
California Conservation Corps	Dept. Fish and Wildlife
State Lands Commission	California Energy Commission
Expo Park, California Science Ctr.	African American Museum
Native American Heritage Commission	Coastal and Mountain Conservancies, Flood Boards

State Administration

- Includes 300 **boards and commissions** that regulate professions, industries, and categories of activities
  - Examples: University of California Board of Regents; Coastal Commission, CalPERS

Discussion Questions

1. If you were to redesign the state's executive branch, which positions would you eliminate and which would you retain?
2. Consider Governor Jerry Brown. What are his informal and formal sources of power?
3. Should the governor have more authority over the other executive offices?

CHAPTER 6

The Court System

California's Court System

- Overview: 3-Tiered Structure
- Types of Cases
- Filling the Bench
- Terms of Office
- Court Administration
- Juries
- Criminal Justice System: Prisons

The Courts: Overview

- Learning Objectives:
  - Recognize how the state court system is organized.
  - Discern the connections between budget cuts and the courts' ability to deliver "fair and equal access to justice for all Californians."

Courts in California

- **Purpose of courts**: "To provide fair and equal access to justice for all Californians."
- **Largest** state system in the nation:
  - About 7,000,000 cases annually
  - 2,000 judicial officers (such as judges)
  - 19,000 court employees
- **Budget cuts have compounded problems**:
  - $1 billion cut from budgets 2009–2014

- Led to unprecedented court **closures**: 22 courthouses and 114 courtrooms by mid-2013
  - Money and capacity have largely been restored but gaps remain
    - People lack easy access to courts, longer delays, and less help available
- NOTE: Those who break **state laws** are tried in the state court system, which is separate from the federal court system
  - If an individual or corporation violates *federal* law or violates someone's *Constitutional* rights, they're tried in *federal* court

Three Tiers: State Court System

SUPREME COURT (seven-member court, San Fran)

Filings: 7,868... 76 written opinions

COURTS of APPEAL (six districts; nine courts)

Filings: 22,084... written opinions: about half

TRIAL COURTS

"Superior courts"(58 courts) Filings: 6,832,710

Source: 2015-16 statistics; see www.courts.ca.gov

Collaborative Courts

- Collaborative courts = "Problem-solving courts"
  - Part of superior (trial) court system
  - About 415 in state
  - Combine judicial case processing, drug and alcohol treatment services, and monitoring
  - Examples: Drug courts, Veterans courts, domestic violence courts, and so on.
  - Help reduce recidivism and prison populations, rebuild lives

Types of Cases

- Learning Objectives:
  - Identify the differences between civil and criminal cases, which include infractions, misdemeanors, and felonies.
- "Litigation" refers to a lawsuit or a legal dispute that is being dealt with through a court
- 90% of all cases never make it to trial

- The government brings cases against individuals for breaking criminal law
  - District Attorneys represent the state of California

Types of Cases, cont.

- **Felonies** (serious, often violent offenses)
- **Misdemeanors** (lesser crimes, would result in less than a year of imprisonment)
- **Infractions** (minor violations of law, such as traffic tickets for which fines are imposed)
- **CIVIL CASES** are brought by individuals or organizations (usually companies) against another person or organization for:
  - **Contract**-related disputes
  - Breaches of property, business, or personal rights ... and commonly result in **monetary compensation**

Filling the Bench

- Learning Objectives:
  - Recognize the governor's influence in the court system through appointments.
  - Describe how a person becomes a judge or justice in California.

Filling the Bench: How judges are appointed

- "**The Bench**" generally refers to judges who make up the courts
  - "Judges" are in superior courts; justices in appellate and superior courts
- **Governor usually appoints** state judges and justices
  - The Governor **fills vacancies** (created by retirements or deaths)
  - State Bar screens the governor's nominees and state **Commission on Judicial Appointments confirms** appointments
- **Governor usually appoints** state judges and justices, cont.
  - The legislature is not involved in court appointments
  - Higher court justices usually have extensive judicial experience
- Higher court justices are often selected because of their background and general ideological orientation
  - Conservative governors tend to select and promote conservative justices; liberal governors tend to do the same for liberal justices
- Judges and Justices are still expected to be **neutral and unbiased**

- The bench skews heavily **male** (66%) and **white** (69%)
- **Judicial retention elections** (voters decide to keep or reject a sitting judge/justice) are becoming **politicized** and more expensive overall

Judges' Terms of Office

- **Appellate Court** and **Supreme Court** justices
  - Appointed by governor, screened by the **Commission on Judicial Nominees**, and confirmed by the **Commission on Judicial Appointments**
  - **12-year terms**, no term limits
  - Must run in **retention election** if first appointed by governor

Judges' Terms of Office, cont.

- **Superior Court** justices (trial courts)
  - Usually **first appointed by governor**, though a few run for **election**
  - Must be a **lawyer with 10 years of experience** to apply or run
  - **Six-year terms, no term limits**
  - **Nonpartisan** office/elections
  - Must **run in a nonpartisan retention election** to be "retained" by the people if the governor first appointed him or her
    - Some judicial elections are contentious and politicized

Court Administration

- Learning Objective:
  - Recognize the chief justice as the head of the court system, and how s/he works with the Judicial Council to keep the courts running.

Court Administration: Running the Courts

- **Chief Justice** (CJ) directs court operations
- CJ chairs the 30-member **Judicial Council**, the administrative body that:
  - Sets **policy, rules, and procedures** for all courts
  - Manages the courts by requesting and handling annual **budgets,** keeping **records, hiring** court employees, and more
  - **Reports** to the legislature and responds to mandates
- Recent Court Policy Changes

- Traffic violators who challenge their tickets avoid paying their fines until a trial is held
- An "ability to pay" (fines) calculator is being tested
- More online "self-help" resources have been funded
  - More information about immigration laws and rights included
- Under consideration: moving all minor traffic violations out of criminal courts and into the civil courts

Juries

- Most citizens are linked directly to courts through **jury duty**
  - **"One day, one trial"** program in effect:
    - Prospective jurors for criminal and civil cases are called to serve on a trial. If not assigned by the end of the day, they are excused and must only respond to a summons once a year until they serve on a jury.
      - » $15/day starting with the second day of service, plus 34 cents/mile one way (for mileage)

Grand Juries

- One in every county, impaneled annually (58 total)
- 19 members (all citizens)
- **Investigate conduct of city and county government**
- Can **indict** public figures for misconduct

Criminal Justice System: State Prisons

- Learning Objectives:
  - Explain why state jails are typically underfunded.
  - Describe current program of "realignment" with respect to reducing overcrowding in state prisons.

Prisons: The Other Side of Criminal Justice

- State prisons are still **underfunded**:
  - Politically unpopular to spend more on existing prisons or to build new ones
  - State prison system currently being overseen by a federal "receiver" because of problems the state has not yet fixed

    - State has increased spending steadily; now $11 billion from the general fund ($13.9b from all sources)
  - **$76,000 spent per year, per inmate**
- State prisons remain **overcrowded**:
  - In 2017, holding steady at 2015 levels
  - In 2015, about 130% above capacity
    - Slightly lower than court ordered 137%
  - In 2011, 185% above capacity
  - In 2013, 150% above capacity
- Courts ordered the release of prisoners if state could not reduce population by other means

Realignment: State's Response to Overcrowding

- Federal **courts ordered reduction** in state's prison population
- State **shifted "triple-non's" to county jails**
  - Triple-non = Adult, low-level *non*serious, *non*violent, *non*sexual offenders
  - More put on parole
  - About 46,000 inmates affected
- Raises questions about fairness and equity, as facilities and resources are different in 58 counties

Discussion Questions

1. Are there ways to "protect" judges from political influence, especially as special interests increasingly try to affect the outcomes of judicial elections?
2. What has been done to reduce overcrowding in California jails? What more could be done?
3. What kinds of reforms might lead to fewer crimes and also create safer societies?

CHAPTER 7

Other Governments

Other Governments

- Overview of Subgovernments
- County Government
- City (Municipal) Government
- Special Districts
- Regional Governments
- Federalism
- Tribal Governments

Subgovernments in California

- **State government alone cannot provide essential services**
- Below the state level, Californians are organized into many "jurisdictions":
  - **Areas governed by authorities** with lawmaking, executive, and/or enforcement powers to **deliver essential services**
    - Counties
    - Cities
    - Special districts
    - School districts
- Mostly invisible, working in background
- Patchwork of governments has been assembled over time as needs have arisen
- Also arise from desire for self-rule or local control
- Some are imposed by the state; others have been created from the "bottom-up"
- Typically struggle for funding; revenues are usually based on fees for services

County Governments

- Learning Objectives:
  - Describe the purpose and functions of county governments.

Size of Counties by Population

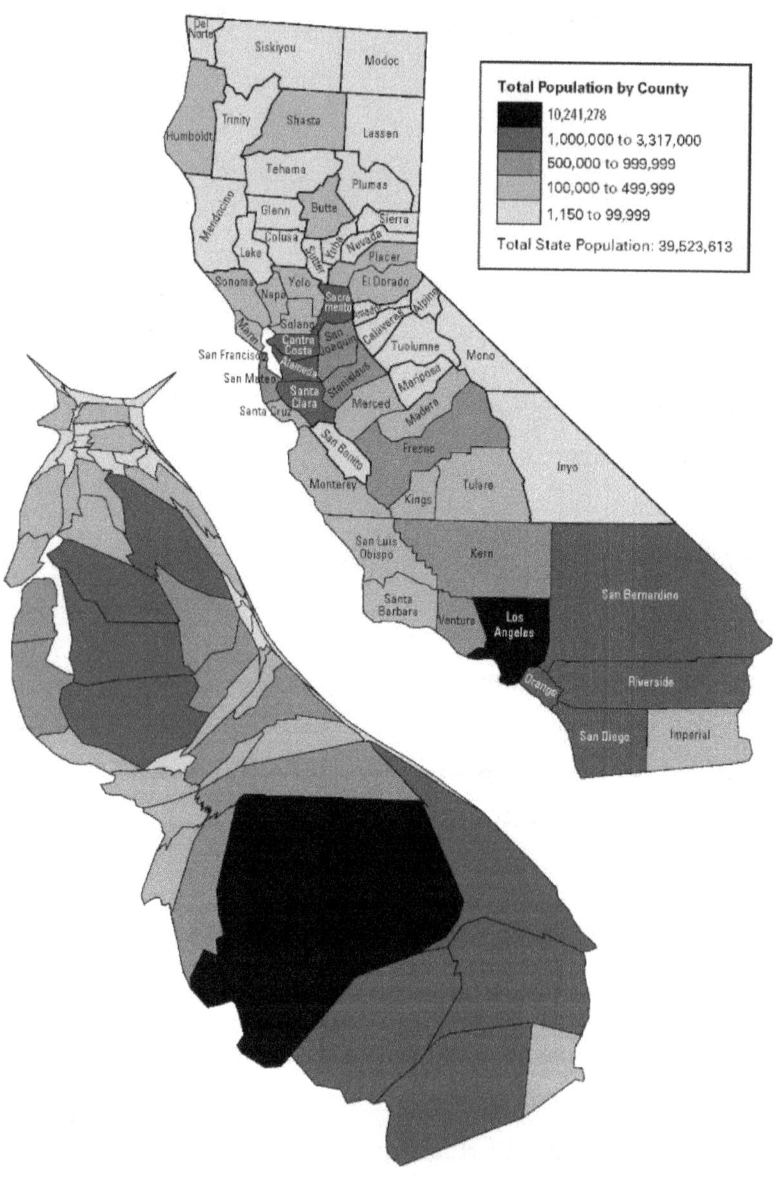

Counties

- **58**, most created by 1879 state constitution
  - Boundaries generally don't change
  - Huge disparities in population:
    - Smallest = Alpine, population 1200
    - Largest = Los Angeles, population 10 million
  - **San Francisco** is the **only combination** city/county
- Created to **carry out state programs**
- Provide essential services similar to services the cities within them provide
  - Primary providers of services to "**unincorporated areas**" (areas not in cities)
- Organize under **charters** or by **state law**
  - 45 are "general law" counties
- General law counties
  - Governed by 5-member elected **boards of supervisors**
    - Have term limits if voters have approved them
  - Other elected officials:
    - Sheriff
    - District attorney
    - Auditor/controller
    - Treasurer/tax collector
    - Clerk/recorder

Counties Provide Essential Public Services

PUBLIC SAFETY	Courts, jails, probation, public defense, juvenile detention, sheriff, fire, and emergency services
PUBLIC ASSISTANCE	Housing, homeless, food stamps, and state welfare programs
ELECTIONS and VOTING	Voting processes, voter registration, and vote counts
TAX COLLECTION	county, city, special district, and school tax collection
ENVIRONMENT and RECREATION	Manage parks, public facilities, open space, waste removal and recycling, air quality, land use, and water

PUBLIC HEALTH	Hospitals, mental health clinics, and drug rehabilitation programs
EDUCATION	Libraries and schools
SOCIAL SERVICES	Adoptions and foster care
TRANSIT	Airports, railways, bus systems, bridges, and road maintenance
VITAL RECORDS	Birth, death, and marriage certificates

Top County Expenses, 2014–15

Public safety, 27.9%
Public assistance, 26.5%
Health and sanitation, 15.3%
Enterprise, 15.6%*

* *Enterprise examples: public utilities; water treatment facilities*

Paying for County Services (Revenue)

- Funds typically in short supply; county officials
- MAIN SOURCES:
  - **STATE** funds, granted through agencies (32.5%)
  - **FEDERAL** GOVERNMENT (15.6%)
  - **PROPERTY TAXES** (19.3%)
  - **ENTERPRISE REVENUE + FEES** paid by users (23.7%)
  - **Other:** Sales **taxes**, licenses, rents, fines, permits (9%)

City/Municipal Governments

- Learning Objective:
  - Describe the purpose and functions of city (municipal) governments.

City or "Municipal" Government

- Cities are also called "**municipalities**"
- 482 cities in California
- Organize under "**general law**" (follow state law) or "**charters**" (like local constitutions)

- Like counties, they provide essential public services
  - Overlap or supplement county services
- Governed by elected five-member **city councils**
- City councils govern with either:
  - A strong **mayor,** who has hiring/firing authority, more control over the budget, or
  - A **city manager**, a hired professional who manages city operations for the council
    - Here, the mayor is only a figurehead
- Councils make law and execute it (possess legislative and executive functions)
  - Local laws = "ordinances"

Cities Provide Essential Public Services

Category	Approx % of annual budget	Types of Services
Public safety	23.5%	Police, fire, emergency; streetlights
Transportation	19.5%	Street repair, construction, maintenance; storm drains; public transit (bus, air, rail)
Public utilities	19%	Electricity, gas, water distribution
Health	13%	Mental and physical / hospital and clinic; sewage, waste removal; cemeteries
Government	9%	Management and support
Culture and leisure	8%	Parks, recreation, libraries, museums, golf courses, stadiums, and auditoriums
Community development	7.5%	Planning, construction, redevelopment, and housing

Cities Need Revenue to Pay for Services

- Strategy: "**Fiscalization** of Land Use"
  - Cities encourage RETAIL businesses and discourage costly housing or service-related construction because cities keep 1% of state sales taxes

- Try to cut expenses by **"contracting out" their services** to neighboring cities or counties
  - For example, use county sheriffs instead of own police force
- Strategy: **Charge extra fees** to housing developers
  - **To pay for infrastructure** that's needed to support new residents
    - Schools, sidewalks, lighting, sewer, and so on.
  - These fees are passed on to new homebuyers as **Mello-Roos** fees
    - Equates to almost $2,000 per year per home (if imposed) for 25 years on average

Special Districts

- Learning Objective:
  - Define "special districts" and list different types, indicating the functions they perform.
- Geographic areas governed by an autonomous **board** for a specific purpose
  - Can **stretch across** cities, counties, and regions
- About **4,700** in California; **2,800** fee-based
- Examples:
  - Mosquito abatement
  - Airport management
  - Water districts
  - Street lighting
- Virtually **invisible** but **essential**
- Provide essential services **not provided by cities or counties**
- Pay for services through **fees** and assessments

Special District: Port of San Pedro

Occupying 43 miles of waterfront, Los Angeles's major port is a prime example of a "special district," generating billions of dollars annually.

School Districts

- Type of special district
- **1,000+** provide K–12 education in California
- 112 Community college districts
- Governed by elected **boards of education**
  - Five elected members
- Funded through state's General Fund
  - Approx. 40% of the budget goes to education
- Other sources of school funding = federal grants, donations, contracts, parcel taxes, and local school bonds

Charter Schools

- Not governed by a school district
  - Organize under a "charter" (like a constitution)
- Are **public** schools
- Organized to offer specialized programs of study:
  - Science based - Performing arts
  - College prep - Foreign language
- **1,100+** provide K–12 education in California

Regional Governments

- Groups that **plan, regulate, and coordinate land-use** and development-related activities across counties and cities
  - Include representatives from local governments, such as mayors, supervisors, and specialists
- "Councils of Governments" (COGs)
  - Plan infrastructure needs for future generations
  - No enforcement authority; make policy recommendations only
- Some regulatory bodies do have enforcement authority
  - Air quality management districts (AQMDs)

As its website shows, SANDAG, or San Diego Association of Governments, is a regional planning body for the San Diego area.

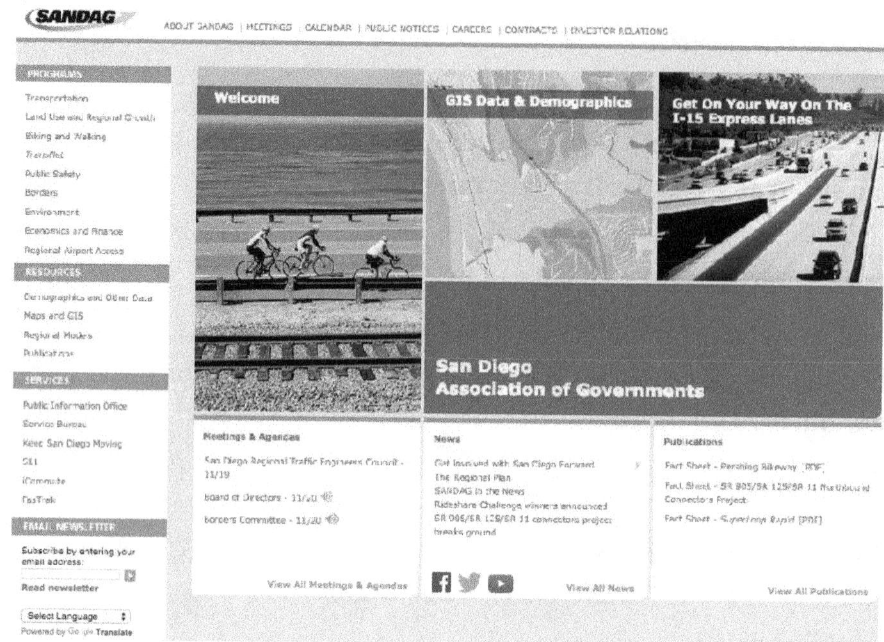

Federalism (U.S. Gov.) and Tribal Governments

- Learning Objective:
  - Describe the relationship between state government and the federal government.

Federalism

- U.S. Constitution recognizes authority of states in matters not given to the federal government
  - Examples: elections, education, and state infrastructure
- Because states retain authority over certain matters, Congress can **entice** the states to do what Congress wants with money (federal funds)
- Because federal law is supreme, by law Congress can also **force** states to comply with federal standards
- Some rules or programs are **mandated** (required) by the federal government, but **no direct funding** provided

- Known as **unfunded mandates**
  - Example: Not reimbursing states for the costs of reducing pollution under the Clean Air Act

- Federal **preemption**: Federal law is supreme, and Congress can, **by law, prevent** California from implementing certain laws or regulation
  - Federal law preempts state laws and constitutions
  - Example of how federal law is supreme:
    - Federal law classifies marijuana as a Schedule 1 drug; it is illegal in the United States
    - Californians voted to "legalize" medical and recreational use of marijuana
    - State officers won't arrest sellers, but federal agents could

- Federal government also **provides critical funding** for state, county, and local programs and services
  - Congress authorizes transfers of federal funds
    - Example: funding for children's health care
  - Money given in form of GRANTS
    - Example: A city can apply for a federal grant to build low-income housing
    - Example: The state receives grants for freeway construction

California's Relationship With Other Governments

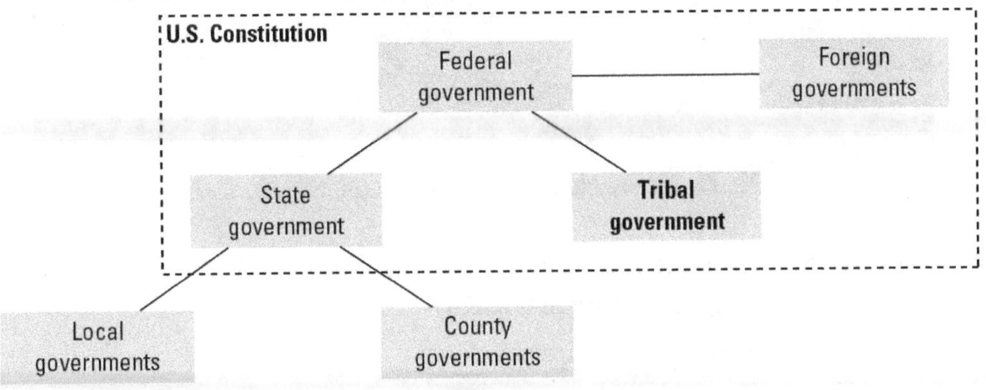

Source: K. Spilde, J. B. Taylor, J.W. Grant II, "Social & Economic Analysis of Tribal Government Gaming in Oklahoma,"(Cambridge, MA: Harvard Project on American Indian Economic Development, 2002). Tribal Governments

Tribal Governments

- Tribes are sovereign entities within the state
  - Receive federal financial support
- 110 recognized tribes within California
  - More are vying for recognition
- Tribes are governed by a multimember Council
- Economic impact today often measured by gaming operations
  - Gaming tribes are big donors to state and federal campaigns
- The Morongo Band of Mission Indians runs a successful tribal gaming operation in Southern California: The Morongo Casino Resort and Spa, located in Riverside County.

Renée B. Van Vechten

- Congress has authorized states to negotiate compacts with tribes operating casinos (Indian Gaming Regulatory Act, **IGRA**)
- States **cannot tax tribes** or require payments
- **States must provide essential services**
  - Examples: law enforcement, road access and repairs, and emergency services
- States can collect money to help offset direct costs/impacts on surrounding communities if negotiated (with tribe's permission)

- Gaming tribes share revenue with nongaming tribes, but poverty persists among those tribes
- State gaming compacts usually subject to referendum
  - Voters rejected one compact in 2014

Discussion Questions

1. Which local governments are responsible for your welfare? List them, along with their responsibilities.
2. What are the advantages and disadvantages of a city's decision to contract services to private entities?
3. What are the negative effects of "fiscalizing" land use in cities?

Chapter 8

The Budget Process

The Budget Process

- California Budgeting 101
- Mechanics of Budgeting
  - Revenue
  - Expenditures, Deficits
- Debt
- Political Constraints on Budgeting
- Tax Burden: Highest in the Nation?

California Budgeting 101

- Learning Objectives:
  - Identify the main steps in the budget process, and the government officials in the legislative and executive branches who play key roles in the process.
  - Identify the legislative rules that directly condition how lawmakers shape the budget.

Constructing the Annual Budget

- State's fiscal year (FY) = July 1–June 30
- Budget process begins at least **18 months in advance**
- Groundwork laid by governor's **Dept. of Finance** (DOF)
  - Initial proposal reflects governor's priorities
- Governor **submits his version to legislature January 10**
- **Legislature's Budget Committees** and subcommittees examine all pieces of the budget bill in spring; reconstruct it

- After tax receipts are calculated, **figures are revised in May**
  - Called the **"May Revision"** (or "May Revise")
- **Negotiations** among legislative leaders and governor help finalize the budget bill
  - Must be passed by both houses with a **simple majority vote** by **June 15**
  - Under Prop. 25 legislators are supposed to forfeit their pay if the budget is late
  - Must be **signed by June 30**
- **Simple majority** vote to pass budget
- **Two-thirds vote needed to raise fees or taxes**
  - This **supermajority** threshold means unless they have a supermajority of seats, the majority party Democrats must obtain consent of some minority party Republicans, who oppose taxes on principle
- **Governor must sign budget**, so negotiations between branches are necessary
  - Main negotiators are "**Big Three**": Governor + Speaker + Senate Pres. Pro Tem (and their staff)

Rules That Matter

- New spending or changed priorities must be followed up with policy changes (in law)
  - Legislature passes "**trailer bills**" to make the budget consistent with statutory (legal) language

Photo: R. Van Vechten

Mechanics of Budgeting: Revenues

- Learning Objective:
  - Identify main sources of state revenue and principal categories of expenditures.

State Revenues (Income)

- State taxes and fees go into the **GENERAL FUND**
  - **$127.6 billion** General Fund budget in FY2017-18
    (includes Rainy Day fund set-asides)
- **Largest sources** of revenue *(including general fund and special funds totaling $178.4 billion):*
  - Personal **income taxes**, "PIT" (50.8%)
    - » Excluding special funds, the PIT is **66.5%** of GF revenues
  - **Sales** and use taxes (23%)
  - Charges, penalties, fees, and licenses (12%)
  - **Car** and **gas**oline **taxes** (8.5%)
  - **Corporation** taxes (6%)

State revenue, FY 2017-18

Includes General Fund + Special Funds ($162.5 b)

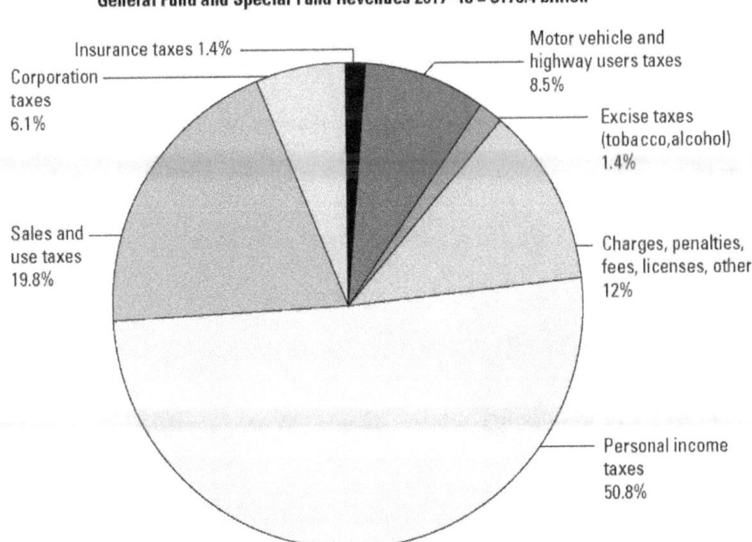

State revenue 2017–18 from all sources = $290.75 billion

Federal government transfers grants $107.5b [37%]
Bond funds $3.3b [1.1%]
Special funds $54.9b [18.9%]
General fund $127.6b [43.0%]

The bigger Picture: All Sources of Revenue, FY 2017-18

General fund budget (excludes $1.7b set-asides)	$125.1 billion
Federal Government transfers/grants	$107.5 billion
Special funds	$54.9 billion
Bond funds	$3.3 billion
TOTAL STATE BUDGET FY 2015-16	$290.8 billion

Mechanics of Budgeting: Expenditures, Deficits

- Learning Objective:
  - Identify different major categories of annual state spending, and largest categories of spending.

State Expenditures, FY 2017-18

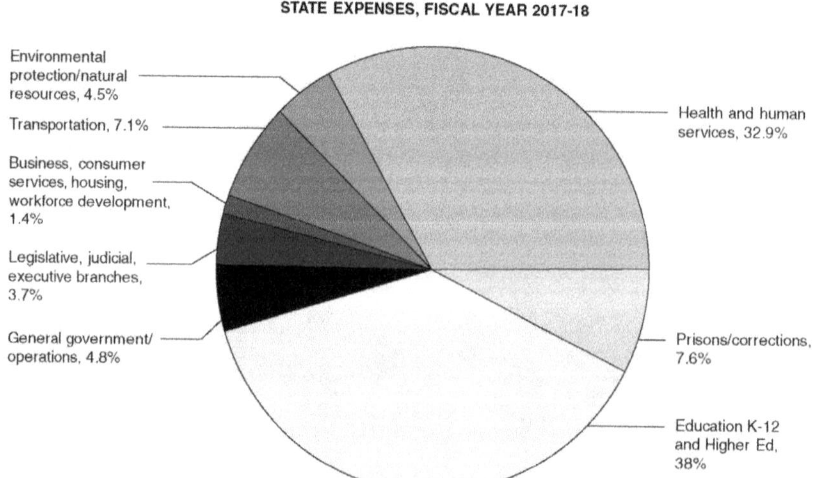

Largest Annual General Fund Expenditures (Spending) FY 2017–2018

Category of Spending	Approx. Percentage
Education	38%
Health and human services	32.9%
Prisons	7.6%
Transportation	7.1%
Environment, natural resources	4.5%

Note: Based on combined revenues from general, special, and bond funds of $183.3 billion.

Education Spending

- Under Prop 98, nearly 40% of general fund budget must be spent on K–14 education
- Per pupil spending is $11,067, still at or below national averages for per pupil spending
- State spends about $69 billion on K–12 and higher education annually

Deficits

- When revenues can't cover spending, **deficits** result
  - During last recession, deficit was $27 billion (in 2009)
  - State borrowed money to cover difference
  - Those debts were repaid under Gov. Brown
  - State has had budget surpluses since 2013
- Deficits are hard to predict
  - If fortunes change unexpectedly and quickly, existing spending plan can't be changed easily

Debt

- Learning Objectives:
  - Distinguish between debt and deficits.
  - Differentiate between deficits and debt and recognize different types of debt carried by the state.

Overview of Debt

- Like consumers, state and local governments **borrow money** to cover expenses

- State treasurer manages state's debt
- State carries different types of debt:
  - Bond debt
  - Unfunded liabilities
  - Budgetary borrowing

General Obligation Bonds: Regular Source of Revenue

Types of debt

- The state **sells bonds** in order to "borrow" money (it promises to pay back what's lent, with interest)
- Must be **repaid in time** (often 5, 20, or 30 years) with interest.
- Typically **cost nearly TWICE their face amount** when interest is added.

  Most common types:
  - *General obligation bonds*
  - *Lease revenue bonds*
- Long-term **loans to cover infrastructure** that shapes quality of life and commerce
- **Voters** must **approve** borrowing over $300k at the ballot box
  - Example: **Proposition 1** (2014) authorized $7.5 billion to be spent on water projects
  - $84 billion in bonds sold, plus $58.4 billion in interest = $142.4 billion to be repaid

Types of Debt

Unfunded Liabilities:

- **Promised benefits** for current and future state retirees
  - Negotiated and set in labor contracts but unfunded or underfunded based on legal obligations

  Types:
  - Underfunded pension payouts for future retirees (state employees), CalPERS and CalSTRS
  - Future health-care liabilities

Budgetary Borrowing:

- Long-term loans or payments deferred to **cover shortfalls** in the annual budget

  Types:
  - *Economic recovery bonds*

- *Internal loans*
- *Deferred payments to local governments and schools, agencies, and other programs*
- *Borrowing from special funds*
- *Unemployment Insurance Fund loans to the U.S. Gov.*

Overview of State Debt

Type of Debt	Approx. Amounts Owed
General obligation bonds	$127 billion
Lease-revenue bonds	$14 billion
Other bond debt (self-liquidating, etc.)	$1 billion
Economic recovery bonds	$27 billion PAID
Budgetary borrowing	$3 billion
Pension liabilities (promised but unfunded)	$83 billion
Plus promised health care for retirees	$95 billion
TOTAL:	$323 billion

Political Constraints on Budgeting

- Learning Objectives:
  - Explain why the annual budgeting process is a political process.
  - Analyze how political factors condition the budgeting choices that legislators and governors make.

Political Constraints/Influences on Budgeting

- **<u>Partisan balance</u>: which party is in charge**
  - **Democrats** are majority in both legislative houses
  - Democrat is in the governor's office (Brown)
- Larger **economic climate**
  - Tough economic times (recession) = less revenue, bigger deficits, and more cuts to state services
  - Economic recovery means more revenues

- **Term Limits**
  - Many lawmakers have little experience with myriad state systems and how they interconnect; difficult to plan or see larger picture
- **Ballot box budgeting**
  - Prop 13 fundamentally changed revenue sources and rules about raising taxes
    - Two-third supermajority to raise taxes and fees, but only a simple majority to lower them
  - Minimum funding levels for education (Prop 98)
  - Limits on "raiding" local tax sources (Prop 1A)
- **Special interests** prevail
  - *"Squeaky wheels get the grease"*
  - Lobbyists proliferate in Sacramento and can be influential at each stage
  - Risk-averse politicians seeking reelection would rather please important groups and constituents than alienate them
- State relies on **volatile revenue sources**
  - Very **high-income individuals** pay the majority of the income tax; the budget relies heavily on their fortunes
    - Top 1% of taxpayers (about 150,000 people) paid ***almost half*** of the state's income taxes
      - » Includes those making $400,000+ per year
    - **Progressive income tax structure** means higher income earners pay higher rates
- **Historical precedents**
  - Prior decisions condition choices of today
    - Difficult to shift tax burdens to keep pace with rapidly changing economic tides
    - Carryover debt can hamper budgeting
- Difficult to predict future
  - All budgeting is based on **predictions** and economic assumptions that can be wrong
    - Estimates can be higher or lower
- **Difficult to adjust quickly to changing circumstances**
  - Inability to cut programs quickly when revenues suddenly fall

    - Promised funding levels are committed far in advance, by law
        - Higher demands (e.g., for unemployment checks) can lead to higher deficits
- **Political climate**
    - Public opinion and pressure to address certain issues shifts over time
        - Crime in the 1980s and 1990s
        - Weather-related events recently: severe drought, flooding from sudden rainfall, devastating, and rampant wildfires
- **Political climate,** cont.
    - Pushback against Trump Administration policies
        - Support among Democratic lawmakers for immigrant-related programs and environmental protection

Highest Tax Burden in the Nation?

- Learning Objectives:
    - Know the general types of taxes that Californians typically pay.
    - Analyze the relationship between an individual's economic status and tax burden.

Californians Pay – and Local and State Governments Rely On – A Variety of Taxes

Type of Tax	Current Basic Tax Rate
Personal income	Marginal rates = 1% to 12.3%; +1% surcharge on income over $1 million
Sales and use	7.25% + local rates
Property	1% of assessed value at sale (+2%/year)
Vehicle license	0.65% of depreciated value; +$100 for alt. fuel cars
Cigarettes	$2.87 per pack of 20
Vehicle fuel	41.7¢/gallon + 2.25% sales tax + local tax + 2¢ UST fee
Corporation	8.84% of net income (higher for some banks)

Sources: Mac Taylor, "Cal Facts, 2016," (Sacramento, CA: Legislative Analyst's Office); Board of Equalization.

Tax Burden Generally

- **Income taxes are progressive**
  - Graduated or **progressive tax structure** means that tax rates increase as one moves up the scale
  - Low-income earners pay about lower than or about the same as those in other states
  - Middle- to high-income earners pay relatively more in California (than in other states)
  - Surcharges are placed on highest income earners
    - +1% on incomes exceeding $1 million
  - Tax credits and deductions lower tax burdens for most

California's Tax Burden *(compared to other states)*

HIGH to MEDIUM HIGH:	LOW:
• **Sales** taxes *(high: 7.25%* • *base + local)* • **Gas** Taxes *(high)* • **Corporate** Taxes *(med.)* • **Income** Taxes *(mixed)*	• **Property** Taxes *(1% of sale price + small adjustments)* • **Excise** Taxes (alcohol, tobacco)

Tax Burden Generally

- **Tax Burden depends on socioeconomic status (SES) and spending habits**
  - Compared to other states...
    - **Sales taxes** are relatively *high*
      - » 8.25% avg. including local, voter-approved sales taxes
      - » Not in top 10 highest states for state + local tax rates
- **Tax Burden depends on socioeconomic status (SES) and spending habits**
  - Compared to other states...
    - **Gas taxes** are relatively *higher (PA was highest in 2017)*
    - **Property taxes** are relatively *low* (among the lowest)
    - **Corporate taxes** are *midrange*
    - **Income taxes** are *lower at bottom* of income scale, *slightly higher in middle,* and *higher at top* of scale

Discussion Questions

1. How should state representatives deal with the fact that taxpayers demand (and need) certain services but are generally unwilling to raise taxes?
2. Should the legislature be empowered to raise taxes, or should tax increases always be subject to a vote of the people?
3. Is moving to a user-fee-based system (where people pay for the services they use) better than a system where all pay into it (through taxes)? What kinds of services could or should not be simply paid for through user fees?
4. California relies heavily on high-income taxpayers for state revenues. Are there more stable sources of revenue that the state should rely on instead?

Chapter 9

Political Parties, Elections, and Campaigns

Political Parties, Elections, and Campaigns

- Overview
  - East-West Divide
  - Progressive Legacy
  - Democratic Stronghold but Weakly Partisan
- Four Dimension of a Political Party
  - Party in the Electorate
  - Party in Government
  - Party Organizations
  - Party in Informal Networks
- Elections: Continuity and Change
- Campaigns

Overview of Political Parties in California

- Learning Objectives
  - Identify the regional strongholds of political parties, including an east-west divide that has been created by natural "sorting."
  - List progressive electoral reforms that have undermined the power of political parties.
  - Characterize the legacy of progressive reforms for California elections and political parties.
  - Know the partisan breakdown of the California electorate.

- Evaluate the strength of the Democratic party in California relative to independents (those without a party preference) and Republicans.

California's East-West Partisan Divide

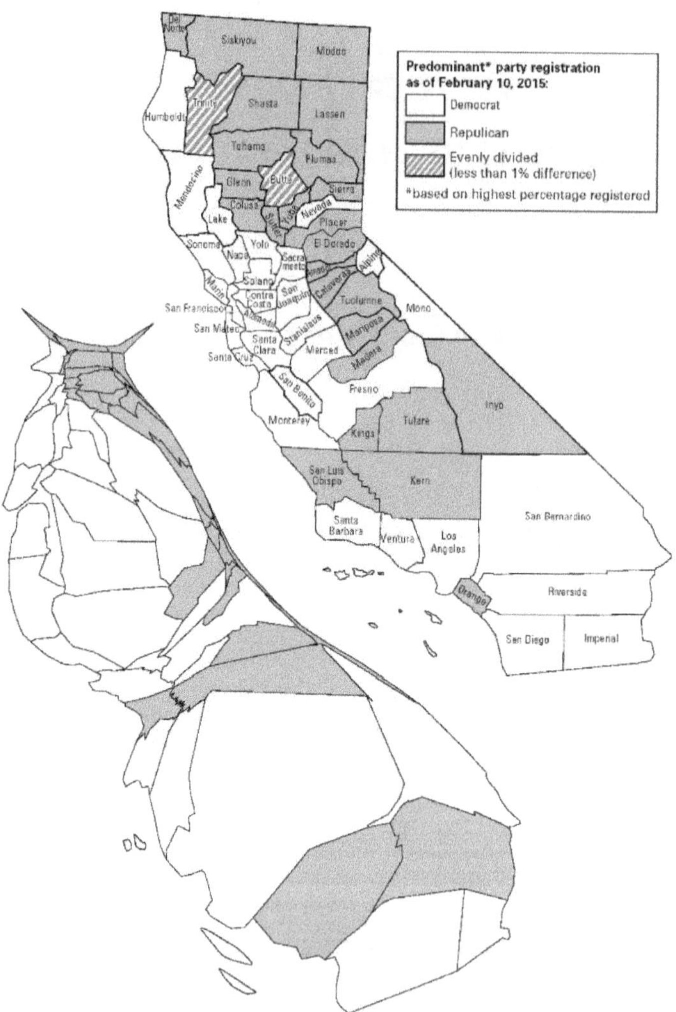

Political Parties Connect Citizens to Government

- In a representative democracy, political institutions **link citizens to politics** through:
  - Elections
  - Political Parties

- Through *elections*, people **hold their representative accountable**, reelecting them as a reward for satisfactory public service
- Through *political parties*, group conflicts are managed; **diverse interests are aggregated**; candidates can be identified with a **political agenda** and also held accountable for their views and actions

Progressive Legacy

- Historically, ***"anti-party" election laws*** have loosened political parties' control over elections
- In early 1900s, progressives established:
  - **Direct Democracy**: *Initiative, Recall, Referendum*
    - Citizens bypass representatives and parties to govern themselves
- **Direct Primary**
  - Citizens rather than party bosses choose nominees for office
- **Cross-filing**
  - Early form of the "open primary" (1910s–1950s)
  - Candidates could run in any party's primary
  - Enabled third party candidates (progressives) to thrive
  - Precursor to current top-two primary system
- **Nonpartisan elections**: candidates' party affiliation does not appear next to their name on the ballot
  - Denies voters a partisan "cue"
  - Still in place for all local and judicial elections

Democratic Stronghold but Weakly Partisan

- **Democrats dominate** the legislative and executive branches
- More people are **registered** as **Democrats** than any other party (45%). However:
  - This is **less than an absolute majority**
  - **24.5% are Independent**, and the category is growing
  - **Seven of 10 would prefer not be registered with a party***
  - A majority think the state needs a (strong) third party
- Only 26% of Californians are registered **Republicans**

Californians Remain Skeptical of Linkage Institutions

- 72% believe that state government is run by a few big interests*
- Majorities believe they make better decisions than government officials
- More and more voters are not affiliating with a major political party: 24.5% today

Party Registration in CA, 2017

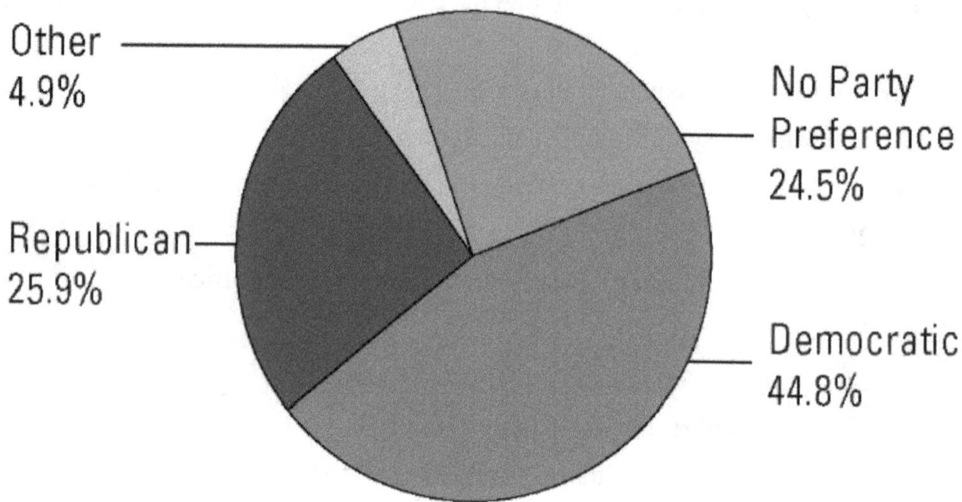

Partisanship in California

- Learning Objective:
  - Define political parties by describing their four dimensions, including: party in the electorate, party in government, party organizations, and party in informal networks.

Defining Political Parties

- Parties have important functions:
  a. Run elections
  b. Organize government
- A party has at least three dimensions or parts:
  1. Party in the Electorate (PIE)
  2. Party in Government (PIG)
  3. Party in Organizations (PO)

Party in the Electorate (PIE)

- Refers to **members who share similar beliefs** about the **role that government should play** in their lives
- Refers to the **generalized sentiment** a party's members share about **what it means to be** a Republican, Democrat, or member of any party

Party in the California Electorate (PIE)

DEMOCRATS	REPUBLICANS
Tend to be: • **Ethnically diverse** (50% White) • **Low-to-middle income** bracket • **Younger** • more **Female** • Slightly over half hold liberal views*	Tend to be: • **White** (77%) • **Higher income** bracket • **Older** • more **Male** • Three of four are **conservative***

Views Among the California Electorate

LIBERAL	CONSERVATIVE
• Want government to **promote equal opportunity in education and workplace** • **Tolerate higher taxes** for more government services; "tax the rich" • Favor greater **access to health care** - Many favor single-payer system • More responsive to **workers** • Favor **looser immigration laws** • Favor steps to curb climate change • Feel government doesn't control guns enough	• Favor **strictly limited government** • **Against taxes** (desire lower taxes and fewer services) • Want government to **stay out of health care** • More responsive to **business** • **Oppose abortion** • Favor strong **anti-immigration** laws • Oppose steps to curb climate change • Favor gun rights

Independents

- "**No party preference**" (NPP) refers to those who decline to affiliate with a political party but are registered to vote (24.5%)
- Tend to be younger, college educated (46% college grads)
- Ethnically diverse group (43% non-White)
- More lean toward (vote for) the Democratic party
- San Francisco has the highest percentage of registered independents (31%)
- Equal proportions (one thirds) consider selves liberal or conservative
  - Evenly split on raising taxes for more services or lowering them for fewer services

Party in Government (PIG)

- Current **elected officials** help build their party's "**brand name**" through lawmaking, taking action, and media visibility
- Leaders and members of a party who ***organize government in order to achieve their policy aims***
- Includes governor, Assembly members, Senators, federal representatives, and local officials
- Parties in California government are strongly ideologically polarized

Party Organizations (PO)

- A party's **organizational** bodies, including **committees**, **conventions**, and **rules**:
  - State Central Committee
  - County Central Committee
  - Regional volunteer clubs
- Help party members ***nominate candidates for election and get them elected***
- Informal networks (interest groups, media, campaign donors) form **alliances** and work "behind the scenes" to influence elections:
  - **Identify** candidates and **raise and spend money** for them
  - **Interact/socialize** with other elites to build networks of support for candidates and officeholders

Elections in California

- Characterize statewide elections in California.

- Describe how California's "top-two" primary elections work.
- Describe how term limits, redistricting, and the "top-two" primary have affected California elections processes and the outcomes of elections.

Overview: Elections in California

- Overall, Assembly and Senate elections tend to be **uncompetitive** (between parties), meaning one party is almost guaranteed to win the seat, based on:
  - Natural "**sorting**": people tend to live near others like themselves, so many districts lean toward one party
- **Primary elections** tend to be competitive among members of the party that will win the seat
- **Democrats** dominate legislative and executive elections
- **Incumbents** possess **great advantages** over challengers
- **Rules** for candidates and voters often change through voter-approved initiatives

Recent Political Changes and Their Electoral Impacts

- **Term limits** for state officials
  - **Turnover** for offices high (slowing somewhat since 2012)
  - **Open seats** are common
  - **Competition** is stronger for all types of offices
- More frequent **special elections** to fill seats vacated by ambitious individuals moving up the political ladder
- **Motor Voter law:** Automatic voter registration
  - Citizens are automatically registered to vote when they renew or get a driver's license (can opt out)
- Unique **primary election system:**

  "**Top-Two**" primary for STATE elections
  - Technically a *"voter preference primary"*
  - ALL VOTERS can select a nominee from among ALL CANDIDATES for each office
  - A version of an"open primary" (also called "jungle primary")
- All candidates for an office listed on ballot
- **TOP-TWO winners in each race advance to the general election** in November, for example:

  - Democrat vs. Democrat for Congress
  - Republican vs. Democrat for state Senate....
  - (Winners don't need to reach 50%)
- Intended to encourage the **election of moderates**, but so far **little evidence** of this has been uncovered
- **Online voter registration**
  - Available since 2012
  - Has encouraged more younger voters to register (but still "under-registered")
  - Matches signature with one on file with DMV
  - Go to: **http://registertovote.ca.gov**
- Rise of voting by mail: over 60% **vote by mail** (VBM) or **absentee** ballot
- Moving toward **ALL VOTE-BY-MAIL ELECTIONS**
  - Special elections and cities with population <100,000 can be all-mailed ballot elections currently
- Experimenting with (and moving toward) regional **voting centers**
  - Neighborhood polling places will be replaced with voting centers
    - Open 30 days before an election
    - Voters will drop off or mail in their ballot
- Vote by e-mail (absentee voter) statistics, 1976–2016

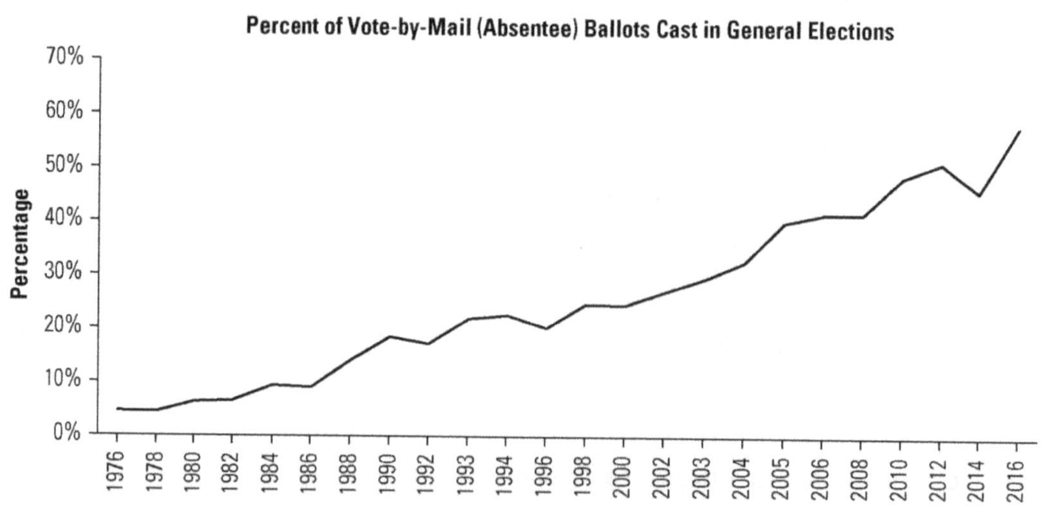

- VoteCal, statewide voter database connecting all county elections offices, now active
- In 2018, same-day registration goes into effect
  - Voters able to register to vote on the day they cast a ballot
- 16- and 17-year-olds can preregister to vote
- Electoral districts now **drawn** by **the California Citizens Commission (CRC)**
  - Districts historically were subject to "gerrymandering"
  - In 2012, the CRC redrew district maps without respect to incumbency or party
    - » Senate, Assembly, Congressional (House), and Board of Equalization maps (wedrawthelines.ca.gov)
  - In 2012, many officeholders had to run against each other

Campaigns in the Golden State

- Learning Objectives:
  - Describe some of the main features of California elections.
  - Recognize which industries and interests tend to dominate campaigns.

Campaigns in California

- **Huge sums** typically needed to reach residents spread across large areas or densely populated (and expensive) **media markets**
  - **Wholesale** campaigning = indirect contact with potential voters, such as through TV ads or mailings
  - **Retail** campaigning = direct contact, "meets and greets," knocking on doors
- **Elections are competitive and costly**
  - Average ASSEMBLY race: $750,000
  - Average SENATE race: $1,000,000
- Open seat elections cost more
- Incumbents are in "**permanent campaign**" mode
- Big **donors** to candidates believe they are **buying "access"** to the politician
- Campaign contributions and expenses must be reported to the **Fair Political Practices Commission (FPPC)**
  - Campaign financing is reported online: http://cal-access.sos.ca.gov
  - Independent spending (spending by outside groups) is rising
    - Donors must be disclosed (reported to the FPPC)

- Individuals are limited to donating $4,400 per candidate
- Small contributor committees can donate $8,800 per candidate
- Political party donations to candidates are not limited

Ballot Campaign Contributors, 2016

Top Contributors SUPPORTING Prop 61	Industry	State of Origin	Total Contributions
AIDS Healthcare Foundation	Non-profit	CA	$18,717068
California Nurses Association PAC	Medical	CA	$264,138
TOTAL, Top Supporters			**$18,981,206**
Top Contributors OPPOSING Prop 61		**State of Origin**	**Total Contributions**
Merck & Co., Inc.	Pharmaceutical	NJ	$9,420,395
Pfizer, Inc.	Pharmaceutical	NY	$9,420,395
Johnson & Johnson	Pharmaceutical	NJ	$9,301,646
Amgen Inc.	Pharmaceutical	CA	$7,670,768
Abbvie Inc.	Pharmaceutical	IL	$6,859,873
Sanofi-Aventis U.S.	Pharmaceutical	NJ	$6,720,945
AstraZeneca Pharmaceuticals	Pharmaceutical	DE	$6,080,535
Allergan USA, Inc.	Pharmaceutical	NJ	$5,079,332
Novartis Pharmaceuticals Corp.	Pharmaceutical	NY	$4,728,302
Glaxosmithkline	Pharmaceutical	NC	$4,528,527
TOTAL, Top Opponents			**$69,810,718**

Discussion Questions

1. Are you more likely to participate in a "mail-in ballot-only" election system?
2. Do you strongly associate with a political party, feel somewhat connected to a party, or apathetic towards parties? What would need to change for you to feel differently?
3. Explore the concept of the "permanent campaign." Do you believe that frequent elections distract representatives from their main duties?
4. What are the advantages and disadvantages of a Top-Two, "open primary" system?

Chapter 10

Political Engagement

Political Engagement

- Citizens and Politics: How Californians Engage Politically
- Predictors of Political Participation and Disengagement
- The Five Californias
- News and Media Habits
- Types of Political Participation
- Major Voting Trends
- Special Interest Groups: Indirectly Connecting Citizens to Government

Political (Dis)Engagement

- Learning Objective:
  - Explain why people do not participate in politics.

Citizens and Politics

- **Political participation** and **civic engagement** encompass far more than the act of voting:
  - Being informed
    - **Mass media** play critical role in linking residents, groups, and government
  - Contacting officials
  - Talking with others about politics
  - and so on

Reasons for Disengaging from Politics, cont.

- **Frustration** or feeling as if one is **wasting one's time**, because one can't make any impact = **low political efficacy**
  - Cycle of frustration: Continuing disengagement → lower levels of efficacy → *higher levels of frustration or apathy*
  - Associated with lower income, less education
    - **Less knowledge** about the system and/or **lower confidence** in one's knowledge is **discouraging**
- **Living in a community** or **culture** where politics is not talked about
- **Lower income, transient** populations: **fewer chances to be contacted or mobilized** for political action
- **Immigrant status**: **Language deficits** complicate participation; **fear of being misunderstood or not taken seriously**
- **Working class**: having **less disposable time** to dedicate to political activities or learn the rules of the system

Who Participates? (Why Don't More People Follow Politics?)

- **Among those who participate:**
  - **Political efficacy is higher**
    - Feeling as if one's actions will matter or make a difference is associated with participating
  - Political interest is higher
    - Note that interest levels are lowest among racial/ethnic minority groups
  - They live in a "**pro-voting**" community/culture
- Among those who participate:
  - They have **higher socio-economic status:**
    - Higher income
    - Educated
    - Older (not younger)
    - Homeowners (deeper roots in a community)
    - Native born
  - Race/ethnicity matters:
  - Whites have highest levels of participation
  - Asian and Latino immigrants less likely to participate

The Five Californias*

- Can better understand **participation** of Californians and the **demands** they place on the system by observing **five** major groupings
- Groups separated by relative levels of human development:
  1. Overall well-being
  2. Access to opportunity
  - Measured by:
    - overall health
    - income
    - education levels

The One Percent (344,000 people)

- Highest human development scores
- Drive and benefit from innovation like information technology
- Access to great health care, stable jobs, and relationships (88% married)
- Extremely well educated (~40% graduate/professional degreed)
- Ethnicity: 51% White, 34.5% Asian American, 9.5% Latino, 1% Black; over 1/3 foreign-born

The One Percent (344,000 people)

- Well-paying careers in management, business, science, and arts
- Annual median household incomes >$114,000.
- 75% of children go to preschool; can afford private schools
- Cluster in Santa Clara County; median home price >$2.1 million

Elite Enclave (5,734,000 people; 15%)

- Access to great health care, stable jobs, and relationships (88% married)
- Well educated (56% college grad; 23% advanced degree)
- Ethnicity: 55% White, 22.4% Asian American, 15.5% Latino, and 3.3% Black
- "Knowledge workers" in management, business, arts, and sciences

Elite Enclave (5,734,000 people; 15%)

- Annual median household incomes >$89,000
- Parents highly focused on getting kids to college

- Reside in low-crime neighborhoods in SF, LA, San Diego, Sacramento, and San Jose
- Can pay bills every month, including child care; bypass poverty

Main Street (14,658,000 people; 39%)

- "Middle-class America"
- 87% high school grads; 34% college degree; 12% advanced
- Ethnicity: 45% White, 30% Latino, 16% Asian American, 4% Black; three-fourth foreign-born
- Mostly office and service sector employees
- Annual median household incomes ~$66,000

Main Street (14,658,000 people; 39%)

- Able to provide enrichment activities for kids;
- Reside in cities, inland counties of Fresno, San Bern, Riverside
- Weak financial security; income barely covers housing and health
- Harder to find child care; many youth are unemployed or not in school

Struggling (16,109,000 people; 42%)

- Barely holding it together
- 73% high school grad; 18% college degree; 5% advanced degree
- Ethnicity: 52% Latino, 29% White, 8% Asian American, 8% Black, and 28% foreign-born
- Insecure high effort/low-reward jobs in sales, service, and office
- Annual median household incomes ~$45,000

Struggling (16,109,000 people; 42%)

- 22% below poverty line; lack of money a constant stressor
- Suburbs and rural areas of No., Central, Southern inland counties
- More exposure to crime, adverse events (long-term care for disabled family member); high unemployment
- Little/no child care, extracurriculars; high youth unemployment

Disenfranchised (1,196,000 people; 3%)

- Marginalized, segregated, excluded socially; live outside the formal economy
- 50% high school grad; 8% college degree; 2% advanced degree
- Ethnicity: 71% Latino, 13% White, 9% Asian American, and 5% Black
- High barriers to employment: no child care, low education, immigration status, prison records, and lack of transportation

Disenfranchised (1,196,000 people; 3%)

- High-effort/low-reward jobs: transportation, service, and production
- Annual median household incomes ~$31,000
- 50% kids in poverty; 30% to preschool; 1/5 youth not in school
- Violent urban areas of Los Angeles; rural San Joaquin (unhealthy air)

The Five Californias

	One Percent California	Elite Enclave California	Main Street California	Struggling California	Disenfranchised California
Life expectancy at birth	86.2	84.3	82.0	79.7	77.6
At least a B.A. degree	71.4%	56.4%	34.5%	17.6%	8.3%
Median personal earnings (2012 dollars)	$ 69,552	$ 48,878	$ 33,975	$ 23,816	$ 17,204
Percentage living below poverty level in past year	6.1%	8.8%	12.6%	22.3%	36.3%
Married-couple family (% of households with children)	87.5%	79.4%	71.7%	62.9%	52.3%
GEOGRAPHIC BREAKDOWN	2 Neighborhood Clusters 344,372 people	42 Neighborhood Clusters 5,733,945 people	102 Neighborhood Clusters 14,658,157 people	110 Neighborhood Clusters 16,109,333 people	9 Neighborhood Clusters 1,195,623 people
POPULATION BREAKDOWN (% OF ALL CALIFORNIANS)	1%	15%	39%	42%	3%

Participation and the Five Californias

- **Human development** distribution allows us to better understand the **capacity of certain groups to advocate for themselves**
- Enormous variation in educational background, basic needs, and stressors creates **different kinds of opportunity structures for political participation**
  - Some people have plenty of time to read newspapers and donate to causes that concern them
  - Others may not understand how politics works and feel intimidated by those who do, or only have time to focus on surviving

News and Media Habits

- Learning Objectives:
  - Identify sources of political news and information.
  - Explain the potential influence of the media on viewers.
  - Describe how media and politics are connected.

Media Habits

Most Californians do not pay much attention to state politics

- The press help mold an audience's attitudes, beliefs, and political understanding
  - Through **framing:** highlighting or ignoring certain elements in the telling of a story
  - Many partisans are skeptical of major news outlets as biased
  - Consolidation among news corporations has reduced number of sources, increasing the possibility of bias
- Partial, brief news stories (promoted by social media) can confuse audience
  - Lack of context promotes misinformation
  - About half of Californians access news online
- <u>Voters</u> tend to be newspaper readers; provides most context
  - *Los Angeles Times, San Francisco Chronicle, Sacramento Bee,* and *San Jose Mercury News* struggle for subscribers

Citizens and Politics: How Californians Engage Politically

- Learning Objectives:
  - List common forms of political participation.

- Recognize progressively more demanding ways to participate politically.
- Describe California's "exclusive electorate," or which subgroups are represented and under-represented in California elections.
- Recognize the differences in voting trends between presidential and off-year elections and state and municipal elections.

How Californians Engage Politically

Candidate
Political activist
Local party activist
Campaign for cause/person
Donate to campaigns/persons
Attend town meetings, join rallies
Call, write, and e-mail official; join a boycott
Influence others how to vote; sign petitions
Influence others how to vote; sign petitions
Display sign, T-shirt, or sticker; vote in elections
Join FB group; discuss politics; work with neighbors
Like/dislike material on Facebook page; follow politician on Twitter

Political Participation Trends

- **Whites** are a minority group, but **dominate** almost every category of **political activity**
  - Diversity of population is not well represented
  - Asian and Latino Americans least likely to *contact public officials* or *donate* to campaigns
  - Whites are most frequent *consumer activists* (changing their purchasing habits for a political reason)
  - Exception lies in *attending public meetings* and *protesting*: major racial/ethnic groups participate at similar levels

Major Voting Trends

- Voting represents a "check" on officeholders
  - Voting is a means to **reject** an incumbent
  - Voting supplies cues to policymakers about what **policies** a constituency prefers
  - A smaller electorate introduces biases into the results
    - The majority of whoever turns out to vote wins!
- California's "exclusive electorate":
  - Voters don't well represent the size or diversity of population
  - **Whites** are well represented
    - Sixty-one percent of electorate/likely voters but 43% of adult population
    - **Latinos are underrepresented** proportionally
      - » Seventy percent of eligible Latinos didn't vote in 2014
      - » Thirty-four percent of adult population but 18% of likely voters
    - Asian Americans make up 15% of population but 12% of likely voters
    - Blacks are 6% of population and 6% of likely voters

Major Voting Trends

- Characteristics associated with voting:
  - Older
    - Youth vote (ages 18–24) historic lows: 8.4% in 2014
    - Rebounded in 2016: 33.4% of youth voted
    - Youth are 22% of likely voters in 2017
  - Homeowners
  - Native-born
  - Higher income

Eligible Youth Voter Turnout, 2014

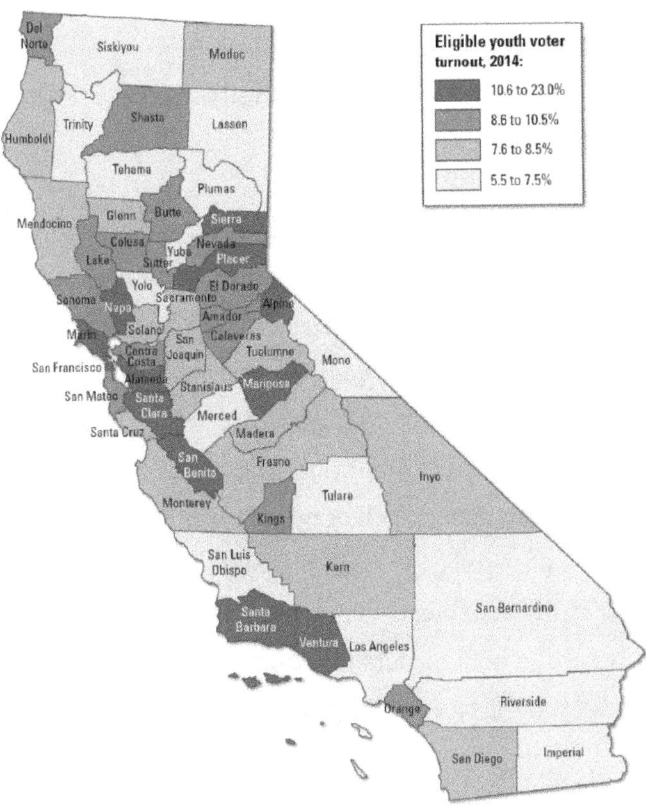

Source: California Civic Engagement Project, UC Davis Center for Regional Change, Table G14-1.

Voting Trends

- **Only a portion of eligible voters vote consistently**
- Among those who vote, **different combinations of voters produce different electoral outcomes**
  - Assembly district voters are different from those who vote for all initiatives, for example
- **Low-turnout elections magnify differences between voters and nonvoters**:
  - **Strong partisans** (with strong beliefs) tend to turn out for all types of elections, while more moderate, occasional voters tend to vote in major elections only

  - **Turnout** (the number of voters) is **highest in presidential elections** or special elections featuring a hot-button issue or celebrity candidate(s).
    - **2012** Presidential election: **55.5% of eligible** voters cast ballots (72.4% of registered voters)
    - **2016** Presidential election: **58.7% of eligible** voters cast ballots (75.3% of registered voters)
- California's "exclusive electorate":
  - Voters don't well represent the size or diversity of population
  - **Whites** are well represented
    - Sixty-one percent of electorate/likely voters, but 43% of adult population
    - **Latinos are under-represented** proportionally
      - » Seventy percent of eligible Latinos didn't vote in 2014
      - » Thirty-four percent of adult population but 18% of likely voters
    - Asian Americans make up 15% of population but 12% of likely voters
    - Blacks are 6% of population and 6% of likely voters
- Turnout is **lower in off-year elections**
  - Averaging 37.5% of eligible voters **(2000-2016)**
  - 2014 Off-year election: **30.9% of eligible** voters cast ballots (42.2% of registered voters participated)
- Turnout is **lowest in municipal** elections
  - Fifteen percent to 35% turnout is common in city/municipal elections

Values and priorities of California voters and nonvoters differ

- They hold distinctly different views about the proper role of government:
  - Forty-seven percent of California registered voters and 70% of people *not registered* would prefer a **bigger government providing more services**
  - Forty-two percent of California registered voters favor a **pro-immigration sanctuary state law** compared to 60% of those *not registered*
  - 55% of registered voters want **stricter gun laws** compared to 71% of those *not registered*

Major Voting Trends

Views about State's Role in Reducing Income Inequality

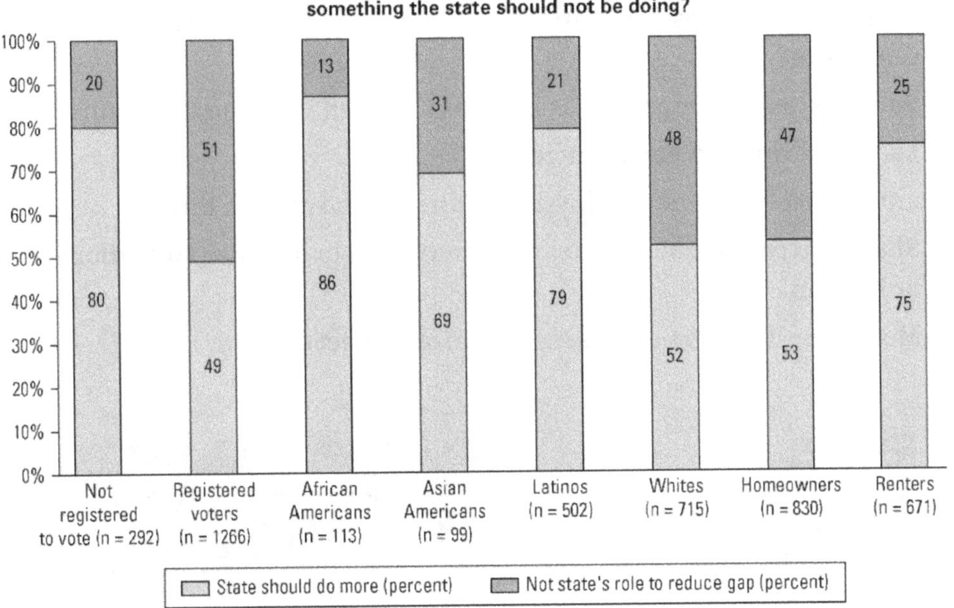

Special Interests / Interest Groups

- Learning Objective:
  - Define the term "special interests" and describe how special interests influence politics, from elections to lawmaking.
- An organized group that tries to influence the government to advance or protect its interests and goals
  - Directly affected by public policy
  - Usually want something
    - from government
  - Link citizens to politics

Nurses descend on the Capitol to convince legislators to support a bill.

- **Examples:**
  - **Professional associations** like the California Teachers Association (CTA)
  - **Business** or **trade associations** like the Chamber of Commerce or California Grocers Association
  - **Single-issue groups** like National Right to Life or Santa Monica Mountains Conservancy
  - **Public-interest groups** such as League of Women Voters or Common Cause
  - **Local governments and agencies**
- Groups connect to the political system indirectly and directly through:
  - **Sharing expertise** about issues that affect them to **mobilize and influence public opinion**
  - **Mobilizing** members or citizens **to vote or contact officials**

Photo: R. Van Vechten

Groups often gather on the steps of the state Capitol where they hold rallies and press conferences to attract attention to their causes.

- Groups connect to the political system ***indirectly*** and through:
  - Employing **lobbyists** who **"educate" politicians** about the effects of a proposed law as witnesses in committees or face-to-face
  - Having lobbyists attend **high-priced fundraisers** (dinners, cocktail hours, golf tournaments, etc.)

Lobbyists and members of special interest groups try to get "face time" with legislators to press their case.

- Groups connect to the political system ***directly*** through:
  - **Organizing members** to press their case to their representatives **in person**
    - Groups organize trips to Sacramento for advocacy activities
  - **Attending committee hearings** for bills and registering their support or opposition

Photo: R. Van Vechten

Members of special interest groups connect with legislators in the Capitol during their "advocacy days."

Photo: R. Van Vechten

Many high-priced lobbying firms are located in buildings directly across the street from the Capitol.

- Groups connect to the political system indirectly and directly through:

  Money:

  - Members make direct **campaign donations** (money goes straight to the candidate)
  - **PACs** (Political Action Committees): members pool their money to donate directly to candidates
  - **Independent campaign spending** (such as making ads without the candidate's knowledge)

Top 10 Spenders on Lobbying in California, 2015–2016

NAME	INDUSTRY	TOTAL SPENT
Western States Petroleum Assn	Oil and gas	$18,718,663
California Hospital Assn	Health services	$11,980,669
California State Council of Service Employees	Labor unions	$11,808,178
Chevron	Oil and gas	$7,179,341
California Chamber of Commerce	Business	$7,033,032
City of Los Angeles + County of Los Angeles	Government	$5,540,934
Kaiser Foundation Health Plan	Health services	$4,525,516
California Teachers Association	Labor unions	$4,449,370
AT&T	Telecommunications	$4,307,774
CA School Boards Assn	Labor unions	$3,981,703

Political Imbalances Among Interest Groups

- Some groups exert **disproportionate** influence
  - The **organized**
  - The **well funded** (and are willing to spend)
  - **Large**, politically **active membership** (e.g., unions, AARP)
  - **Big economic interests** (large employers, companies)

- Some groups **barely register** on the political scale
  - Resource-poor and unorganized interests

Discussion Questions

1. If "money is the mother's milk of politics," as Assembly Speaker Jess Unruh claimed in the 1960s, then how politically influential can underfunded, "poor" groups (such as university students) be in California?
2. Does the government bear responsibility for educating its citizens and encouraging more participation?
3. Latinos are among the least politically active group but the fastest growing segment of the population. What are the implications of these trends for California's political future?

Chapter 11

Paradoxes, Policy, and Exceptionalism

Paradoxes, Effective Government, and Exceptionalism

- Learning Objectives:
  - Explain the paradoxes that characterize California politics.
  - Argue for and against labeling California politics as "exceptional."

Paradoxes in California Politics

- Voters do not trust government to make good decisions, yet collectively are incapable of making all the decisions needed to run one of the world's largest countries
- Voters don't trust politicians, but they generally do not trust other voters either
- Initiatives are often intended to make government work better, yet new rules often make it more difficult for elected officials to work more efficiently
- Californians would like to take the politics out of politics.
- Californians expect the public good and their personal needs to be met simultaneously
- Californians demand much from government and generally do not want to pay for expanded services, expecting greater and greater efficiency for less and less state spending

Public Policy and Political Issues That Will Define California's

- Learning Objectives:
  - Define "effective governance."
  - List major categories of political problems that will define California's future.
  - Describe the political issues that politicians will likely encounter and need to address to ensure effective governance.

- Identify ways to reform California government to achieve more effective government.

Planning for Tomorrow

- California will grow critically in the coming decades
  - 40 million by 2020; 50 million by 2050
- By 2025, one in seven will be over age 65
- State already has a $500 billion backlog in infrastructure projects (roads, schools, etc.)
- Unfunded liabilities (promises to retirees) threaten future budgets and long-term economic stability
- California is a majority Latino state
  - ...Yet Latino immigrants are less integrated into the political system than whites and other ethnic/racial groups and have lower high school and college graduation rates

"Exceptional" Governing Challenges to Consider

- California faces many of the **same issues** as other states
- But **scale, scope, and volume of issues** exceed those in almost all other states
- **Hybrid democracy** also sets the state apart: the people compete with representatives over control of certain issues

Policy Issues to Consider: Education

- Per-pupil spending remains below national average *(depends on calculation terms)*
  - Was raised in 2017–2018 to $11,067 per student
- An educated workforce is necessary to support a service-based economy
  - How will the state prepare itself for a global economy? What would the economy look like *without* a well-educated workforce?
  - Wide achievement gap between Whites and Asian Americans (on the one hand) and Latinos and African Americans (on the other). How to close the gap?

Policy Issues to Consider: Immigration

- Largest immigrant population in nation: 27% of Californians born outside the United States

- What happens to a "shadow" population who have no documents but no other homeland?
  - California is a "sanctuary state" as of 2017
    - Local law enforcement barred from aiding federal officials in deporting non-violent undocumented immigrants
    - Approx. 2.5 million people are undocumented
- Public benefits are continually questioned
  - Yet low-skilled, unemployed, low-educated groups and individuals generally require *more* state services to move up the socioeconomic ladder

Policy Issues to Consider: Environment

California's **natural resources are a backbone** of the state's economy

- State continues to **regulate greenhouse gases** with AB 32 and SB 32
  - **Carbon cap-and-trade program** has expanded
  - Increases the cost of doing business and prices
  - Governor Brown: pushing back against federal policy by partnering with global leaders (China)

Climate change fundamentally affects natural resources, from oceans to forests, from mountains to deserts

- Climate change brings **uncertainty, erratic weather patterns** that are difficult to plan for
  - Too much water in some areas = **flooding**
  - High heat and too little water in some areas = **drought,** air **pollution, wildfires, and less biodiversity**
  - Important **industries cannot quickly adjust**: agribusiness, tourism-based businesses (e.g., ski resorts), construction, and so on suffer
  - **Costs for emergency services, cleanup, and recovery from natural disasters** can be budget-busters
    - Earthquakes, floods, and fires can cause billions in damage
- Growing population **demands more water**; long-term solutions are elusive
  - Meeting demands requires changes in individual behavior; conservation
- Delivery systems are at capacity; **scarcity** is the norm; **costs** will continue to rise (and voters will continue to resist higher fees)
- **Wetlands are degraded**; restoration needed statewide

- Major systems (such as the Delta) have highly **vulnerable levees** that could fail and need repair, but such projects are prohibitively costly
- Even heavy rains from weather events like El Niño cannot repair damage from 5+ years of drought
- **Overreliance on groundwater**
  - Management plans now just getting underway
  - Sources are depleted; leads to subsidence of land, damage to infrastructure
  - Forces rebalancing of rights among environment, agriculture, and people (and business)
- Delta is imperiled: ecosystem is failing; inland farmers demand water; critical source of Southern California drinking water
  - Will $19 billion tunnels help address water supplies?

Policy Issues to Consider: Transportation

- California's 50,500 miles of state highways and roads and 13,100 bridges are the most travelled in the nation, and the most congested
  - Many **roads/highways are nearing the end of their useful life** and need to be rehabilitated, but spending falls well short of what's needed ($2.8 billion annually)
- Backlog of **local street repairs**
  - $82 billion estimated in repairs
- Higher gas taxes now in effect (12¢/gallon, 20¢/gal for diesel); will taxes be repealed through a referendum?
- **Airports, railways, and seaports** need continual updating to accommodate larger populations, higher demand, and higher environmental standards
  - Significant source of **pollution**
- Public transit is underutilized
  - **Costs for building new systems are astronomical**:
    - **High-speed rail** from San Diego to San Francisco now estimated to be between $70 and $100 billion
      - » Construction is underway but funding is only partial

Policy Issues to Consider: Business and Labor

- **California's economy depends on a thriving business sector**

  - Many businesses are heavily regulated
    - Democratic lawmakers tend to favor labor rights over businesses
  - AB/SB 32 puts more pressure on big industries such as manufacturing, transportation, and construction
- Support for labor (public employees) translates to billions of dollars of **unfunded liabilities**
  - State is obligated to pay contracted pensions, health benefits, and so on

Policy Issues to Consider: Poverty, Health, and Inequality

- Gaps among the "five Californias" continues to widen
  - "Rich," "middle income," and "poor" have different levels of political participation and sometimes different ideas about government's appropriate roles
- California depends **heavily on federal spending** to address health care, education, housing, and welfare needs of citizens
  - Federal spending cutbacks on social programs threaten to increase gaps, not close them

Discussion Questions

1. Do you consider California politics to be "truly exceptional"? Why or why not?
2. What would it take for California government to become a model of efficiency and planning? What political, social, and economic factors need to change, in light of current demographic trends?
3. What will it take to reduce the state's backlog of infrastructure needs, and what should be prioritized?
4. What other policy areas not mentioned in the chapter pose great political challenges?
5. Should California be a sanctuary state?

About the Author

Dr. Roger Lang Cohen is a university lecturer in Southern California. He loves the beach when he is not working. As a citizen of both the United States and New Zealand, he is a political and philosophical activist.

CPSIA information can be obtained
at www.ICGtesting.com
Printed in the USA
FSHW012215310120
66677FS

9 781988 557250